AF263610

JAPANESE
WOODBLOCK
PRINTS 1680–1980

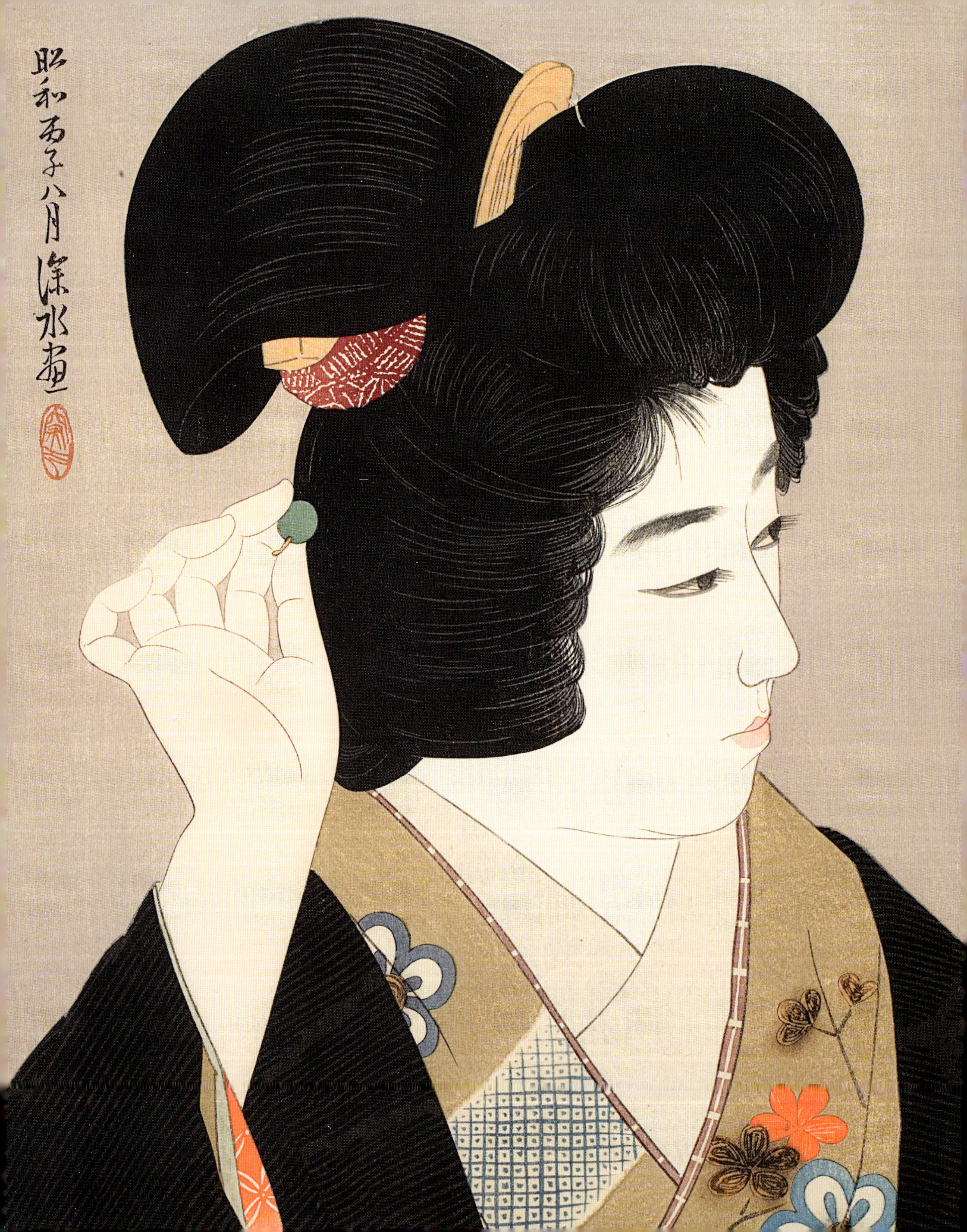

昭和丙子八月
深水画

JAPANESE WOODBLOCK PRINTS 1680–1980

WORCESTER ART MUSEUM

Director's Foreword by Matthias Waschek
Introduction by Fiona Collins
Edited by Fiona Collins

Contributions by Fiona Collins, Quintana Heathman Scherer, and Sarah E. Thompson

Worcester Art Museum, Worcester, Massachusetts,
in association with D Giles Limited

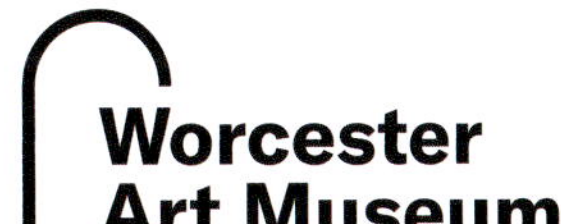

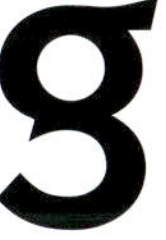

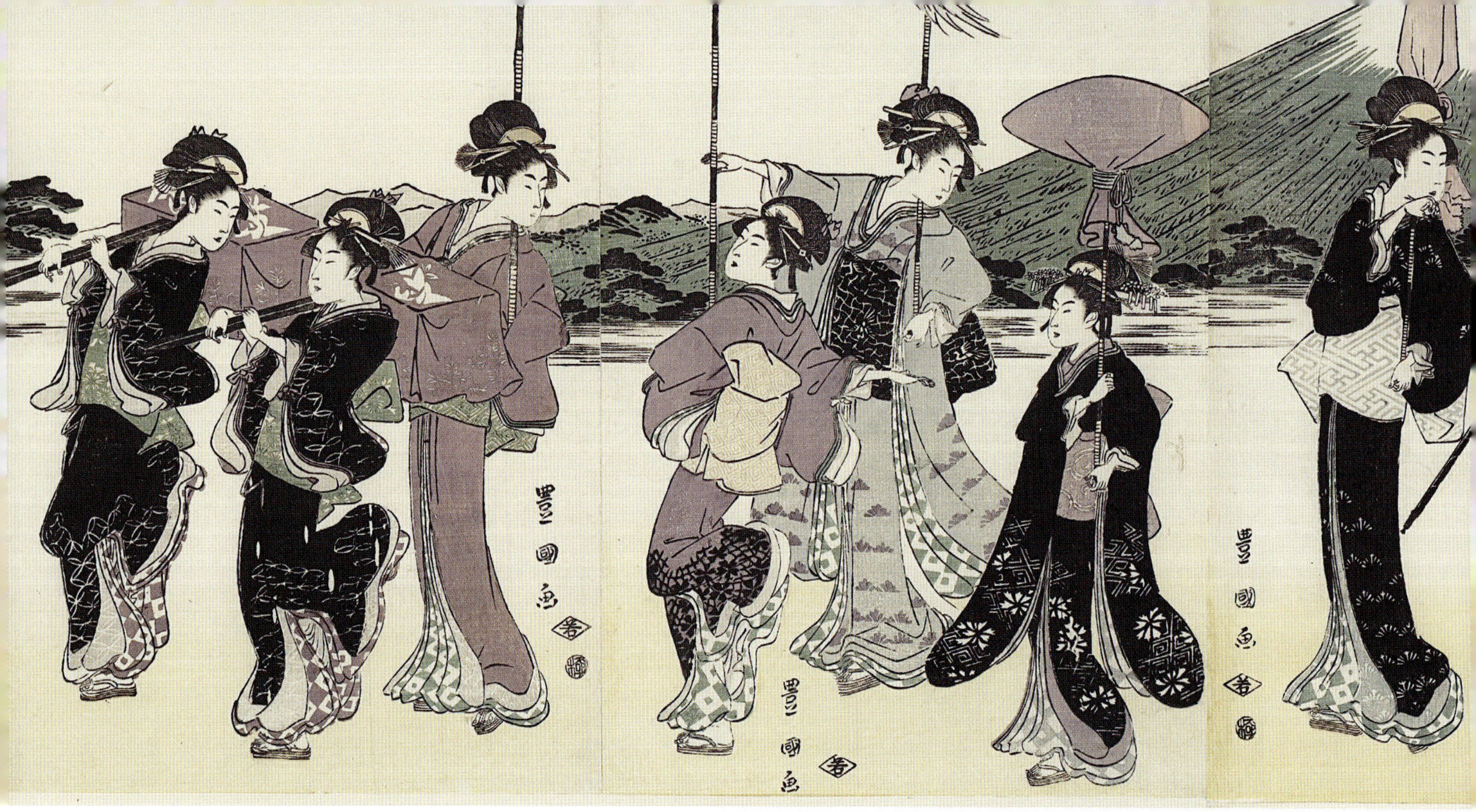

Japanese Woodblock Prints, 1680–1980: Worcester Art Museum is made possible by grants from the E. Rhodes and Leona B. Carpenter Foundation and the Japan Foundation Exhibitions Abroad Support Program.

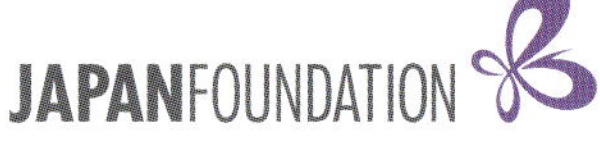

This catalogue accompanies the exhibition *Reflections of a Changing Japan: The Evolution of Shin Hanga* on display at Worcester Art Museum, March 29, 2025 – June 29, 2025

© 2025 Worcester Art Museum

First published in 2025 by GILES

An imprint of D Giles Limited
66 High Street,
Lewes, BN7 1XG, UK
https://gilesltd.com/

ISBN: 978-1-913875-91-6

For Worcester Art Museum:
Edited by Fiona Collins, Curatorial Researcher of Asian Art

For D Giles Limited:
Copy-edited and proofread by Sarah Kane
Designed by Helen Swansbourne
Produced by GILES, an imprint of
D Giles Limited

Printed and bound in Italy

All measurements are in centimeters and inches; height precedes width precedes depth.

Front cover: Yoshida Toshi, *Stone Garden*, 1963 (detail)

Back cover: Katsukawa Shunsen (Shunkō II), *Geisha Tying her Sash while Holding a Roll of Tissues between Her Teeth*, ca. 1815–20 (detail)

Frontispiece: Ito Shinsui, *Pupil of the Eye*, 1936 (detail)

Above: Utagawa Toyokuni I, *Mitate-e Daimyo Gyoretsu*, ca. 1796 (detail)

Page 132: Katsushika Hokusai, *Under the Wave off Kanagawa*, ca. 1831 (detail)

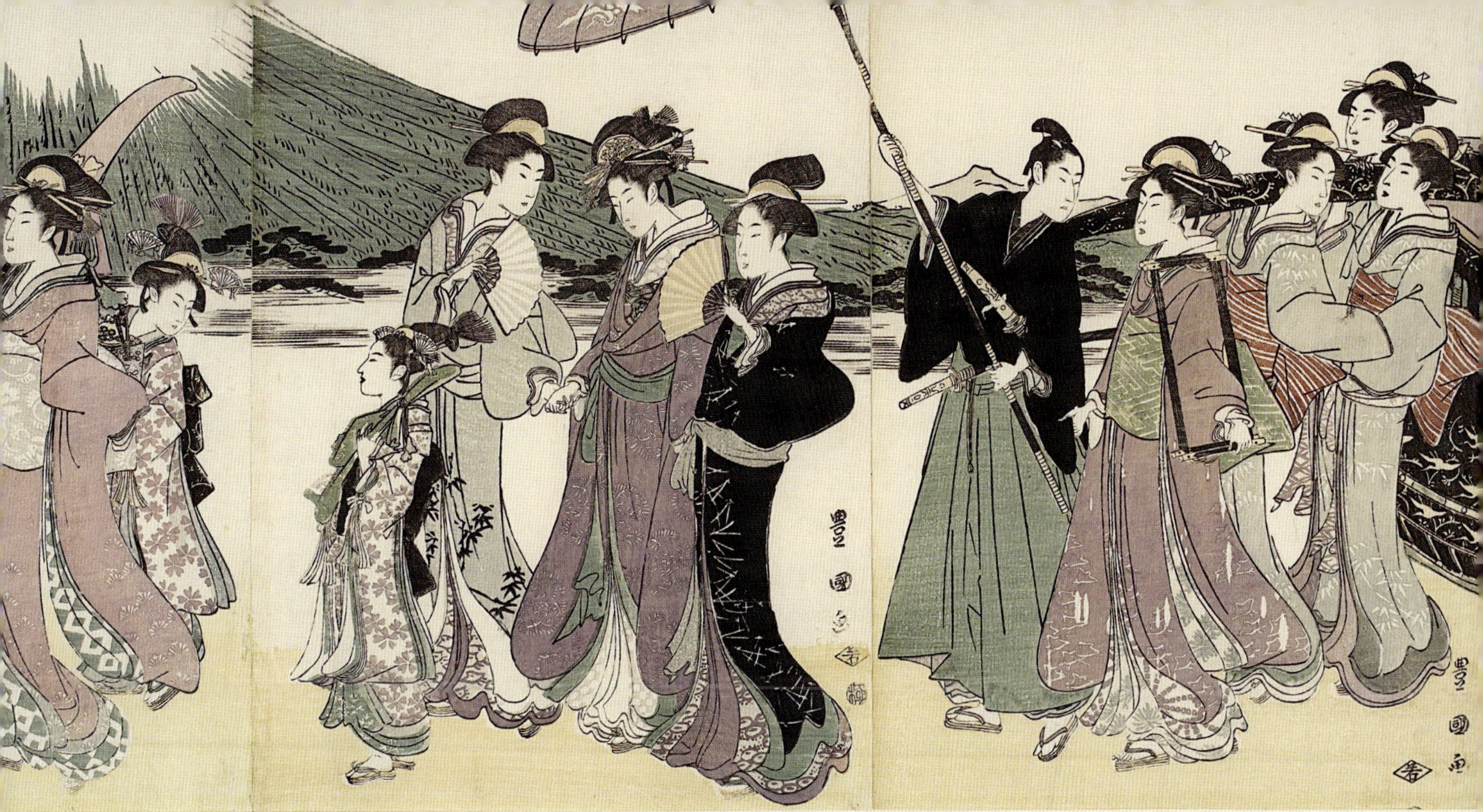

CONTENTS

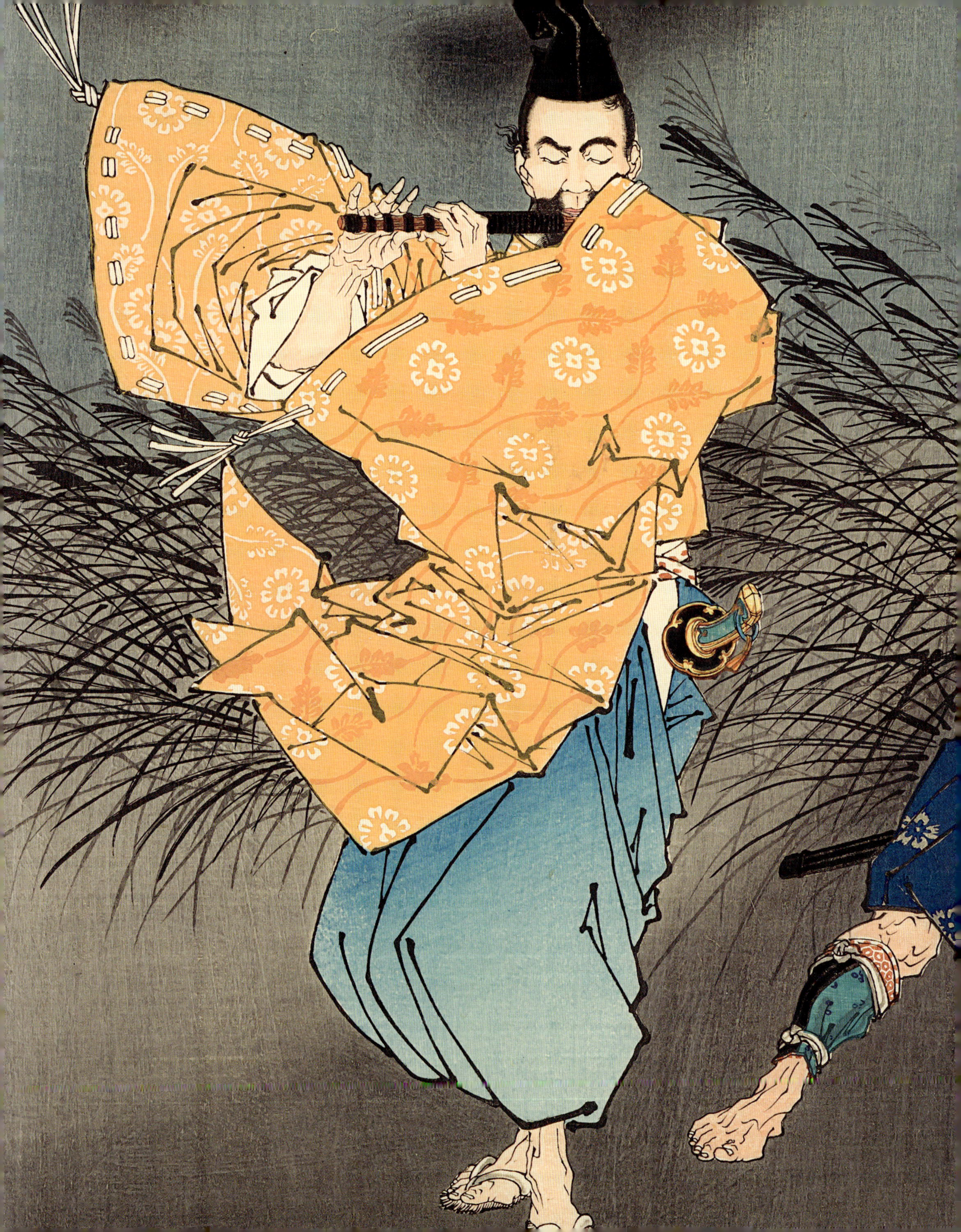

DIRECTOR'S FOREWORD

n 1901, only a few years after the Worcester Art Museum was founded, local businessman and collector John Chandler Bancroft (1835–1901) gave over 3,000 Japanese prints to our growing collection. Bancroft had studied art in Paris and, as early as 1863, was among the first Americans to collect *ukiyo-e* woodcuts. His keen artistic eye and intent are evident in the wide array of exceptional works he assembled, which include rare early pieces by *ukiyo-e* trailblazers like Hishikawa Moronobu and Okumura Masanobu, as well as later masters such as Kitagawa Utamaro, Katsushika Hokusai, and Utagawa Hiroshige. Notable for its scope and quality, it remains the earliest collection of Japanese prints to be gifted to an American museum. Over the years, the museum has expanded its collection to include significant modern and contemporary prints, such as extensive holdings of works by Tsukioka Yoshitoshi and Yoshida Toshi.

This catalogue draws from the great depth and breadth of the museum's Japanese woodblock print collection, presenting a selection of highlights arranged chronologically from the medium's rise in popularity in early modern Japan through the twentieth century. This progression enables viewers to appreciate the art form's diverse styles and functions across the centuries, its technical evolution, and the ways in which the prints' designs fuse traditional and modern elements.

I would like to express the museum's and my personal gratitude to Fiona Collins, Curatorial Researcher of Asian Art, who has taken the lead for this project, with expertise, initiative, and a strong sense of team work; the multidisciplinary team of Japanese print scholars—Sarah Thompson of the Museum of Fine Arts, Boston and Quintana Heathman Scherer of Kanagawa University—for their insightful contributions; Dan Giles and his team for their work on the catalogue design; and Claire Whitner, Director of Curatorial Affairs and James A. Welu Curator of European Art, for her invaluable guidance throughout the project.

MATTHIAS WASCHEK
Jean and Myles McDonough Director

Tsukioka Yoshitoshi, *The Painting "Fujiwara Yasumasa Playing the Flute by Moonlight," Exhibited at the National Painting Exhibition in the Autumn of 1882*, February 12, 1883 (detail)

ACKNOWLEDGMENTS

The development of this catalogue would not have been possible without the contributions of numerous dedicated colleagues. First and foremost, I am grateful to the E. Rhodes and Leona B. Carpenter Foundation and the Japan Foundation for their confidence and extraordinary generosity. For their support in this project, I am deeply appreciative of Matthias Waschek, Jean and Myles McDonough Director, and Claire Whitner, Director of Curatorial Affairs and James A. Welu Curator of European Art.

The researchers who contributed essays to this volume—Sarah Thompson and Quintana Heathman Scherer—each brought their different areas of expertise to provide a framework for understanding the diverse group of objects featured. The entries for each object were informed by former Curators of Asian Art at the Worcester Art Museum Vivian Li, Louise Virgin, and Elizabeth Swinton, and their invaluable research on the Japanese print collection. This project equally benefited from the invaluable insights of other specialists, particularly Patricia Graham, Kendall Brown, and Watanabe Shoichiro. Thank you to the artists and their families who granted permission to include the wonderful works in the twentieth-century section of the catalogue.

The outstanding staff of professionals at the Worcester Art Museum made this catalogue possible. Images were ably managed by Gareth Salway, Director of Museum Services; Rose Perriello, Exhibitions Registrar; and photographer Steve Briggs. Christine Proffitt, Senior Manager of Institutional Giving, shared her enthusiasm for the project and deftly worked with its supporters. Thank you to Yagnaseni Datta, Sohail and Mona Masood Assistant Curator of Asian and Islamic Art, for her invaluable insights and editing expertise during the development of the catalogue. Finally, I am grateful to Nancy Kathryn Burns, Stoddard Curator of Prints, Drawings and Photography, and Olivia Stone, Assistant Curator of Prints, Drawings and Photography, for their feedback and constructive advice, as well as Anne Greene, Preparator of Works on Paper, whose long dedication to the care of the Japanese print collection inspired and directed my inquiry.

FIONA COLLINS

Yoshida Chizuko,
Muroji Stone Road,
1953 (detail)

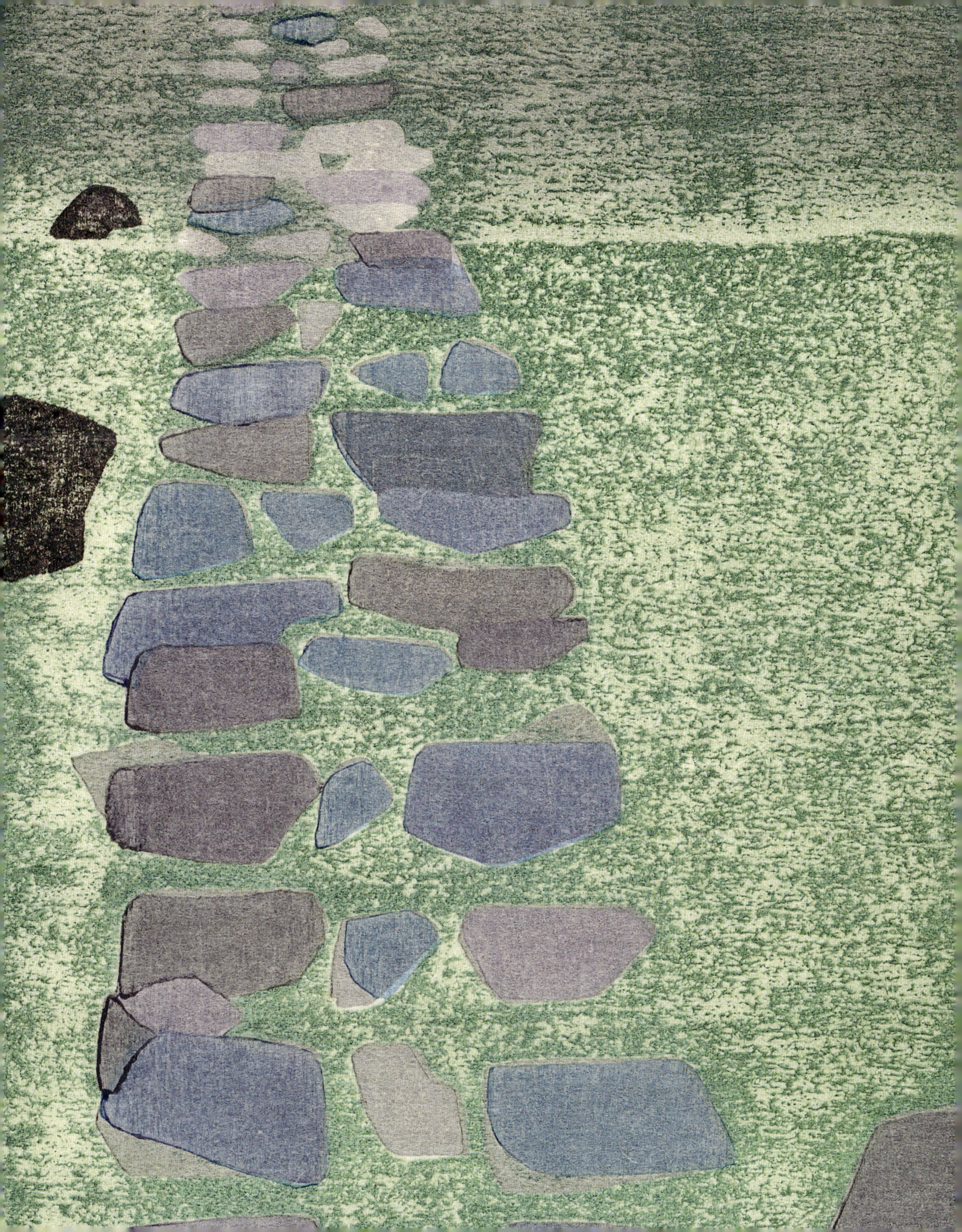

On 7 December 1900, John Chandler Bancroft's son, Professor Wilder D. Bancroft (1867–1953), wrote to Stephen Salisbury (1835–1905)—one of the founders of the recently established Worcester Art Museum—that his father wished to bequeath his collection of Japanese art, including over 3,000 woodblock prints. Bancroft passed away less than two months later, on 3 February 1901, at the age of sixty-six. This donation was the earliest of its kind in the United States and is still notable for its high quality and state of preservation.

Like many of his contemporaries, John Chandler Bancroft's passion for Japanese art, both as an artist and collector, began in Europe. After withdrawing from Harvard Law School in 1863, he spent six years in Dresden, Dusseldorf, and Paris, studying drawing and landscape painting surrounded by some of the most notable artists of the day. It was during these travels that he was first exposed to Japanese prints among the aesthetes of the urban *bohème*. Returning to the United States with the outbreak of the Civil War, he settled near Newport, Rhode Island, where he frequented the studio of impressionist painters William Morris Hunt (1824–1879) and first met John La Farge (1835–1910), the latter with whom Bancroft formed a lifelong friendship bound by mutual interests in art criticism, modern color theory, and, above all, the "exoticism" of Japanese woodblock prints. In 1863, Bancroft and La Farge began purchasing Japanese prints from Abiel Abbot Low (1811–1893), president of the New York Merchants'

Association and a major figure in New England's Asian trade.

The focus of Bancroft's collection was *ukiyo-e* (pictures of the floating world); produced in Japan's Edo period (1603–1868)—an era of peace and restricted interactions with the rest of the world— they drew on classical art, literature, and evolving trends in popular design to generate reflections of the urban population's dreamlike experiences. The incredible vibrancy and expressive power of *ukiyo-e* prints was driven largely by the introduction of new technologies, materials, and methods of production in the Edo period, which enabled the genre to transcend its commercial and religious origins in the first decades of the seventeenth century to become a dynamic vehicle for artistic and literary expression. Gradually, print subjects expanded to include portrayals of folktales, Buddhist iconography, sartorial expressions, the natural world, theater, courtesans, and other modern cosmopolitan subjects.

The Worcester Art Museum's Japanese woodblock print collection has since been greatly enriched by subsequent curators. It now also reflects significant evolution of the medium in response to Japan's profound cultural transformation during the Meiji and Taishō periods, marked by increased international trade, industrialization, and nationalism. In recent years, the museum has also expanded its collection's scope by focusing on postwar prints produced from the 1950s to the present. The works featured in this publication demonstrate the remarkable range of styles, techniques, and themes that have characterized Japanese woodblock print-making throughout its history, offering readers a journey through the art form's rich and diverse heritage.

The volume features an essay by Sarah E. Thompson, who explores the development of Japanese woodblock printing as an artistic medium. Thompson pays particular attention to the collaborative nature of Japanese woodblock print production in the Edo period before introducing later deviations from this method, including *shin hanga* and *sōsaku hanga*, which marked significant shifts in the creative process and allowed artists to exert greater control over their work. Complementing Thompson's piece is an essay by Quintana Heathman Scherer, which examines the ways in which Japanese woodblock prints from the Edo period onwards have reflected the evolving urban and rural landscapes of Japan. Scherer traces the country's transformation from a feudal society with thriving urban *demimonde*, through the significant cultural shifts of the twentieth century. The essay honors Bancroft's passion for landscape prints, and, using objects in his collection, investigates the ways in which societal and cultural shifts influenced the portrayals of traditional subjects in woodblock prints.

FIONA COLLINS

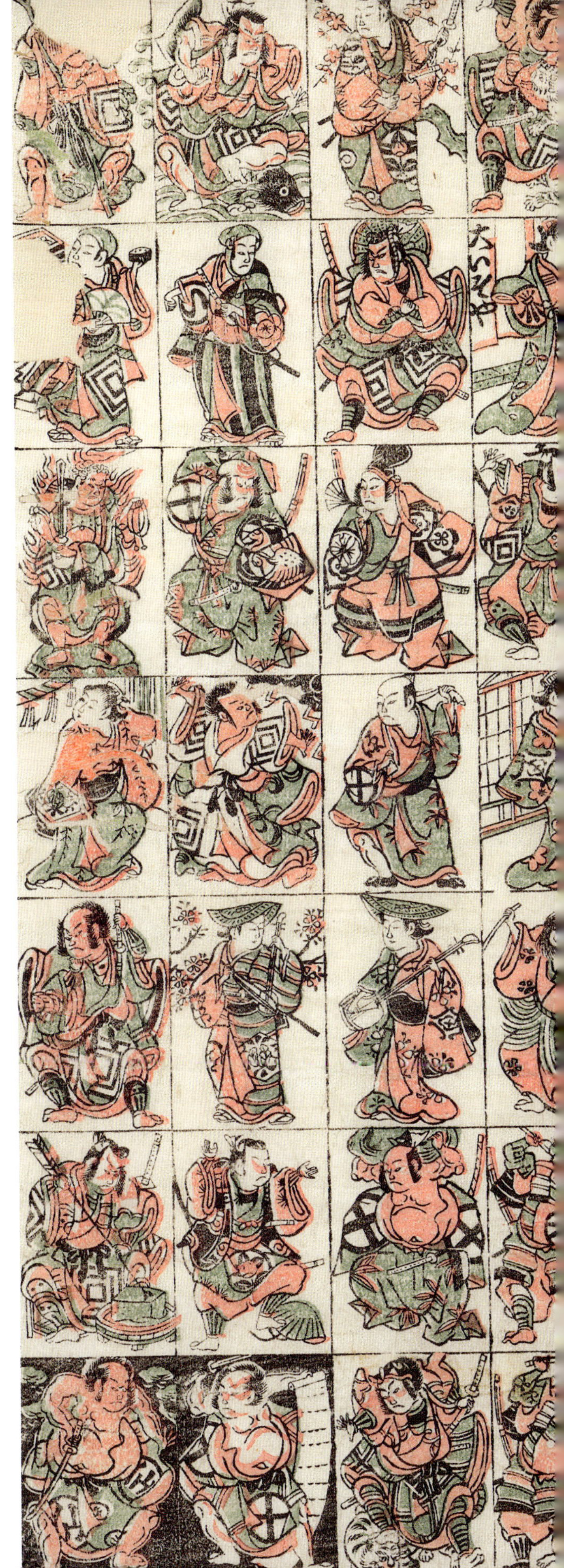

Torii Kiyomitsu,
*Thirty-five Small
Portraits of Actors
in Various Roles*,
1750 (detail)

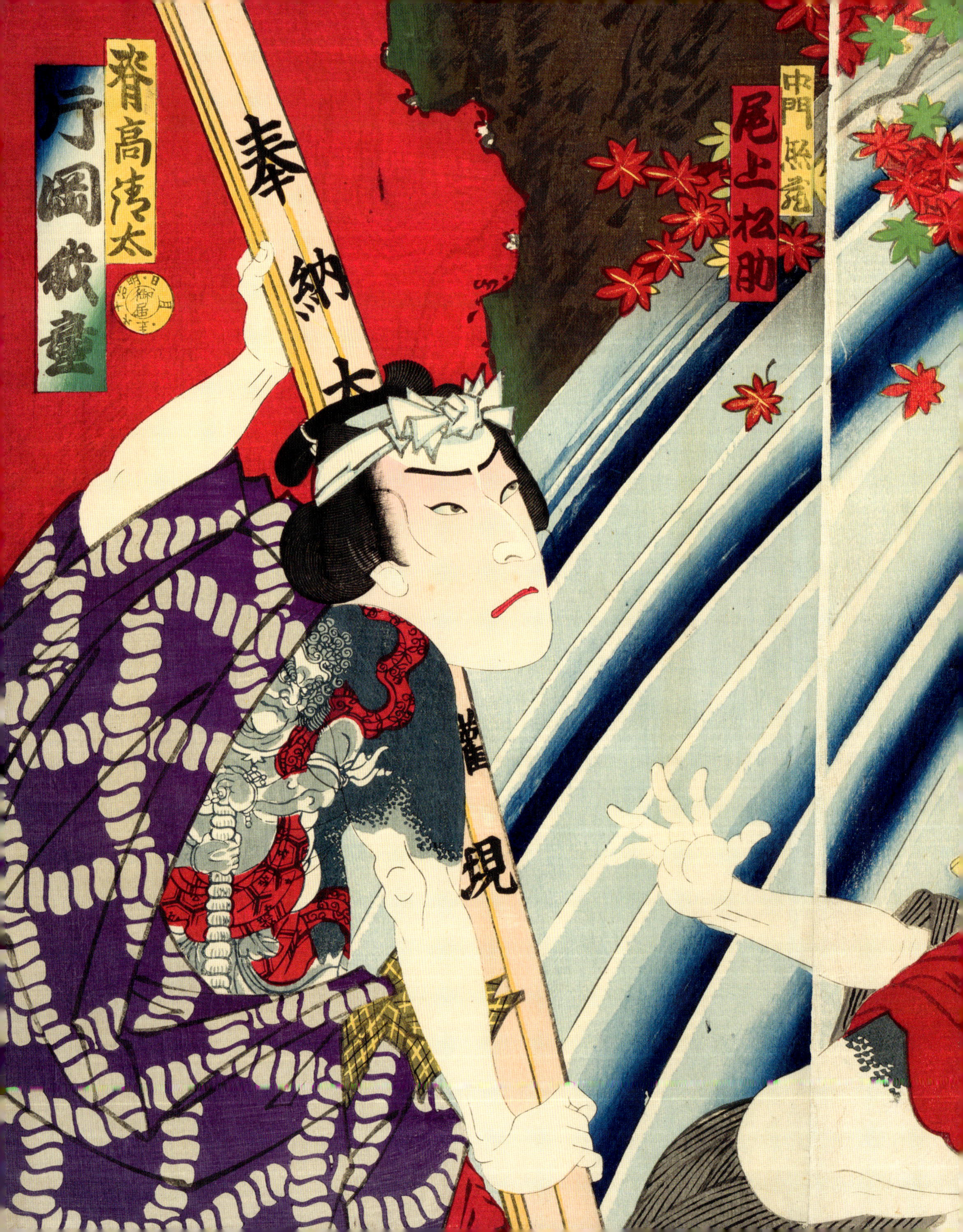

脊高清太
片岡我童
中門照光
尾上松助
奉納大

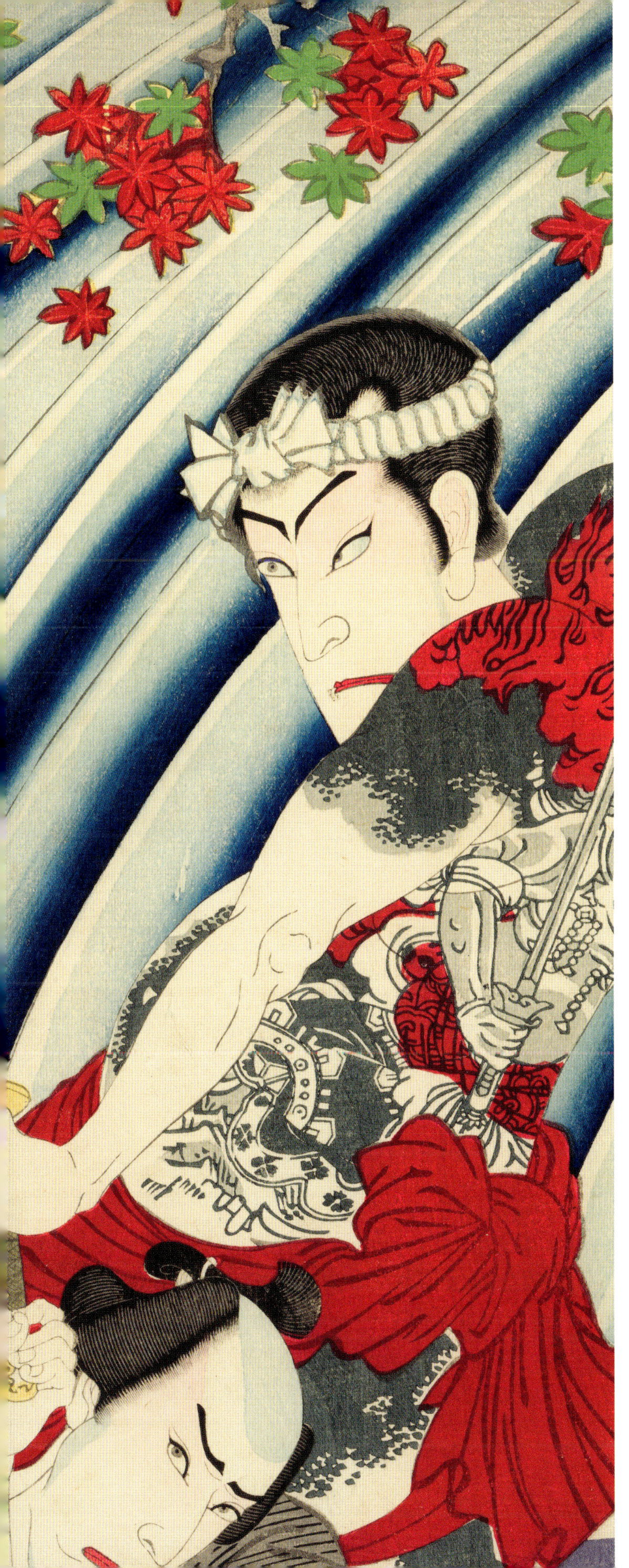

THE TECHNOLOGY OF JAPANESE WOODBLOCK PRINTS

SARAH E. THOMPSON

The use of hand-carved woodblocks to produce multiple impressions of texts and/or pictures has a long history in Japan, from the eighth century CE to the present. Until the twentieth century, printing was a collaborative process, done initially for religious and political reasons, and later for commercial ones. Full-color printing, using a separate block for each color, was inspired by earlier Chinese examples and became common from 1765 on. The version of the process that developed in Japan appears to have been the most efficient and affordable color-printing technology in the world for about a century, prior to the rise of color lithography in Europe in the late nineteenth century. In the early twentieth century, after the function of color woodblock prints as a way of documenting popular culture had been taken over by other media, the prints came to be regarded as a fine art form, often produced entirely by a single artist.

The earliest known use of printing in Japan was the grand imperial project known as the "Million-Pagoda Invocations" (*Hyakumantō darani*), consisting of one million miniature wooden pagodas, each with a short prayer printed on a slip of paper that was rolled up inside the pagoda, produced on the orders of the reigning empress from 764 to 770. Despite this early start, however, printing in Japan developed only very slowly over the following centuries. Printing of devotional texts and images was carried out in Buddhist temples; and after the introduction of the Zen Buddhist sect from China, secular Chinese books for educational purposes were also sometimes printed.

The basic method of preparing woodblocks for printing purposes has remained essentially the same throughout history. A hand-written text or an artist's drawing, on thin paper, is glued face down to a wooden block and dampened with water or a drop of oil, so that the ink lines show clearly through the paper. (If necessary, a little of the paper might be rubbed away from the back at this point.) The block cutter then carefully cuts away a thick layer of wood all around the inked lines, leaving the lines in relief. Expert block cutters can do this so skillfully that the result is a perfect mirror image of the original text or drawing.

The carved woodblock is placed face up on a low table in front of the seated printer and inked as evenly as possible. The printer then carefully places a sheet of paper face down on the block and rubs the back of the paper with a smooth, circular pad, known in Japanese as a *baren*, to take an even impression. No printing press is needed. For the color-printing technique that developed in the eighteenth century, the block of black ink outlines, known as the "key block," was carved first and then used in the same way as the original drawing to make a separate block for printing each color.

The commercialization of printing that began in the seventeenth century added a fourth participant to the process already established by earlier publications. Now, in addition to the artist or calligrapher, the block cutter, and the printer, the publisher became the most important figure of all, the one who hired the other three to produce his products and then sold the results in a bookstore. It was the publisher rather than the artist, calligrapher, or author of a book who had the final say in matters of subject matter, design, and production quality.

Commercial publishing of books intended for the general public became a viable business with the growth of major cities—Edo (modern Tokyo), Kyoto, and Osaka—and the rise of a newly affluent, literate middle class. The consolidation of the rule of the Tokugawa shoguns (hereditary military dictators who ruled in the name of the emperor) in 1615 ended over a century of civil war and ushered in an era of relative peace and prosperity, when urban commoners such as merchants and artisans could accumulate disposal income. Initially the center of printing was Kyoto, the old capital where the emperor still resided; but in the course of the seventeenth century, Kyoto was overtaken by the shogun's city of Edo, now the center of government and commerce.

Woodblock-printed books were published in all of the major Japanese cities, but single-sheet pictorial prints were a specialty of Edo. Individual prints began to be produced toward the end of the seventeenth century as a spin-off from heavily illustrated popular books. Competition between the publishers drove technological change, at first in the form of methods of hand coloring. There were two main types of hand coloring used before the development of color printing, in addition to monochrome prints called *sumizuri-e* (ink-printed pictures). The earliest examples, made from the 1690s to the late 1710s, were called *tan-e* ("red pictures") because the main pigment used was red lead (*tan*), which produced a bright orange-red color.

In about 1718–19, a new kind of print came into fashion, smaller in size but with a wider range of colors, the most prominent among them being a rose-red color made from safflower (*beni*), hence the term *beni-e* ("pink pictures"). Some of the *beni-e* were also called *urushi-e*, literally "lacquer pictures," although there was no actual lacquer involved, because they used a hand-applied shiny black color made by mixing ink with glue. Another special effect sometimes used on *beni-e* prints was gold-colored brass filings, sprinkled over the paper in imitation of the flecks of gold sometimes used to decorate paintings.

Experiments in color printing began in the 1740s, inspired by the beautiful Chinese art books that had been printed in full color in the previous century and were made available in Japan after the ban on importing foreign books (part of the shogunal policy of restricting Japan's access to the outside world, to consolidate their own power) was partially lifted in the 1720s. Since no Japanese were allowed to travel abroad, and the Chinese who came to Japan were merchants rather than printers, the Japanese had to use reverse engineering to reinvent the process for themselves. The key is in the *kento*, guide marks carved in exactly the same places on the edges of each block, so that the printer can place the paper in perfect alignment for each color.

Pictures printed in two or three colors in addition to the black outline—sometimes with the colors overlapping each other to give the illusion of still more colors—were initially in competition with the hand-colored prints but eventually won out. The early color prints came to be called *benizuri-e* (pink-printed pictures) to distinguish them from the hand-colored *beni-e* (although occasionally the term *beni-e* is used, confusingly, for all prints that emphasize the colorant *beni*, whether hand-colored or printed).

The breakthrough to full-color printing, defined as five or more colors in addition to the key block outlines, came in 1765 (or perhaps the very end of 1764) when a group of wealthy merchants who socialized with each other in amateur poetry clubs sponsored the development of practical, large-scale color printing in order to create pictorial calendars for the year 1765 as New Year holiday gifts for their friends. Following the private print runs, publishers appear to have removed the calendar information and printed new editions of the lovely full-color designs for sale to the public. The new prints became known as *nishiki-e* (brocade pictures), an Edo product comparable in their gorgeous, colorful appearance to the famous brocade fabrics of Kyoto.

The *nishiki-e* prints were so satisfactory in combining ease of large-scale production with relative affordability that they continued to be the main visual component of the popular culture until the beginning of the twentieth century. Over this time, print runs gradually went up from hundreds to thousands of impressions, and the prices of individual prints went down. For deluxe editions, or the privately commissioned prints known as *surimono*, special techniques such as metallic pigments, embossing, or shiny backgrounds made with ground mica (stenciled on after the color printing was done), might also be used.

Although the basic technique of woodblock printing remained the same, the nineteenth century saw several innovations in the colorants used. In the late 1820s, the imported synthetic pigment known in English as Prussian blue became cheap enough to use in prints as well as in expensive paintings (suggesting that it may have been manufactured in China as well as Europe). The availability of a beautiful blue color that did not fade quickly was a major factor in the rise of landscape prints in the 1830s. At the beginning of the Meiji era (1868–1912), the pinkish safflower red (*beni*) that had been the standard red colorant for well over a century was replaced by the brighter red of cochineal carmine, an imported colorant made from insects; and, in the 1870s, various synthetic aniline dyes came to be widely used to create the brilliant colors that are considered typical of the era.

By about 1905, woodblock printing as an expression of the popular culture was being replaced by lithographic prints and photographs, in new media such as magazines and postcards. Its revival as a fine art form shortly after that took two forms: *shin hanga* ("new prints") and *sōsaku hanga* ("creative prints"). *Shin hanga* were made by the traditional collaborative process and depicted familiar subjects, but in a new, realistic, Westernized style; whereas *sōsaku hanga* were designed, carved, and printed entirely by the artist and could depict any subject in any style. Japanese printmakers strongly favored the woodblock method through the 1960s, with other print media gradually becoming popular from the 1970s on. Today, woodblock continues to be one of the many different expressive media available to artists making prints.

Further reading

Brown, Kendall. "Prints and Modernity: Developments in the Early Twentieth Century." In Amy Reigle Newland, ed., *The Hotei Encyclopedia of Japanese Woodblock Prints* (Amsterdam: Hotei Publishing, 2005), 277–93.

Hockley, Allen. "Suzuki Harunobu: The Cult and Culture of Color." In Julia Meech and Jane Oliver, eds., *Designed for Pleasure: The World of Edo Japan in Prints and Paintings, 1680–1860* (Seattle and London: Asia Society and Japanese Art Society of America in association with University of Washington Press, 2008), pp. 82–99.

Kornicki, Peter. *The Book in Japan: A Cultural History from the Beginnings to the Nineteenth Century* (Leiden: Brill, 1998; paperback edition, Honolulu: University of Hawai'i Press, 2001).

Salter, Rebecca. *Japanese Woodblock Printing* (London: A. & C. Black, 2001; paperback edition, Honolulu: University of Hawai'i Press, 2002).

Smith, Henry D., II. "Hokusai and the Blue Revolution in Edo Prints." In John T. Carpenter, ed., *Hokusai and His Age: Ukiyo-e Painting, Printmaking, and Book Illustration in Late Edo Japan* (Amsterdam: Hotei Publishing, 2005), 234–69.

Smith, Henry D., II. "The True Colors of Meiji Prints: Science Tells a Different Story." *Impressions: The Journal of the Japanese Art Society of America* 44, Part 2 (2023): 126–51.

Kitao Shigemasa and Katsukawa Shunshō, *Courtesans of the Ōkaneya*, 1776 (detail)

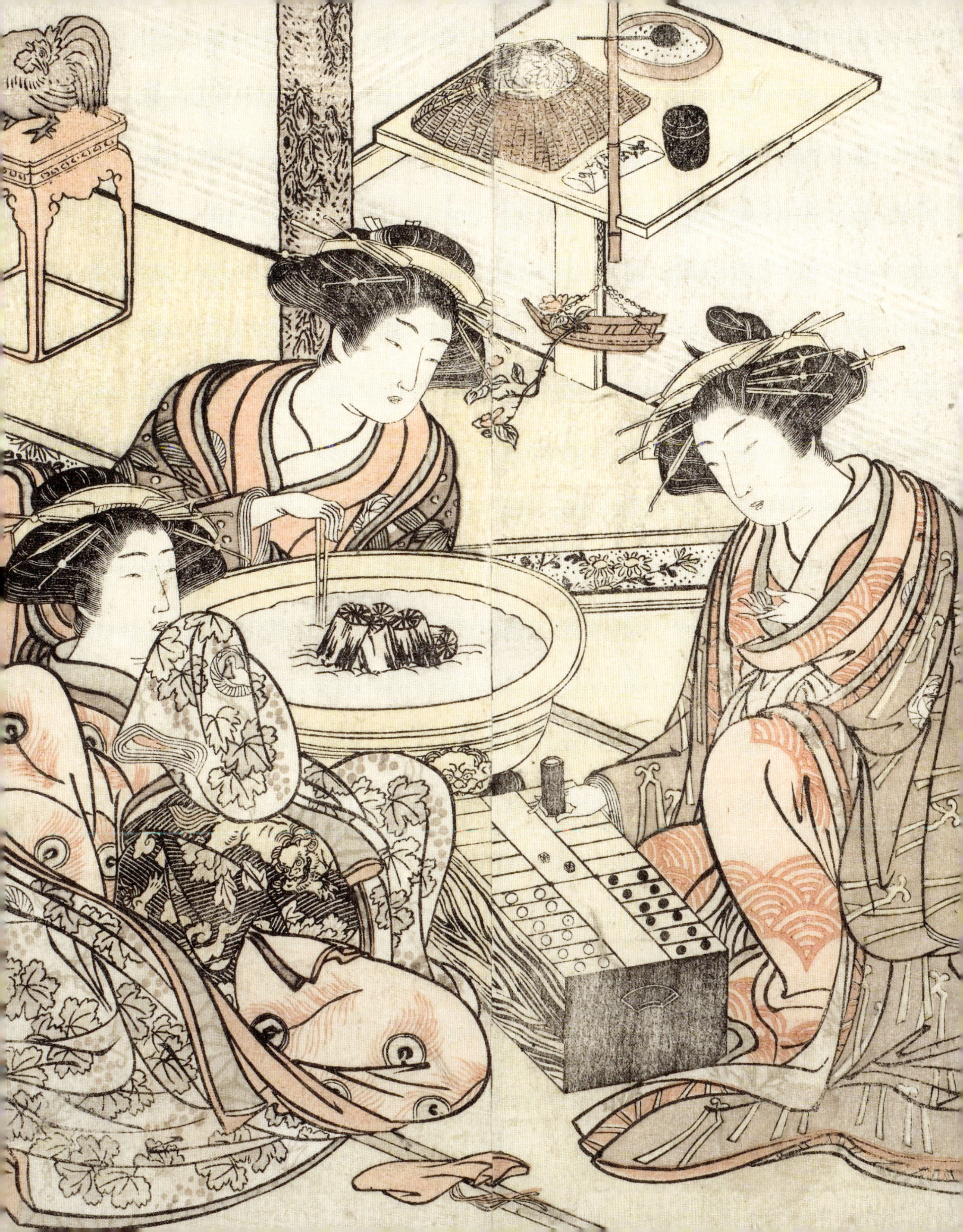

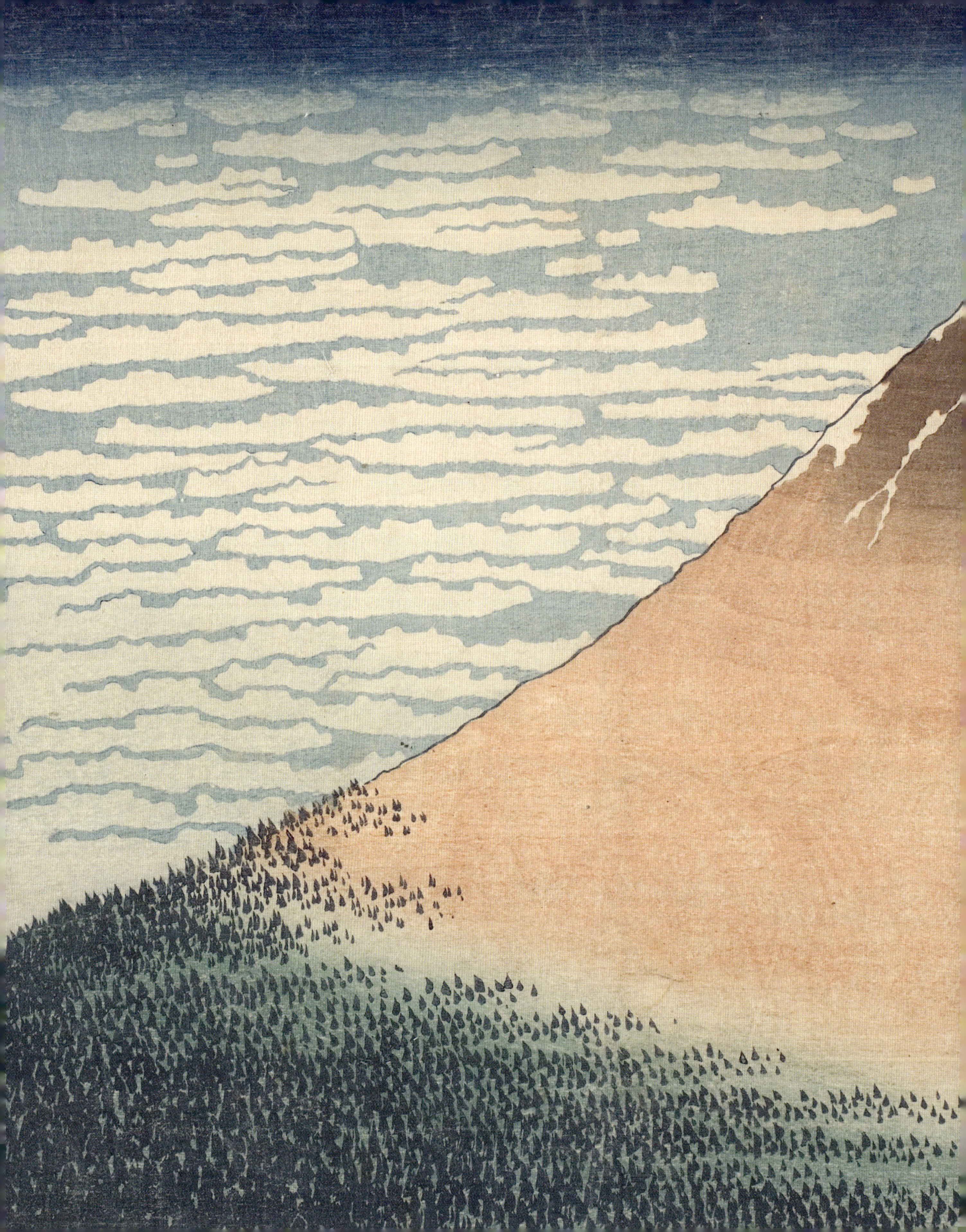

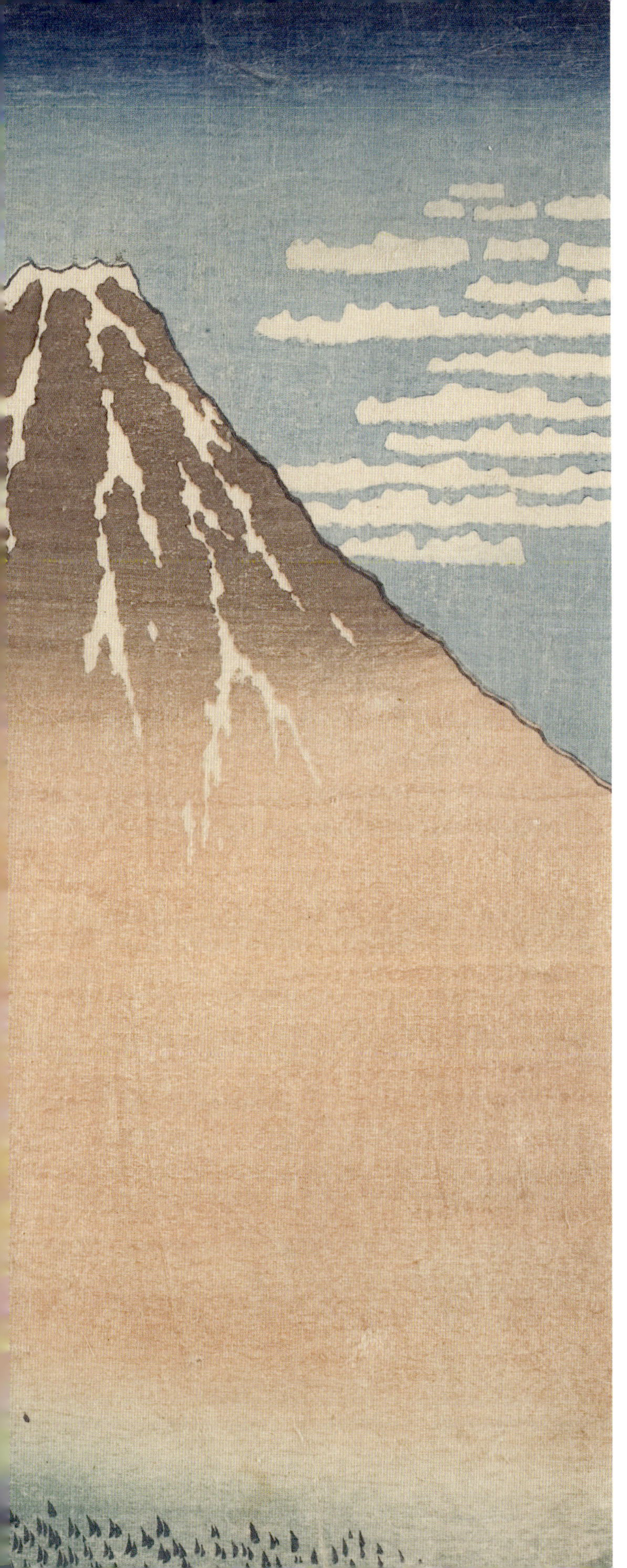

FAMOUS PLACES: JAPANESE WOODBLOCK PRINTS AT THE WORCESTER ART MUSEUM

QUINTANA HEATHMAN SCHERER

At the start of the seventeenth century, Edo, now known as Tokyo, was a quiet castle town. That would all change when Tokugawa Ieyasu became shogun, Japan's supreme military leader, and chose the city as his seat of power. To maintain control over his vassals around Japan, he implemented the *sankin-kōtai* policy that required regional feudal lords called *daimyo* (and their numerous retainers) to spend alternate years in Edo. The growth of this new population resulted in the city developing rapidly into a place of major political and cultural importance.

As the city grew, a sophisticated urban culture emerged. The shogun's official neo-Confucian policies divided people into rigid classes, but a growing economy meant that the commoners at the lower strata of society prospered. In this new space, the *ukiyo* developed—a world of urbane pleasures such as the kabuki theater and the Yoshiwara licensed brothel district. The term represented the mentality of the Edo *chōnin* (townspeople); *ukiyo* is a homonym for the Buddhist term referring to a "world of sadness," with the characters changed to mean a "floating world," where one enjoyed the fleeting and earthly pleasures of human life. As the *ukiyo* developed, so did *ukiyo-e* ("pictures of the floating world"), artworks celebrating the lively character of city life.

Many places associated with this floating world soon became *meisho*, literally a "named place" or famous site. Before the Tokugawa rise to power and the growth of Edo, most *meisho* were associated with the lengthy poetic history of places in and around the imperial court of Kyoto.[1] As *ukiyo-e* developed, these celebrated sites of early modern Edo became staple subjects of the genre, a tradition that continued to influence woodblock printing into the modern period.

Early spaces in the floating world

In the earliest days of *ukiyo-e* print publishing, the celebrities of the kabuki stage and the beautiful courtesans of the Yoshiwara reigned supreme. Their visages were a staple of the woodblock print industry, but the spaces these stars inhabited were soon celebrated as well. Perhaps no one place in Edo captivated the imagination of the public more than the Yoshiwara, the licensed brothel district located in the northern outskirts of the city. A remote, walled area whose finest establishments were accessible to only the wealthiest and most cultured patrons, the Yoshiwara and its inhabitants quickly inspired content for guidebooks, single-sheet prints, and erotica—the earliest products of the *ukiyo-e* print industry. Guidebooks to the Yoshiwara provided useful information for Edo's new inhabitants as well as locals who needed aids to navigate the arcane customs of the brothels. Early *ukiyo-e* images centered on idealized young beauties (*bijin*) of the pleasure quarters, appealing to potential patrons of the high-ranking prostitutes or those who could not make the journey themselves.

The first plate in this catalogue is an impression from "Appearance of the Yoshiwara" (*Yoshiwara no tei*), a set of album prints published 1681–84 by early *ukiyo-e* innovator Hishikawa Moronobu. These prints give viewers a sense of the journey to the quarter and titillate them with pictures of experiences that were out of reach for average people. Titled *Merrymaking in a House of Assignation*, it provides a glimpse into an upscale *ageya*, a teahouse where courtesans could meet their clients. In Moronobu's print, a party can be seen in a luxuriously appointed room, enlivened by song and dance. The Yoshiwara was one of Moronobu's defining subjects, and the images in *Yoshiwara no tei* were derived from an earlier narrative guidebook, a common practice in *ukiyo-e* prints that reinforced certain sites and motifs within the genre.[2]

Later works, such as the book *A Mirror of Beautiful Women of the Green Houses Compared* (*Seirō bijin awase sugata kagami*), illustrated by Kitao Shigemasa and Katsukawa Shunshō, make use of the introduction of full-color printing (*nishiki-e* or "brocade prints") to create sumptuous images of this rarified place. The pages of the book provide stunning views of lavishly decorated interiors, perpetuating the upscale image of important Yoshiwara brothels and their courtesans. Each figure is accompanied by text that is purportedly in their own handwriting, to give viewers a sense of personal access to these famous prostitutes (see p. 42).

A codified courtesan ranking system and annual critiques encouraged brothels to enhanced their reputations. As such, the production of publications like this one was likely supported by the brothels themselves, a shrewd collaboration with *ukiyo-e* publishers as they sought to enhance the romantic appeal of the place, setting it apart from their unlicensed competition.[3] Such prints not only romanticized the harsh realities faced by the women working in the sex industry of the Yoshiwara but also burnished the reputation of the district in the minds of locals and tourists alike.

Urban landscapes: new perspectives of Edo in the eighteenth century

As the eighteenth century progressed, Edo grew, reaching a population of 1.3 million by 1720 and 1.34 million by the beginning of the nineteenth century.[4] The locales depicted in *ukiyo-e* expanded, with more sites of urban amusements singled out for praise. Additionally, as *nishiki-e* printing was introduced to single-sheet printing around 1765, more elaborate, colorful prints created engaging images of the new cosmopolitan world. Though landscape scenes had frequently been a part of earlier printed travel guides, in single-sheet prints the introduction of newly imported techniques helped popularize the *meisho-e* (images of famous places).

For example, Utagawa Toyoharu, founder of the Utagawa school, used Western-style single-point perspective originally adapted from imported foreign artworks, which were brought in limited numbers to Nagasaki, creating *uki-e* ("floating images" or perspective prints) of popular outdoor urban spaces and architectural settings. In his view of Ryōgoku Bridge, the unusual perspective amplifies the hordes of people, numerous shops, and lively attractions, creating a charming, chaotic scene (fig. 1).[5] The viewer is prompted to marvel not only at Toyoharu's innovation but also the site's characteristic crowds, which were celebrated in contemporary texts as being so large that all the houses of the provinces appeared to have emptied onto the bridge.[6]

Famous shops and restaurants also appeared frequently in prints, their popularity a testament to the importance of commercial pleasures and pastimes in the urban landscape. In Torii Kiyonaga's triptych of fashionable young people out for a stroll on New Year's Day (pp. 44–45), the artist uses the same technique as Toyoharu to depict the Surugachō area of Edo. The broad, shop-lined street recedes in *uki-e* fashion into an auspicious view of Mount Fuji, while a local shop's signage is placed conspicuously, the logo of the famed Echigoya shop clearly visible. It advertises fine silk and cotton garments, undoubtably similar to the beautiful kimono worn by the attractive figures in the foreground. Echigoya, which was founded in 1673, appears frequently in prints of the area, and its popularity continued into the modern period when it would develop into the Mitsukoshi department store.[7]

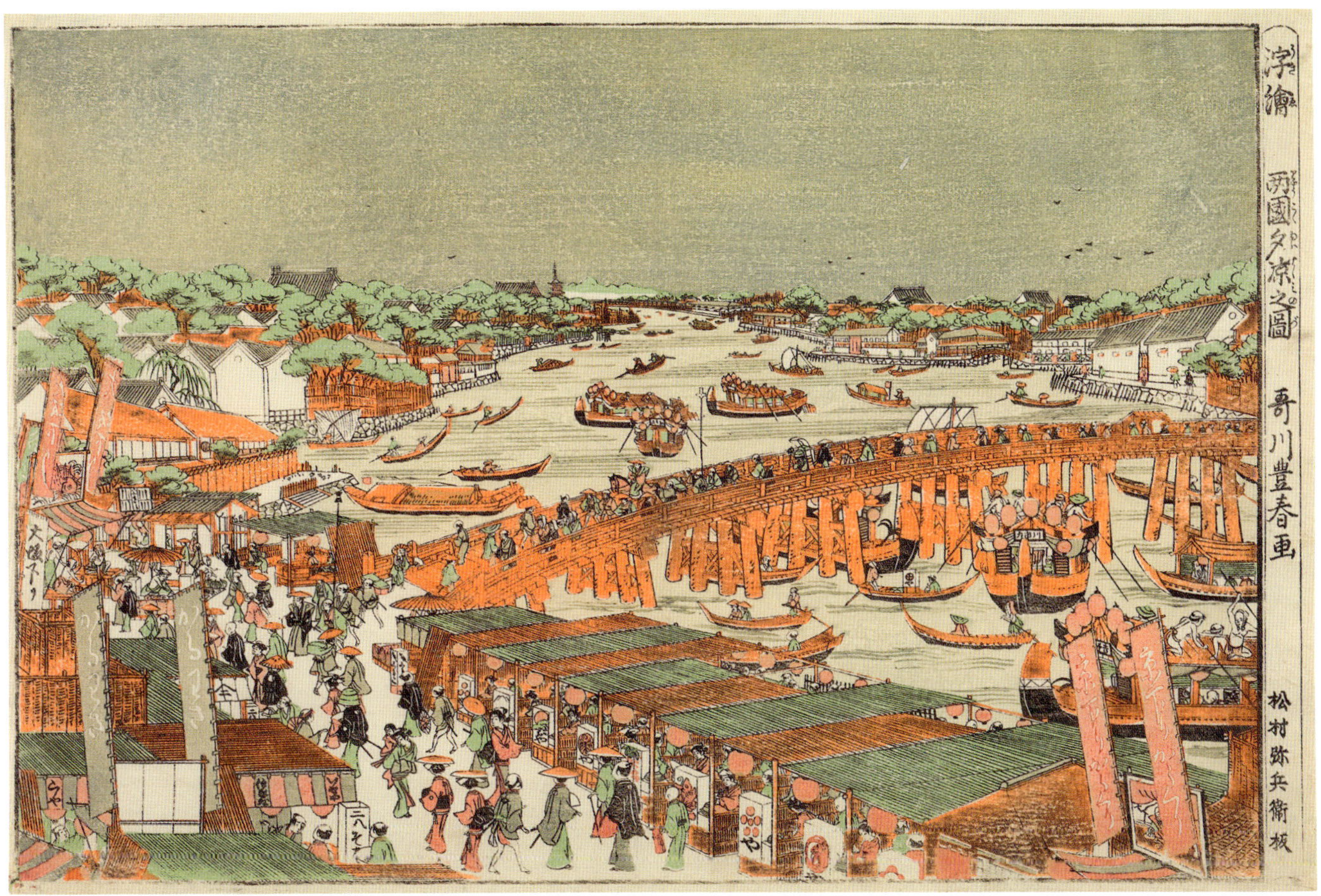

Nineteenth-century landscapes: journeys through Japan

Artists such as Katsushika Hokusai and Utagawa Hiroshige took *meisho-e* in new and unusual directions in the nineteenth century, creating inventive compositions and making excellent use of the now highly developed color-printing technologies. Invigorated by townspeople's increasing interest in domestic travel, these artists (and their savvy publishers) increasingly included images of popular destinations along the country's major highways. Their now-iconic prints of *meisho* have proven to be enduring images of Japan.

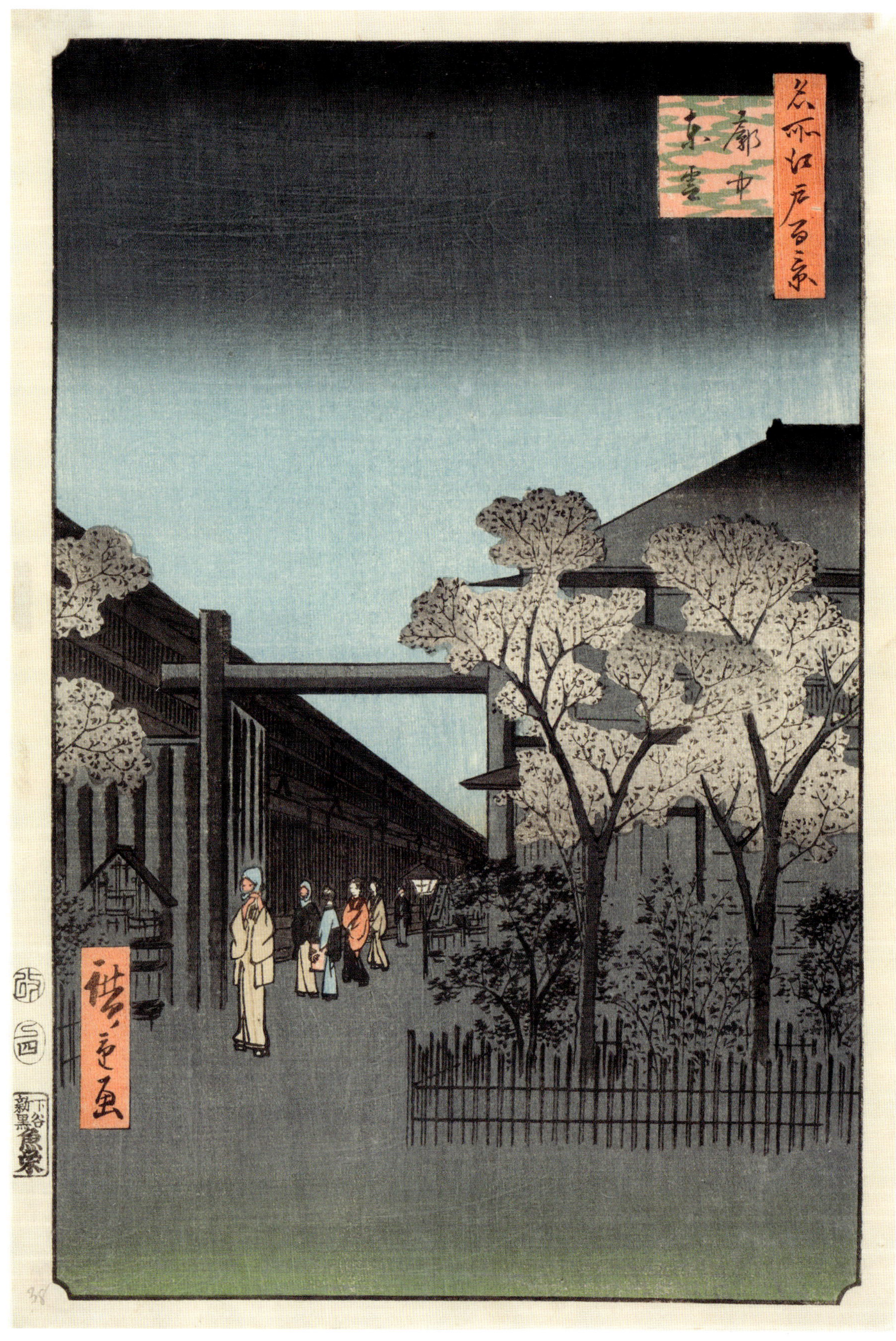

Katsushika Hokusai, whose imaginative and amusing designs have inspired innumerable artists around the world, is perhaps best known for his images of Mount Fuji. A sacred mountain long celebrated in poetry and painting in Japan, the iconic landmark was a significant focus for Hokusai, though he designed his "Thirty-six Views of Mount Fuji" (*Fugaku sanjūrokkei*) much later in life. The series eschews established approaches to the landscape and instead becomes a vehicle for Hokusai's creativity, as well as a means of showcasing the newly imported *bero-ai* or Prussian blue pigment. Hokusai's prints show the mountain from different locales and in different seasons. Fuji is sometimes almost hidden, a small feature in the backdrop to human activities, while in other prints it takes center stage. One such example is *South Wind, Clear Sky (Gaifūkaisei)*, where the iconic shape of the mountain fills the composition, rendered in gentle shades of pinkish red as the sun lights up the slope at dawn (see p. 76).[8] Hokusai's inventive approach to this classical *meisho* resonated with the print-buying public—the series was so popular that an additional ten prints were published, including many of the most recognizable images of Japan today, such as *The Great Wave*, which now appears on the Japanese 1,000-yen bill.

During the same period, Utagawa Hiroshige breathed new life into the *uki-e* style used by Toyoharu and others by creating an exaggerated version of forced perspective to create dramatic contrasts between foreground and background. His first popular series featured images of the famous stations along the Tōkaidō Eastern Sea Road. At the end of his life, he turned his attention to Edo in his ambitious "One Hundred Famous Views of Edo" (*Meisho Edo hyakkei*), which includes an impressive 118 famous sites. Its production extended after his death, with the last prints completed by his student, Hiroshige II. In *Plum Estate at Kameido (Kameido Umeyashiki)* (see p. 87), the view of the popular Umeyashiki gardens is interrupted by a tree branch belonging to the famous Sleeping Dragon Plum in the extreme foreground. The dramatic composition is further enlivened by the striking reddish pink sunset sky rendered in skillfully executed *bokashi* gradation. Other prints from the series, such as *Dawn inside the Yoshiwara (Kakuchū shinonome)*, used forced perspective and evocative colors similarly to create fresh images of familiar, iconic sites of Edo, in this case the Yoshiwara's main gate. Instead of the bustling quarter frequently depicted, the scene is one of quiet moodiness as customers and courtesans part in the morning silence (fig. 2).

The new world of the modern woodblock print

After the arrival of American Commodore Matthew Perry, Japan ended its official policy
of national seclusion in 1854, and Japanese prints were exported widely around the world
in the nineteenth and early twentieth centuries. Foreign artists and collectors alike were
charmed by *ukiyo-e*, which famously influenced impressionist painters and fed the craze
for all things Japanese (*japonisme*). *Meisho-e* were particularly desirable: Hiroshige was
a favorite of Worcester Art Museum's John Chandler Bancroft, an amateur landscape
artist himself. Hiroshige's innovative approach to landscape composition and color was
also inspirational to later foreign artists, such as James McNeill Whistler and Vincent
van Gogh.[9]

The Meiji (1868–1912) and Taishō (1912–1926) periods rapidly introduced new print
technologies, global influences, and artistic inspirations. Woodblock print designers
embraced new subjects as Japan entered the Meiji period, not only including images of
modern customs, but also of war as Japan engaged in several international conflicts.
However, woodblock print technology was increasingly outdated, as photography and
lithography became the new standard for inexpensive printed material. Furthermore, as
artists around the world began to reevaluate the role of the artist and art in society,
print artists also sought ways to center self-expression in a medium that had traditionally
been a collaborative production process between the artist, carver, printer, and publisher.
Thus, the woodblock print medium was sent in numerous directions, with some artists and
publishers returning to traditional modes, while others sought new forms.

One of the most popular print movements to emerge in the early twentieth century was
shin hanga ("new prints") guided by publisher Watanabe Shōzaburō, who revived *ukiyo-e*
traditions in an effort to appeal to foreign collectors. Produced in a collaborative manner,
the subjects harkened back to Edo period conventions, featuring mainly images of beautiful
women and idyllic landscapes—often without the intrusion of the reality of a modern Japan.
The artists hired by Shōzaburō had fresh approaches to the long-established subjects,
which proved popular with foreign customers. Yoshida Hiroshi, an influential *shin hanga*
artist, used his training in Western-style painting to create fresh images of the Sumida
River (see pp. 110–111). Taking on a watercolor-like quality, the famed river of Tokyo is
depicted at different times of day through subtle changes in the color schemes in multiple

versions. The Sumida River was an established *meisho*, and frequently appeared in Edo period *ukiyo-e* prints, but Yoshida Hiroshi's versions make clever use of the woodblock technology to show the natural variations of the landscape.

Still, woodblock print artists began to increasingly move further from the conventions of *ukiyo-e*. Approaches to art creation were changing globally, and print artists began to assert control over the printmaking process of *ukiyo-e* and s*hin hanga.* Print subjects and styles changed as well, with artists eschewing the conventional, *ukiyo-e* inspired, carefully executed landscapes and beauties, instead embracing the expressive and abstract trends seen more broadly in artmaking. *Sōsaku hanga* ("creative print") artists of the early twentieth century handled print production independently as a way of changing the woodblock medium from a commercial process to one of artistic self-expression. Even Yoshida Hiroshi, who enjoyed success as a *shin hanga* artist publishing with Shōzaburō, began his own publishing studio in the 1920s to oversee the entire printing process carefully, a methodology later adopted by other members of his family.

Sōsaku hanga works were often deeply personal and even abstract, reflecting an artist-centered approach. However, personal expression and landscape could still be deeply intertwined. In 1945, immediately after the ending of World War II, sōsaku hanga artists in the Nihon hanga kyōkai (Japanese Print Association) published the portfolio *Tōkyō kaikō zue* (rendered in English as "Scenes of Last Tokyo"). Individually, the prints are a nostalgic look at prewar Tokyo, yet untouched by the Allied bombings and the hardships of war, such as Hiratsuka's Un'ichi's print of Sukiyabashi (see pp. 31 and 114). However, the portfolio, along with its introduction written by the artist Onchi Kōshirō, places an emphasis on sites of imperial importance, making landscapes into symbols of the trauma of the war and the political ideology of the day.[10]

In the postwar period, abstraction in woodblock prints became increasingly influential, and Yoshida Hiroshi's daughter-in-law Yoshida Chizuko—influenced by *sōsaku hanga* innovators as well as modernist principles—took an aesthetic approach that differed greatly from earlier artists in her family (see p. 117). Her depiction of the Muroji Temple, a religious site long famous for accepting female worshipers, transformed a stone path into a study in abstracted geometric forms and colors. Though technically still a "named place," the true focus of the work is not the landscape, but Chizuko's deft use of color, shape, and texture. Works such as these were championed by many American print enthusiasts and were quickly collected abroad—the Worcester Art Museum's impression entered the collection in 1954, just a year after it was printed.

These modern interpretations of subjects that have inspired artists since the early years of *ukiyo-e* represent the latest development on a continuum. Even as they embraced new modes of representation, Japanese woodblock prints recalled the rich history of depicting cultural sites that have been focal points in Japan's history. Their enduring appeal among foreign collectors, both individual and institutional, ensured that their legacy expanded far beyond Japan's borders, becoming a nexus of international artistic and cultural dialogues. As their influence continues to exponentially grow and change, the medium's historical and aesthetic continuity remains a significant aspect of its appeal, bridging traditional and modern styles to captivate new audiences while honoring its heritage.

NOTES

1. For more on *meisho-e* and the development of landscape painting, see Chino Kaori, "Meisho-e no seiritsu to tenkai," in *Nihon byōbu-e shūsei 10: Keibutsuga, Meisho keibutsu*, ed. Takeda Tsuneo (Tokyo: Kōdansha, 1980), 115–21.

2. As David Waterhouse makes clear, the images in *Yoshiwara no tei* are derived from Moronobu's *A Guide to Love in the Yoshiwara* (*Yoshiwara koi no michibiki*), a narrative guidebook published in 1678. For further discussion of Moronobu's depictions of the Yoshiwara in print and painting, see David Waterhouse, "Hishikawa Moronobu: Tracking Down an Elusive Master," in *Designed for Pleasure: The World of Edo Japan in Prints and Paintings, 1680–1868*, ed. Julia Meech and Jane Oliver (Seattle and London: Asia Society and Japanese Art Society of America in association with University of Washington Press, 2008), 33–55.

3. As Julie Nelson Davis argues, Shigemasa and Shunshō's book was a luxurious, collaborative work whose main purpose was to enhance the image of the Yoshiwara and benefit the brothels therein. See Julie Nelson Davis, "Picturing Beauties," in *Partners in Print* (Honolulu: University of Hawaii Press, 2015), 61–107.

4. Yazaki Takeo, *Social Change and the City in Japan, from Earliest Times through the Industrial Revolution* (Tokyo: Japan Publications, 1968), 134. Naito Akira, *Edo: The City that Became Tokyo* (Tokyo: Kodansha, 2003), 178.

5. As argued by Timon Screech, the introduction of Western single-point perspective was seen less as a method of creating naturalistic landscapes and more as a novel method of exaggeration. Timon Screech, "The Meaning of Western Perspective in Edo Popular Culture," *Archives of Asian Art* 47 (1994): 58–69.

6. Hiraga Gennai, *Nenashigusa* (*Rootless Weeds*), in *Hiraga Gennai Shū*, ed. Tsukamoto Tetsuzō (Tokyo: Yūhōdō Shoten, 1917), 263.

7. *Mitsui Takatoshi to Echigoya: Mitsuika sōgyōki no jigyō to bunka* (Mitsui Memorial Museum, 2023), 3.

8. It has been noted that the gentle pink color, such as in WAM's impression, is likely to be earlier than the brighter red impressions, representing the initial artistic intentions. Roger S. Keyes, "Pink Fuji: The Print Hokusai Saw," *Impressions* 29 (2007–8): 68–75.

9. See Fiona Collins, "The Floating World through the Eyes of John Chandler Bancroft: The Founding of the Worcester Art Museum's Japanese Print Collection," *Orientations Magazine*, March/April 2024.

10. According to Lawrence Smith, Onchi's introduction and the selection of locations important to the imperial state makes the portfolio a work that could speak to the Japanese reader as a "coded message," reinforcing the revered status of the emperor. Lawrence Smith, *Japanese Prints during the Allied Occupation, 1945–1952* (Chicago: Art Media Resources, 2002), 23–26.

Un'ichi Hiratsuka, *Sukiya Bridge*, from the series "Scenes of Lost Tokyo", 1945 (detail)

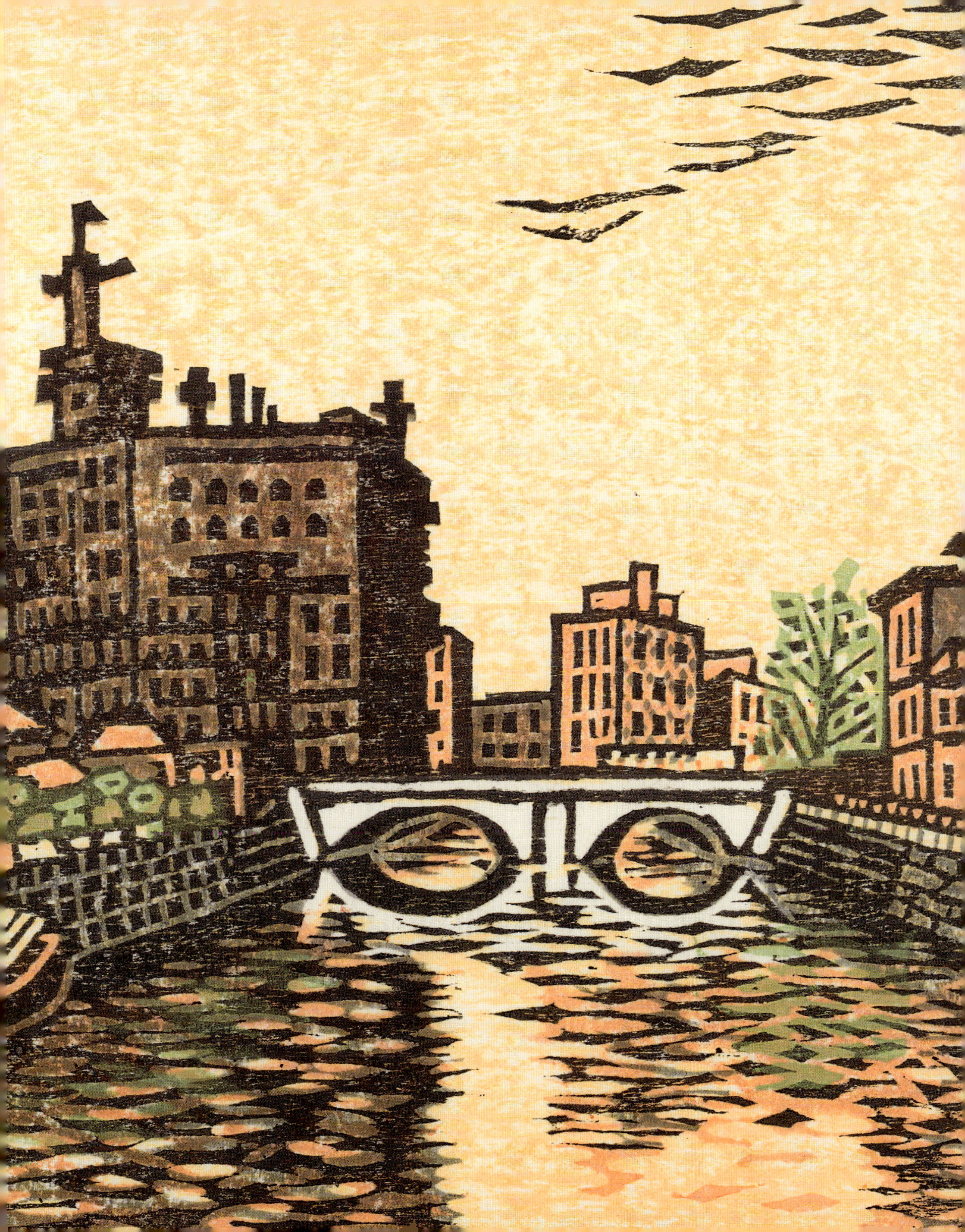

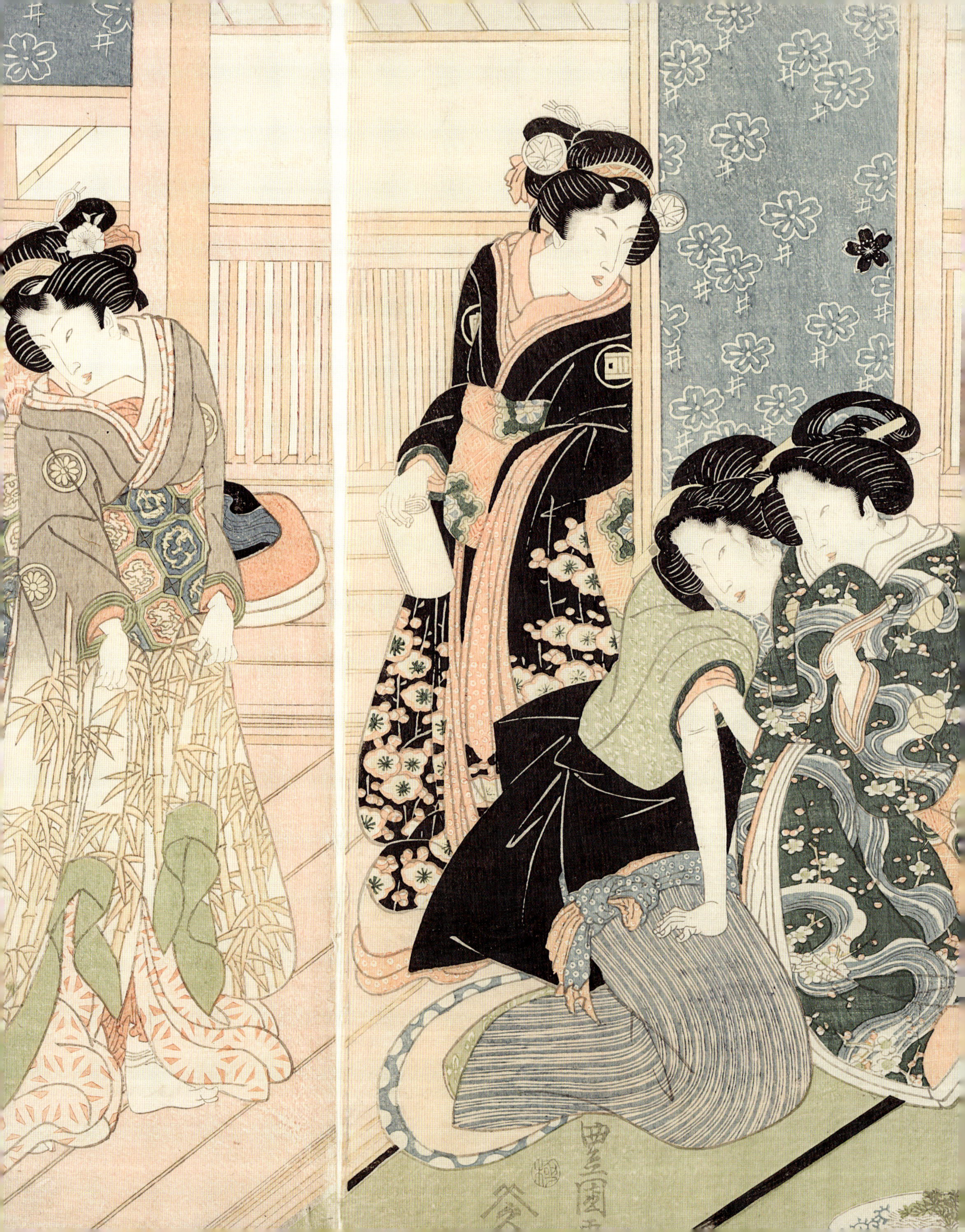

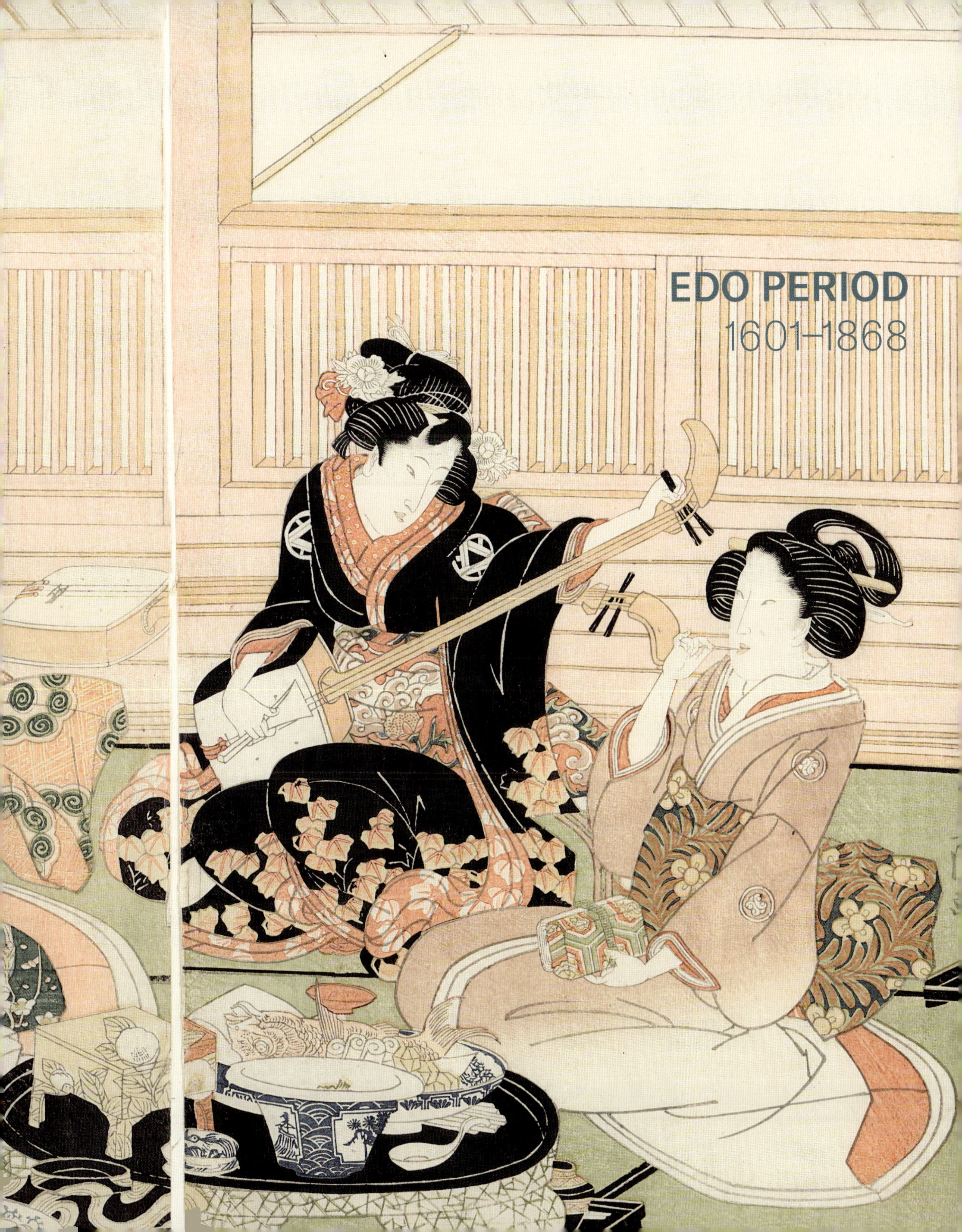
EDO PERIOD
1601–1868

HISHIKAWA MORONOBU

(1618–1694)

Merrymaking in a House of Assignation, from the series "Appearance of the Yoshiwara", 1681–84

Publisher: Yamagataya Ichirōemon
Woodblock-printed album sheet
Ōban: 26.2 × 37.3 cm (10⁵⁄₁₆ × 14¹¹⁄₁₆ in.)
John Chandler Bancroft Collection, 1901.59.2250

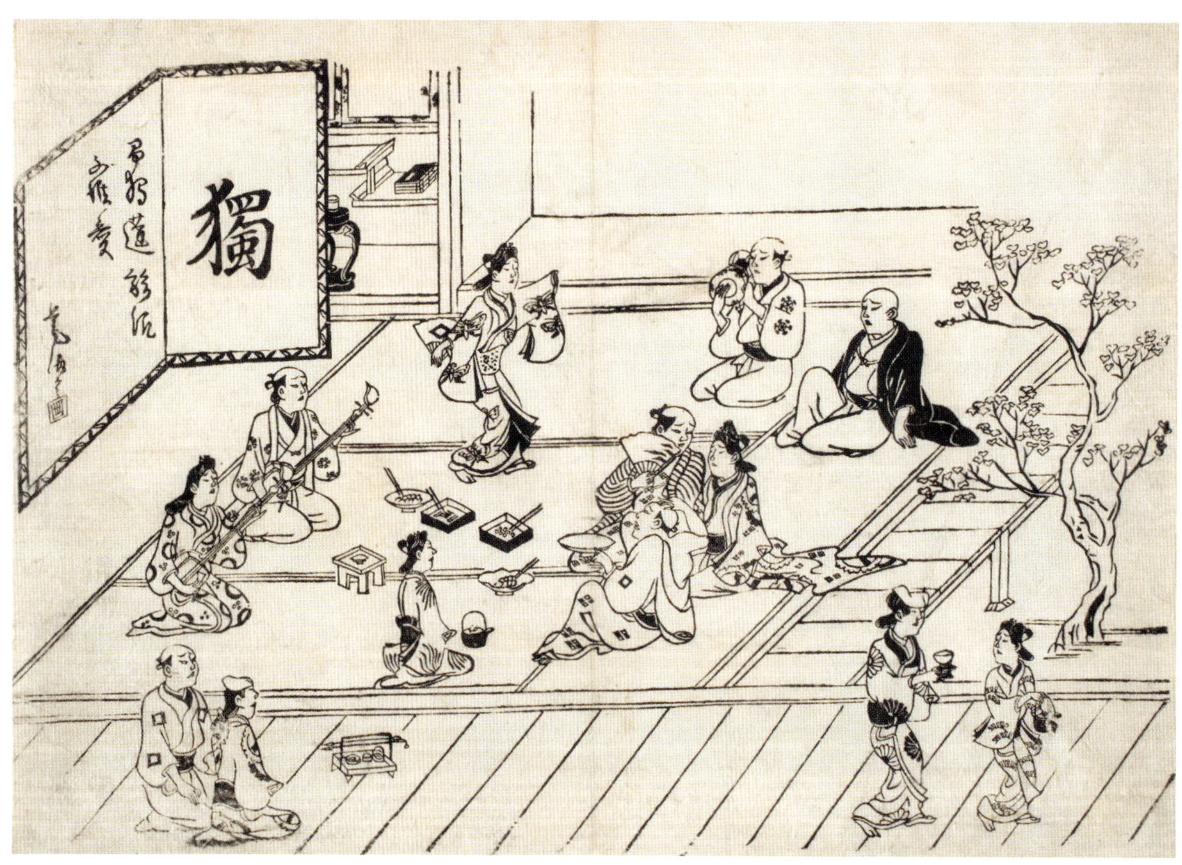

Before the Edo period, woodblock printing was predominantly used by religious institutions such as Buddhist temples to print prayers and sutras. The technique continued to be used occasionally for functional, artistic, and commercial purposes until the seventeenth century. Hishikawa Moronobu was among the first to embrace print as a vehicle for _ukiyo-e_, a genre which centered on quotidian subjects from Edo's urban demimonde known as "the floating world."

Merrymaking in a House of Assignation comes from a series of twelve prints centering on the Yoshiwara, the licensed "pleasure quarters" of Edo where one could pursue entertainment in establishments like brothels, theaters, and teahouses. Its subject is a lively banquet whose diversions include a captivating woman dancing in front of a two-panel folding screen and musicians playing a _tsuzumi_ shoulder drum and two shamisen. Moronobu masterfully portrays this scene in suspended animation, with all of the figures captured in the midst of conversation or in midstride, conveying a sense of dynamic energy and joy. It was created using the earliest form of printmaking in Japan—_sumizuri-e_, black and white images printed using a single woodblock.

TORII KIYONOBU I

(1664–1729)

Actor Sawamura Kodenji I as Tsuyu no Mae, 1698, third month

Publisher: Hangiya Shichirōbei
Woodblock print with hand-applied color
Ō-ōban: 53.2 × 30.9 cm (20¹⁵⁄₁₆ × 12³⁄₁₆ in.)
John Chandler Bancroft Collection, 1901.59

Torii Kiyonobu's prints—renowned for their vibrant, graphic style and idealized figures—were heavily influenced by his work creating large signs advertising kabuki, a popular theatrical art form that blends drama, music, dance, and elaborate costumes and was enjoyed by urban audiences during the Edo period. This large sheet with hand-applied color, considered the earliest extant *yakusha-e* (print portraying a kabuki actor) in the world, depicts the star *onnagata* (male actor specializing in female roles) Sawamura Kodenji I in his captivating performance in the drama *Kantō Koroku,* which debuted during the third lunar month of 1698 at the Nakamura theater in Edo. He is in his role of Tsuyu no Mae, caught in the moment that the character performs a poignant *kyoran,* or lunatic dance, triggered by the unyielding societal expectations that prevent her from being with the one she loves. Torii Kiyonobu's composition masterfully captures the way the actor's robes flowed while performing the dance, and underscores the character's physical and emotional isolation, with the Tadasu Shrine (where the play is set) floating in the background like a mirage. Although the figure is highly stylized, the multiple black circles adorning Kodenji's robes can be recognized as his unique actor crest.

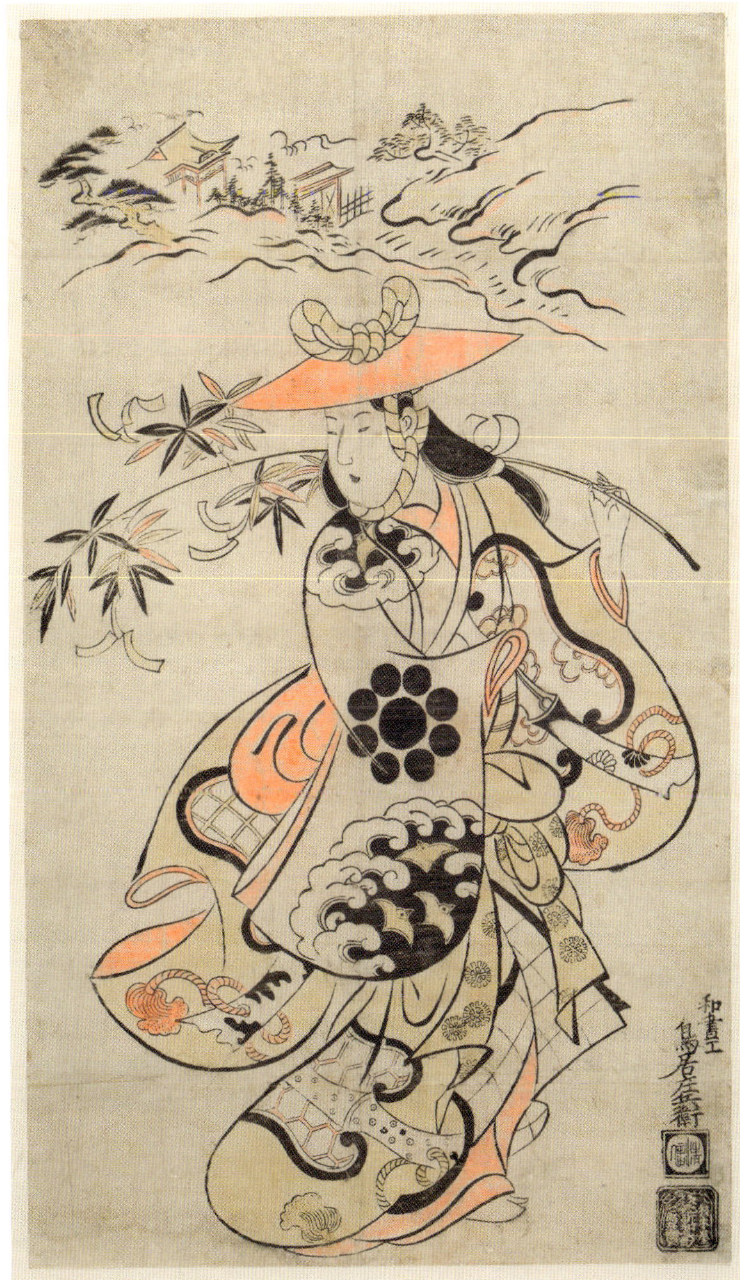

ATTRIBUTED TO SUGIMURA JIHEI

(active ca. 1680–1703)

Retrieving the Jewel from the Dragon King's Palace, ca. 1685–ca. 1690

Woodblock print with hand coloring
52.7 × 60.4 cm (20¾ × 23¾ in.)
John Chandler Bancroft Collection, 1901.59.2

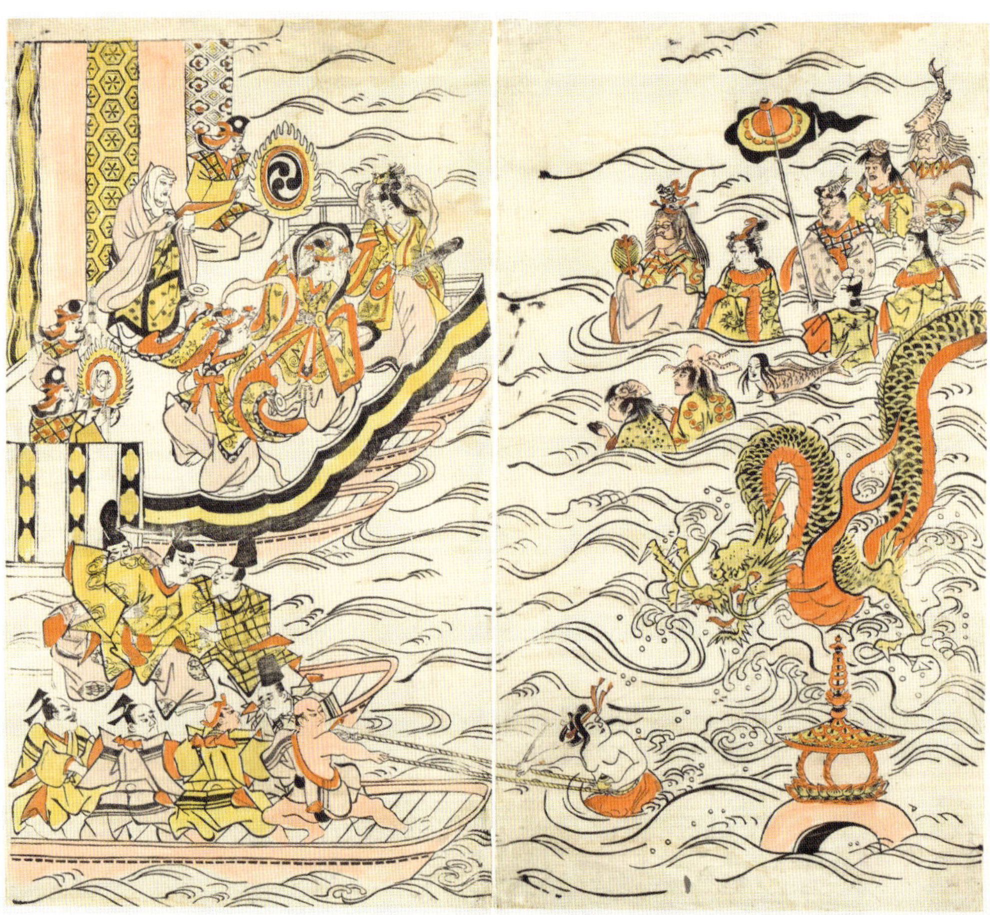

This hand-colored print called a *tan-e* illustrates the climactic moment of the famous *Tamatori monogatari* (*The Tale of the Taking of the Jewel*). In the story, a mythical emperor of the Chinese Tang dynasty (618–907) sent three rare treasures as an offering to the Kofuku temple in Nara. One of these was a magic wishing gem, or *tama*. When the ship carrying the offerings was sailing through Japanese waters, the Dragon King emerged from his dwelling in the deep sea and stole the gem. The young hero

Kaminari asked his lover, a shellfish diver, or *ama*, to use her skills to enter the underwater palace and retrieve it. This print shows the moment after she resurfaces from her mission, the *tama* in her left hand, and is pursued by the Dragon King and his army of hybrid creatures. Kamatari watches with concern as a nearby boat pulls his lover to safety. This legend inspired the Noh play *Ama*, which emphasizes the sacrifice of the diver, popularly known as *tamatori-hime* or the "jewel-taking princess."

OKUMURA MASANOBU

(1686–1764)

The Demon Queller Zhong Kui (Shōki or Sho Ki), ca. 1745

Woodblock print: ink on paper
Hashira-e: 62.2 × 9.5 cm (24½ × 3¾ in.)
John Chandler Bancroft Collection, 1901.1201

According to legend, the spirit Zhong Kui, or Shōki, as he was
known in Japanese, earned the title of "demon queller" after
he drove away the evil phantoms that had been haunting the
dreams of the Chinese emperor Xuanzong (685–762 CE) of
the Tang dynasty. In this print, Okumura Masanobu chooses
to depict Zhong Kui in the moment before he charges at the
demons. The figure is captured in midstride, his intense gaze
locked on an unseen target before him, as his exaggerated
features crackle with palpable rage. To maximize the sense of
movement and energy within the limiting pillar-print format,
Masanobu added *nikawa* glue to the ink to enhance the bold
black lines. Although this *urushi-e* ("lacquer picture") method
had been used in painting and ceramics for centuries, he is
believed to be the first to adapt it to print.

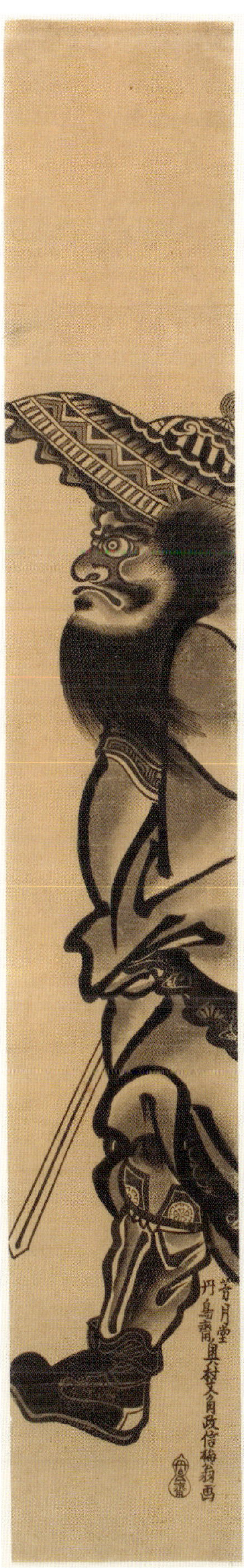

ATTRIBUTED TO FURUYAMA MOROMASA

(1712–1772)

A Flower Show, early 18th century

Woodblock print with brass filings and hand coloring
Ōban: 30.5 × 55.2 cm (12 × 21¾ in.)
John Chandler Bancroft Collection, 1901.59.114

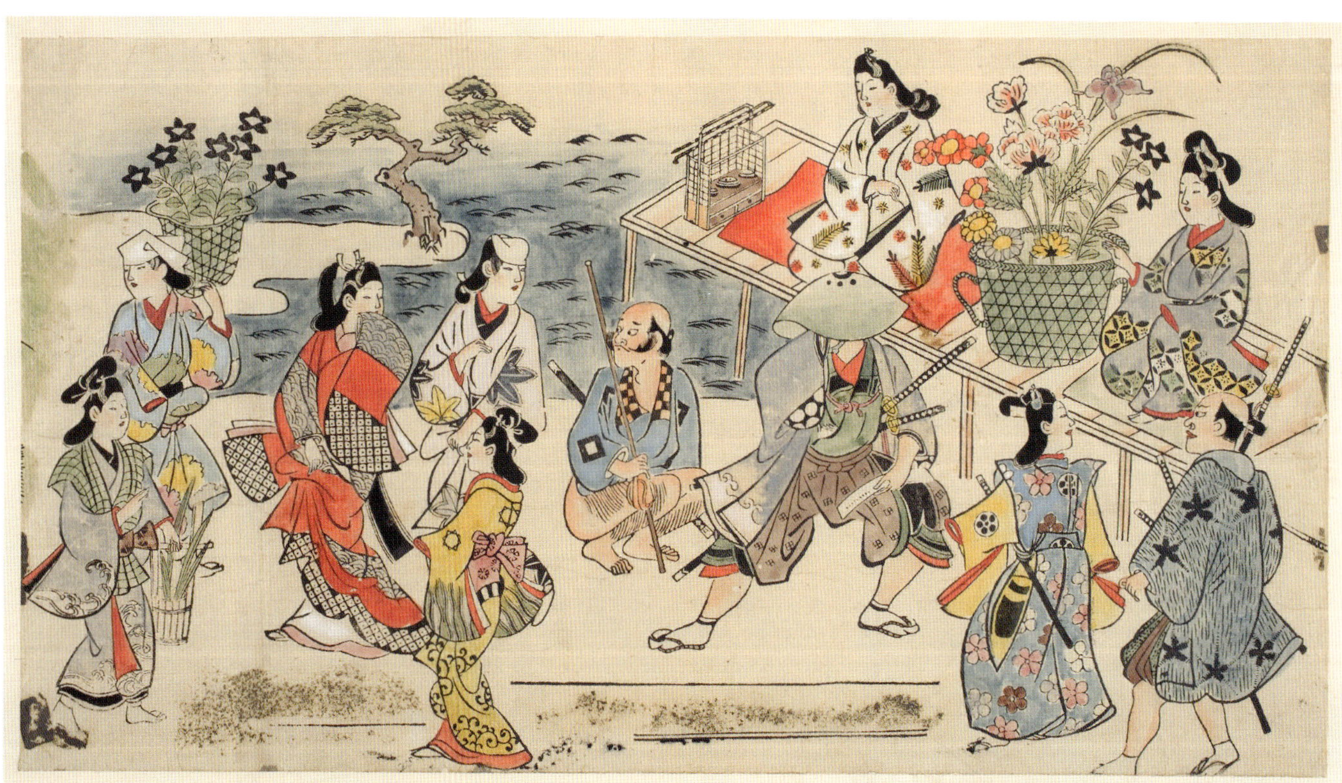

Elevated on a long wooden platform, two elegant women sit on mats; between them is a basket filled with autumn fruit and flowers such as chrysanthemums, persimmon, bellflower, and irises. A tray with smoking accessories occupies the left end of the platform. This arrangement might be a visual parody of the gifts of flowers made to the early shoguns—heads of Japan's military government—many of whom were avid gardeners, by the lords subservient to them.

A Flower Show is an example of a Japanese print in which colors were applied by hand rather than through woodblock printing. It is notable for its wide range of colors; in the early 1790s, hand-painted elements were generally limited to orange, black, and green inks, which may suggest that the print was colored sometime after it was printed.

ISHIKAWA TOYONOBU

(1711–1785)

Playing Battledore and Shuttlecock at New Year, 1750s

Publisher: Iseya
Woodblock print (*benizuri-e*): ink and color on paper
Vertical *ō-ōban*: 44.1 × 31.2 cm (17⅜ × 12⁵⁄₁₆ in.)
John Chandler Bancroft Collection, 1901.74

The highly stylized forms set against
negative space seen in this print are
typical of Ishikawa Toyonobu's mature
style. The subject is a pair of young
people playing *hanetsuki* (in English,
battledore and shuttlecock), an activity
similar to badminton. They stand facing
one another, their eyes on the airborne
hane. This image was probably created
in celebration of New Year's, indicated by
the symbols on both paddles associated
with the holiday—red-flowered plums
and treasure connected to the Seven
Gods of Good Fortune. It is a *benizuri-e*,
an early form of multi-block color printing
using predominantly red *beni* (safflower)
pigment and hues of green or yellow.

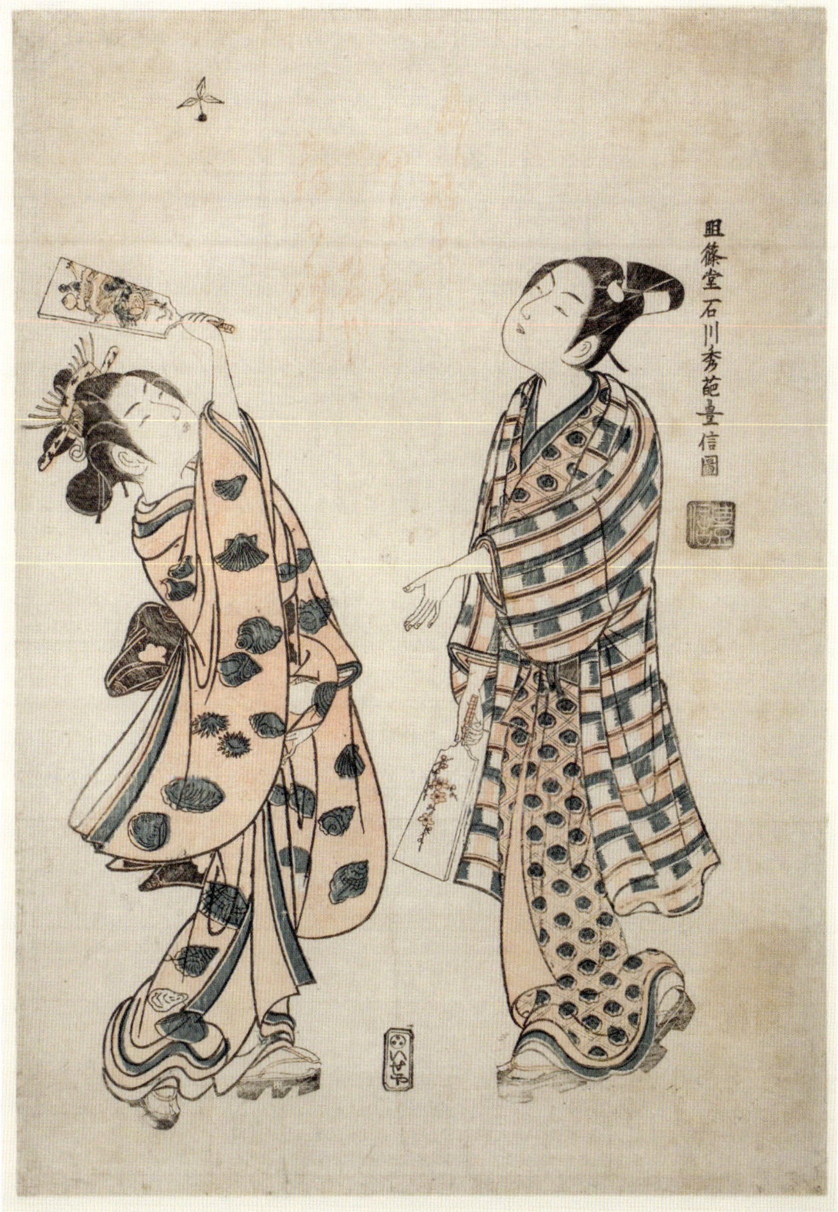

TORII KIYOMITSU

(1735–1785)

Thirty-five Small Portraits of Actors in Various Roles, 1750

Woodblock print (*benizuri-e*): ink and color on paper
Sheet: 31 × 14.5 cm (12³⁄₁₆ × 5¹¹⁄₁₆ in.)
John Chandler Bancroft Collection, 1901.346

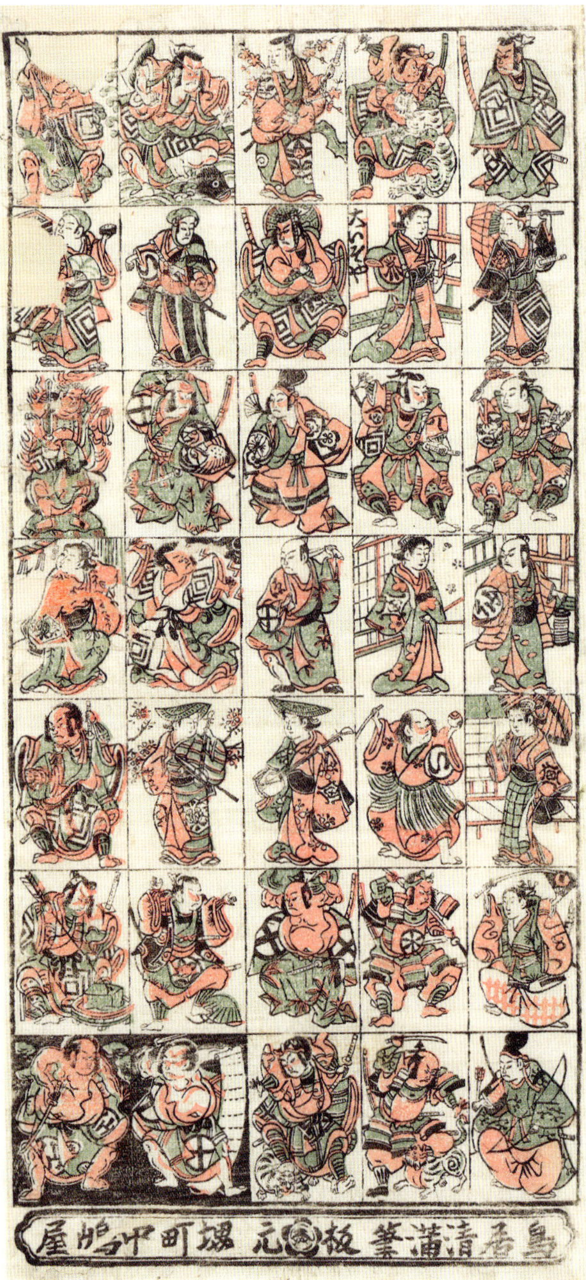

This small print functions much like a cast sheet: each figure represents a kabuki actor who will be performing at a theater in the upcoming season. They strike poses and are highly individualized despite their minuscule stature.

SUZUKI HARUNOBU

(ca. 1725–1770)

Three Fashionable Women as the Three Sake Tasters, ca. 1766

Woodblock print: ink and color on paper
26.3 × 19.4 cm (10⅜ × 7⅝ in.)
John Chandler Bancroft Collection, 1901.59.2070

Suzuki Harunobu pioneered the multi-block color printing technique known as *nishiki-e*, which allowed for the creation of vibrant, polychromatic prints. He quickly developed a signature palette characterized by soft, muted colors and delicate pastels achieved through the skillful layering of colors and the mixing of pigments.

In this print, Harunobu presents a playful reimagining of the classic tale in which Confucius, Gautama Buddha, and Laozi gather around a barrel of sour wine, agreeing that although their philosophies differ, they are all united by their shared visceral experiences of the world (in this case, a dislike for the brew.) They are replaced by three beautiful women evocative of famous female poets from ancient times Yō Kihi, Ono no Komachi, and Murasaki Shikibu—further emphasizing the idea that wisdom can be found across different cultures and eras.

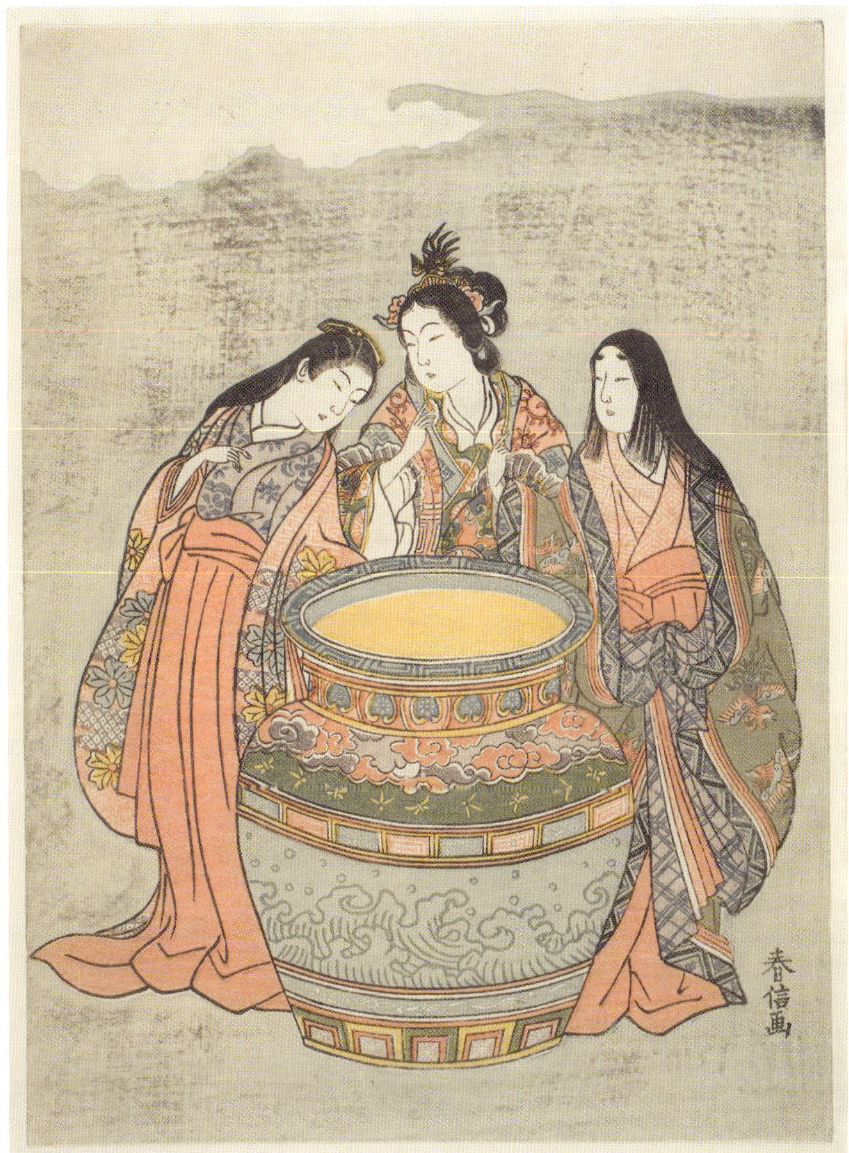

KITAO SHIGEMASA (1739–1820)
AND KATSUKAWA SHUNSHŌ (1726?–1792)

Courtesans of the Ōkaneya, from "A Mirror of Beautiful Women of the Green Houses Compared," Vol. 2, 1776

Publishers: Tsutaya Jūzaburō and Yamazaki Kimbei
Woodblock print: ink and color on paper
21.6 × 30.2 cm (8½ × 11⅞ in.)
John Chandler Bancroft Collection, 1901.59.2711

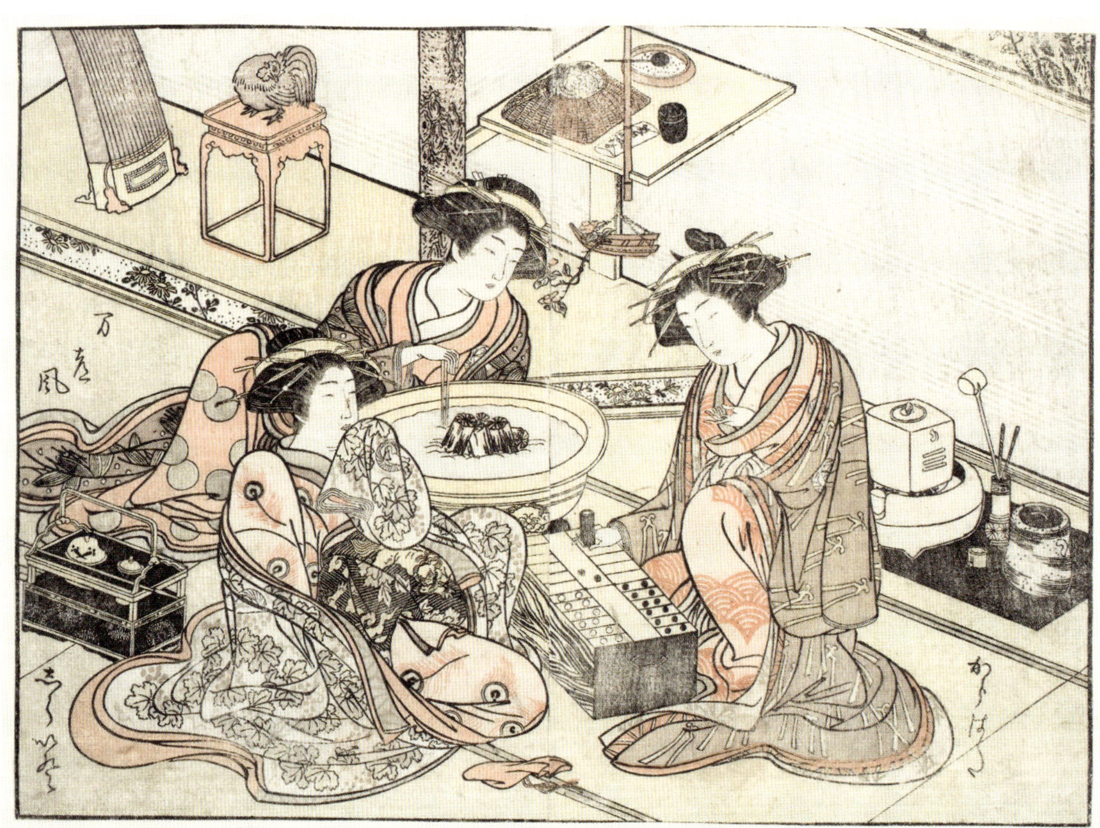

During the Edo period, licensed pleasure quarters in cities were frequented by clients known as *tsū*, or men of great refinement. Sometimes also referred to as "sophisticates," these individuals represented the pinnacle of urbane gentility, possessing specialized knowledge in literature, the arts, performance, beauty, and fashion. Prints and paintings crafted for this discerning audience were designed to appeal to viewers who prided themselves on being familiar with the cultural codes of pleasure districts like the Yoshiwara and invited them to examine and categorize the "types" of women typically found there, along with their skills in poetry, calligraphy, and music, as well as the intricacies of their dress, hair, and makeup. One notable publication of this type, *A Mirror of Beautiful Women of the Green Houses Compared*, is celebrated as one of the most exceptional works in the history of illustrated books, and portrays the district's actual inhabitants—in this case the Ōkaneya brothel. Each woman featured was an actual courtesan, with her name penned by her own hand beside her image.

The collaboration between Kitao Shigemasa and Katsukawa Shunshō on this publication resulted in printed images of remarkable quality and stylistic coherence. While some scholars have attributed some of the designs to Shigemasa and the rest to Shunshō, there is no definitive consensus on the division of labor between the two artists.

UTAGAWA TOYOHARU

(1735–1814)

Perspective Picture of the Great Kagura Ceremony at Ise, ca. 1773

Publisher: Nishimuraya Yohachi (Eijudō)
Woodblock print: ink and color on paper
25.4 × 38.1 cm (10 × 15 in.)
John Chandler Bancroft Collection, 1901.514

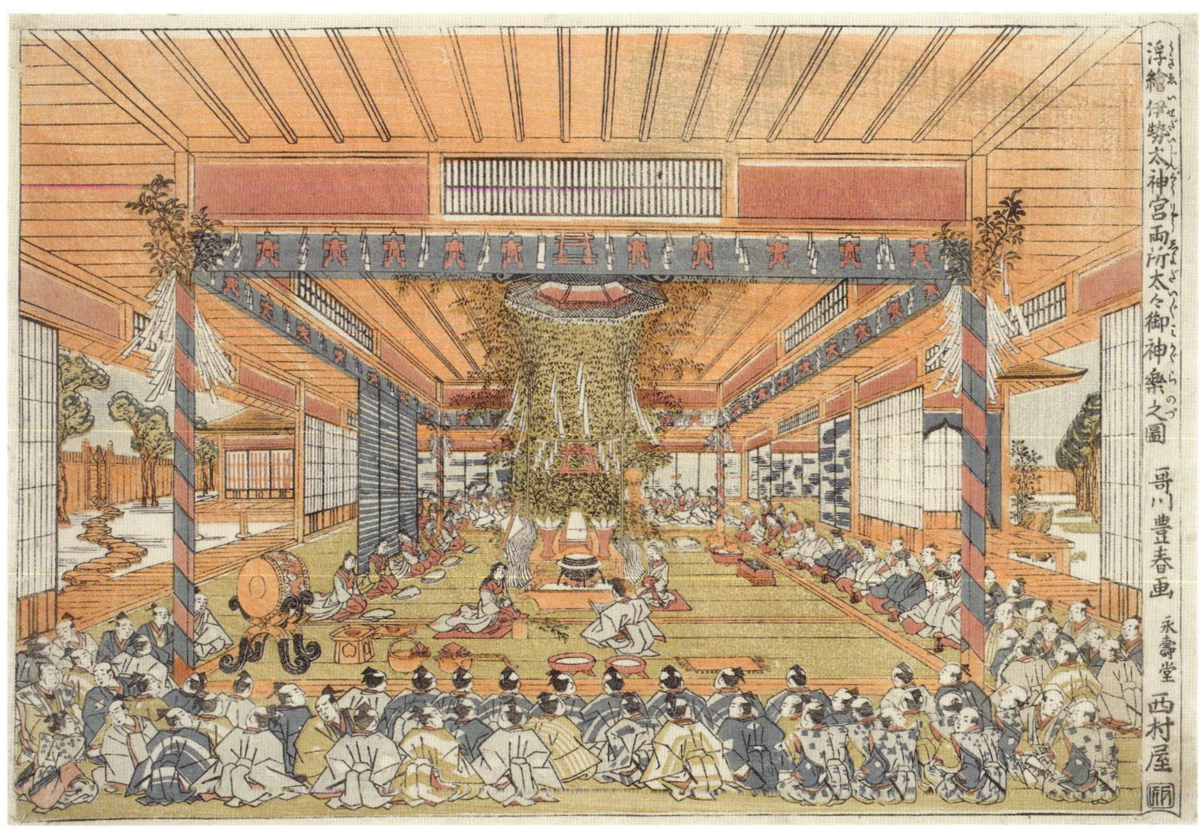

A *kagura* is a Shinto ceremony, usually performed in the eleventh month of the Japanese lunar calendar, in which sacred sake is served before the gods. Although the details of the rites vary depending on which institution performs them, the proceedings usually involve drawing water from a local source, which is then offered to the gods and used in the ritual purification of worshippers in attendance. Feasting and festivities follow, after which masked dancers invite the gods to leave the site. The *kagura* depicted in this print takes place in a hall of the Ise shrine, one of the holiest and most ancient Shinto sites in Japan.

It is unclear why Toyoharu chose to use one-point perspective in this picture, but, because it was considered an illusionary device in Japan—as opposed to an accurate means of depicting spatial recession—it is possible that he was trying to capture the otherworldliness of the event.

TORII KIYONAGA

(1752–1815)

The Echigoya on New Year's Day,
ca. 1787

Woodblock print: ink and color on paper
37.8 × 74.9 cm (14⅞ × 29½ in.)
John Chandler Bancroft Collection, 1901.83

In the eighteenth century, Torii artists, known for their actor prints, also explored other genres, such as street scenes and depictions of everyday life, as evidenced in this print. It portrays a group in front of the Echigoya, a renowned kimono shop established in Edo in 1673, often featured in *ukiyo-e* prints. It later evolved into the modern-day Mitsukoshi department store, which catered to the fashion-conscious townspeople of the Edo period. The signage at the store's entrance proclaims that they offer ready-made products for immediate purchase, rather than solely made-to-order items, appealing to a wider customer base by accepting cash payments.

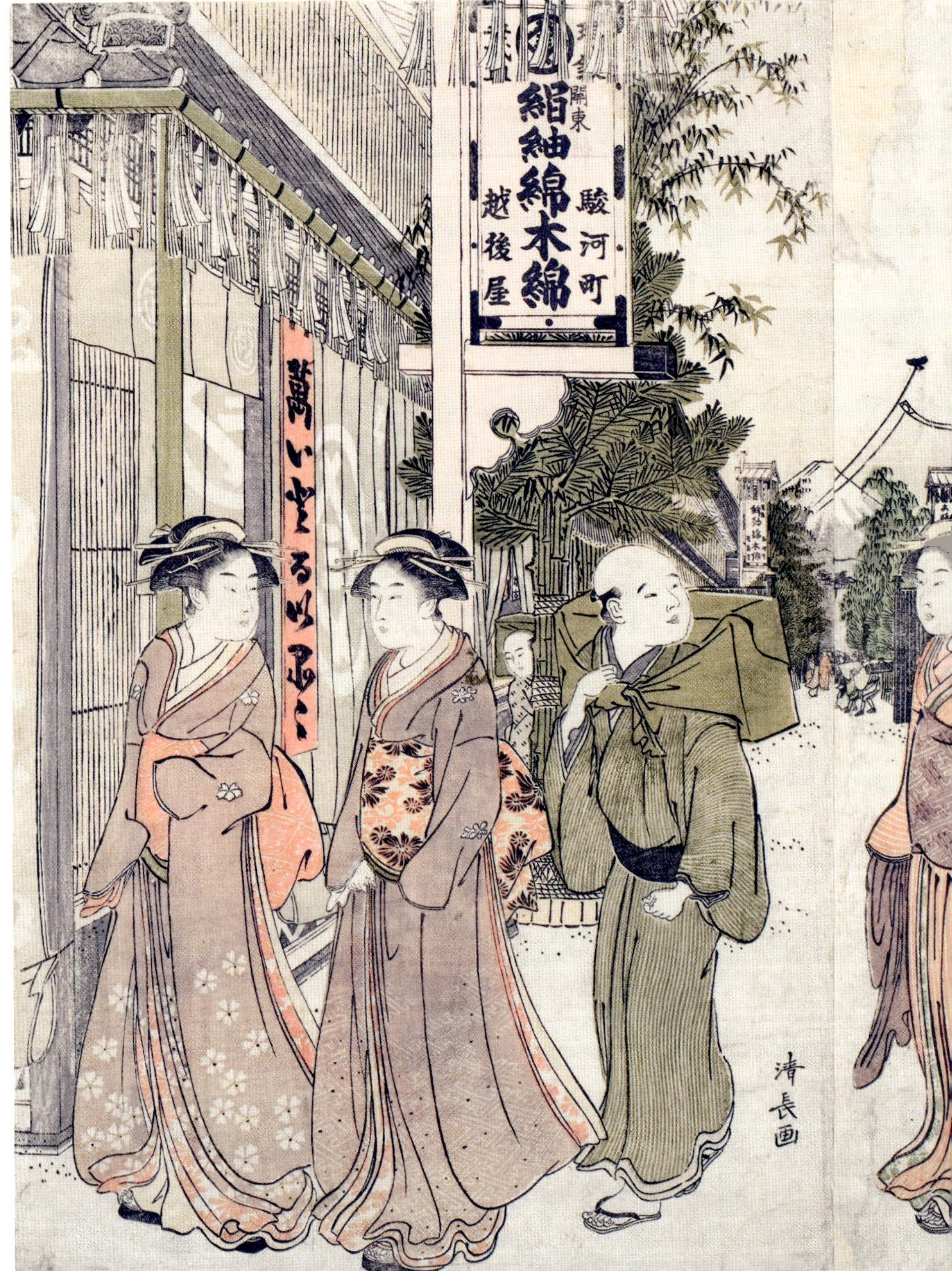

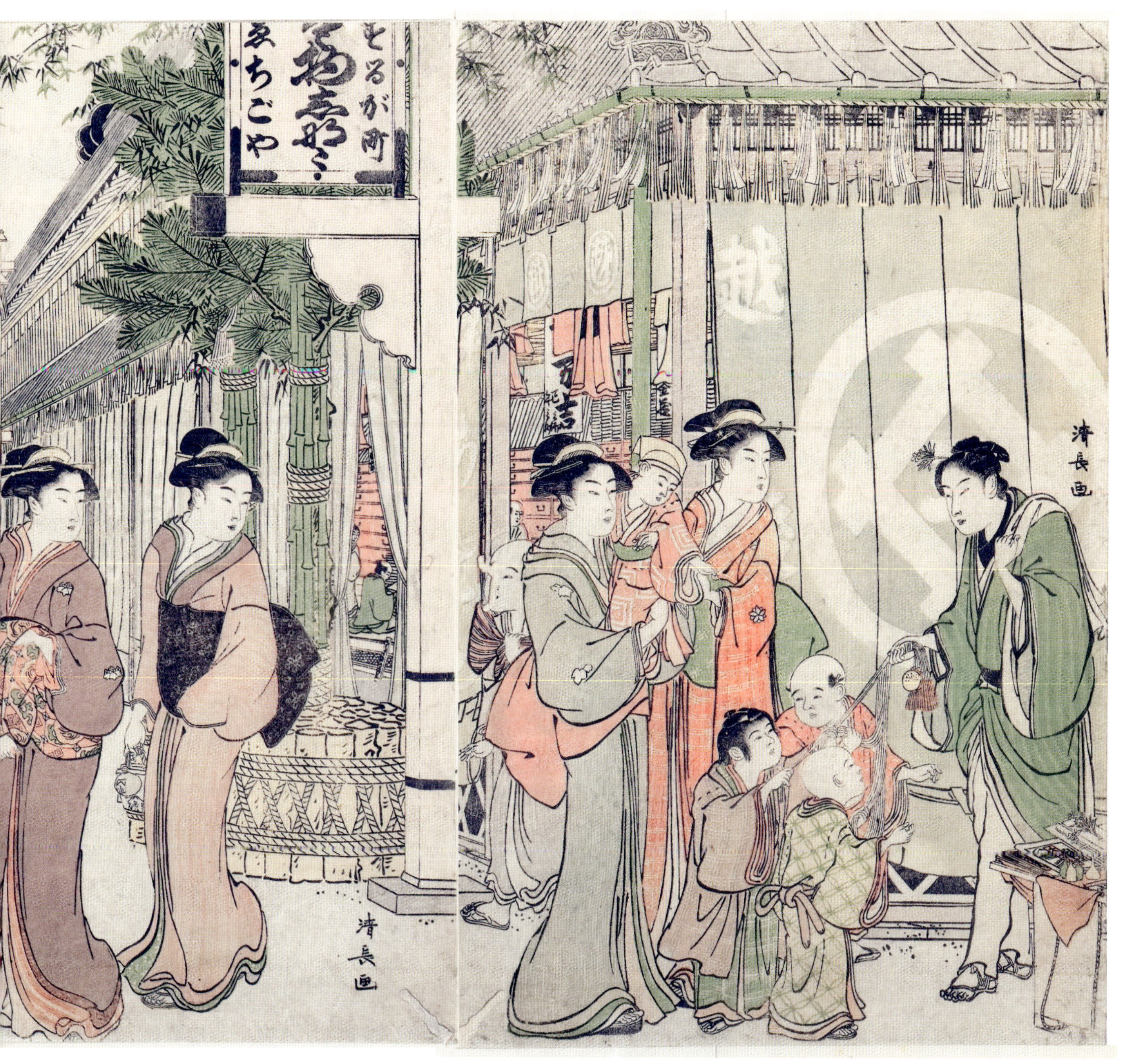
するが町
福寿好○
みちごや
越
清長画
清長画

KITAGAWA UTAMARO I

(1753–1806)

Needlework, 1794–95

Publisher: Uemura Yohei
Woodblock print: ink and color on paper
Vertical *ōban* triptych; 37.4 × 76.1 cm
(14¾ × 29¹⁵⁄₁₆ in.)
John Chandler Bancroft Collection, 1901.118

In this intimate scene, a group of women sort through their silk sashes, mending and folding them as they go. Around them, their children play, one lying in his mother's lap while playing with her fan, another using a mirror to show a frightened cat his reflection, and the last looking at the contents of a small insect cage. The coziness of the tableau is completed by the pot of tea sitting behind them.

Although the subject of this print is decidedly quotidian, and its palette muted, Utamaro uses an array of techniques to convey the textural spectrum of the fabrics. From the rougher weave of woven cotton to the silvery silk worn by the woman to the left, to the delicate and transparent silk held up to the light on the left, these sensory details imbue this print with his trademark sensual touch.

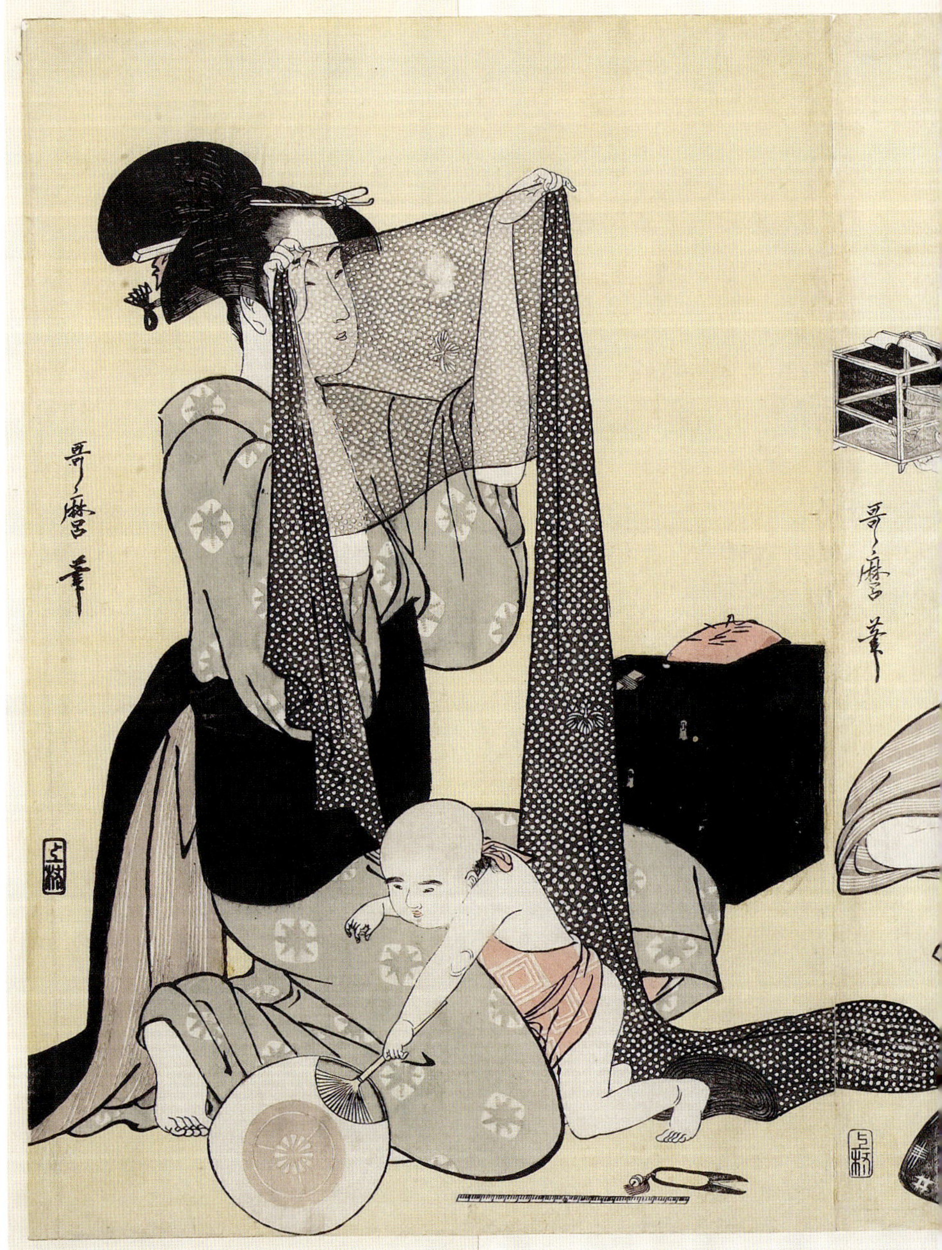

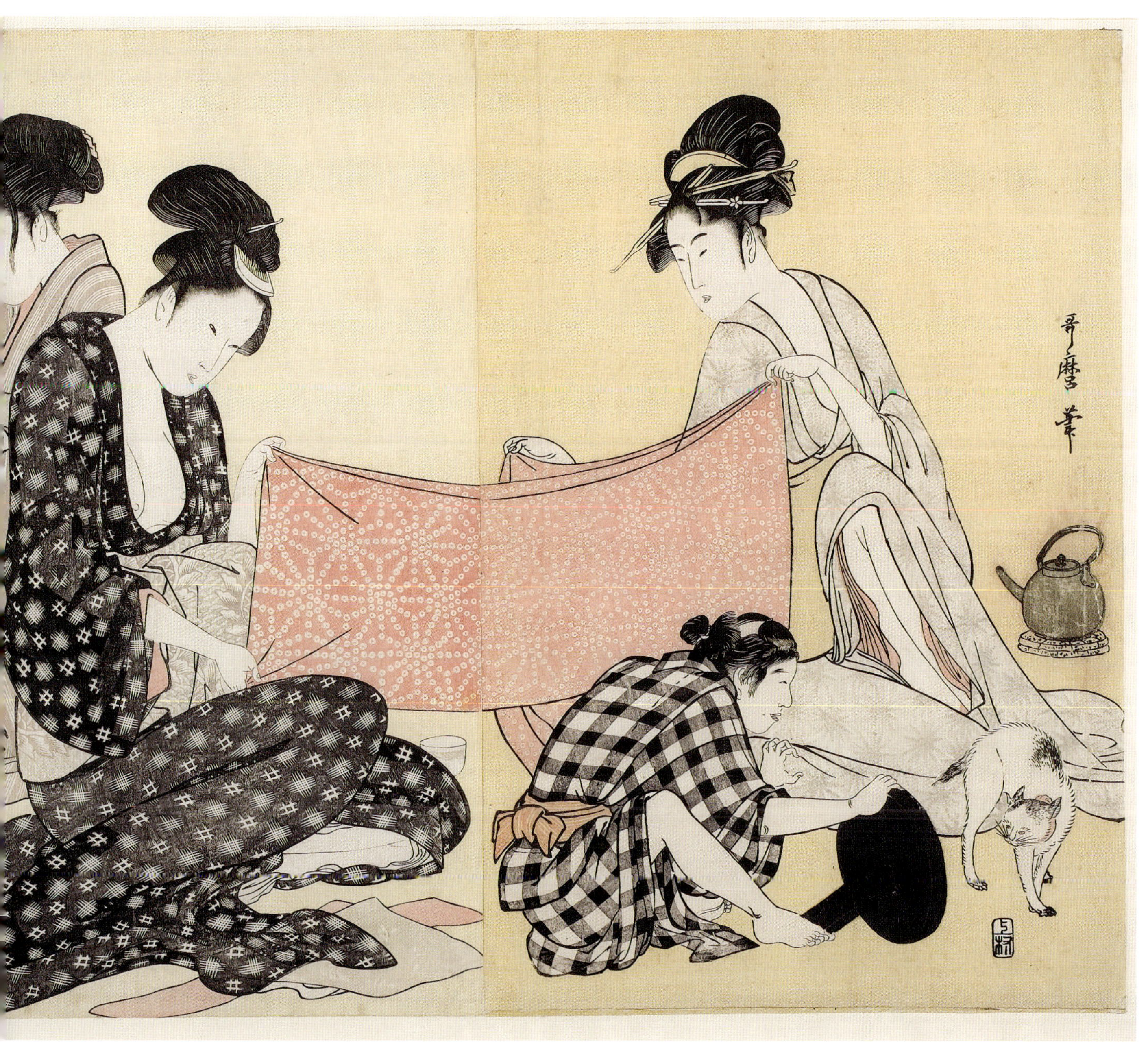

CHŌKŌSAI EISHŌ

(active 1793–99)

The Hand Mirror, ca. 1796

Woodblock print: ink and color on paper
37.5 × 25.1 cm (14¾ × 9⅞ in.)
John Chandler Bancroft Collection, 1901.534

Eishō specialized in the portrayal of tall, willowy women. The
garb this woman wears is highly fashionable, with wide *obi* belts
and a kimono worn such that it gapes at the nape of her neck.
Like his contemporary Utamaro, Eishō used a combination of
hand painting, diluted inks, and strategically placed streaks left
by the printer's instruments, for example, to convey the variance
in texture of the garments, from the shimmer of the silk to the
rough woven texture of cotton.

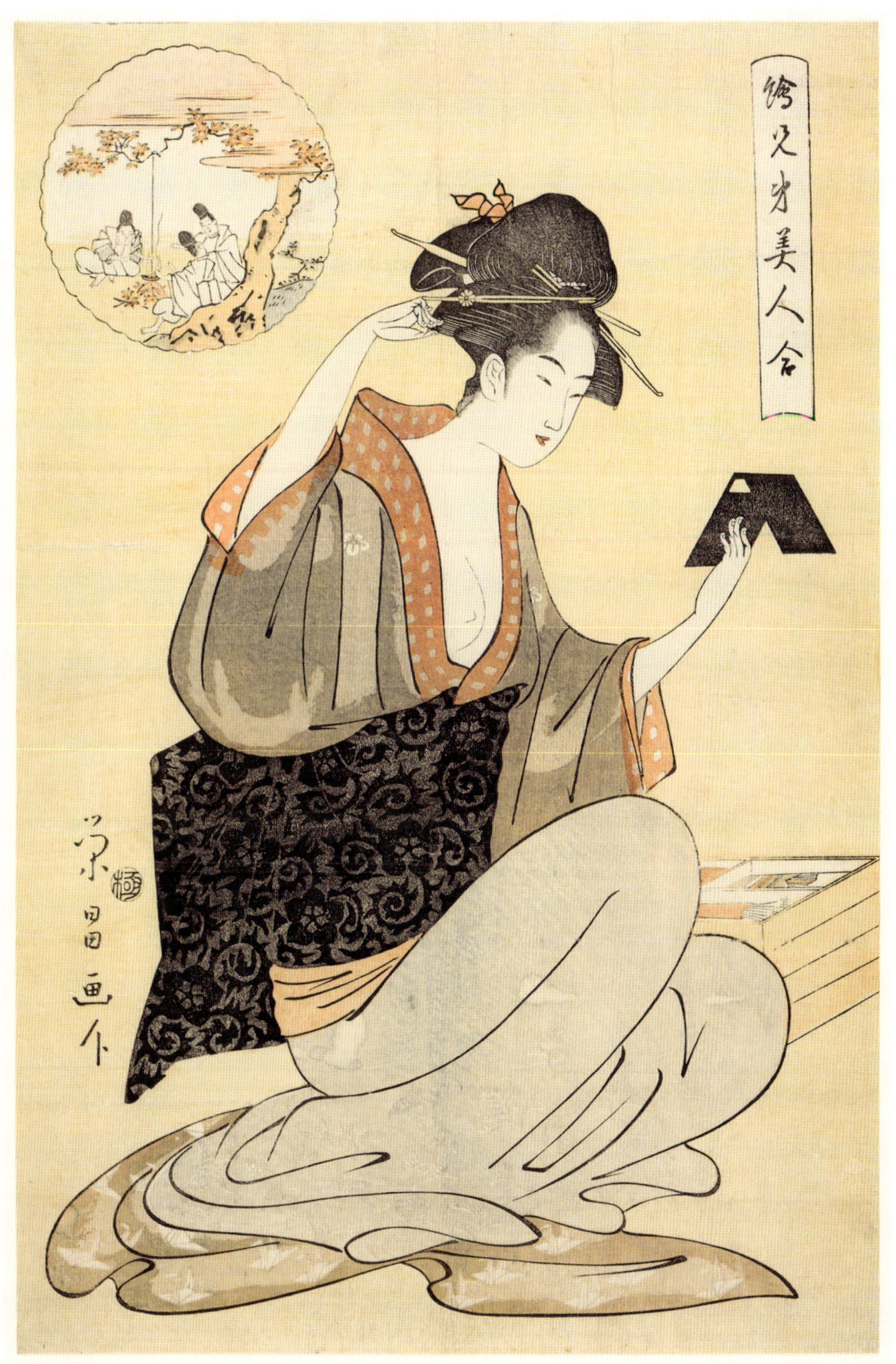

UTAGAWA TOYOKUNI I

(1769–1825)

Mitate-e Daimyo Gyoretsu, ca. 1796

Publisher: Wakasaya Yoichi
Woodblock print: ink and color on paper
37.8 × 125.7 cm (14⅞ × 49½ in.)
John Chandler Bancroft Collection, 1901.59.2293

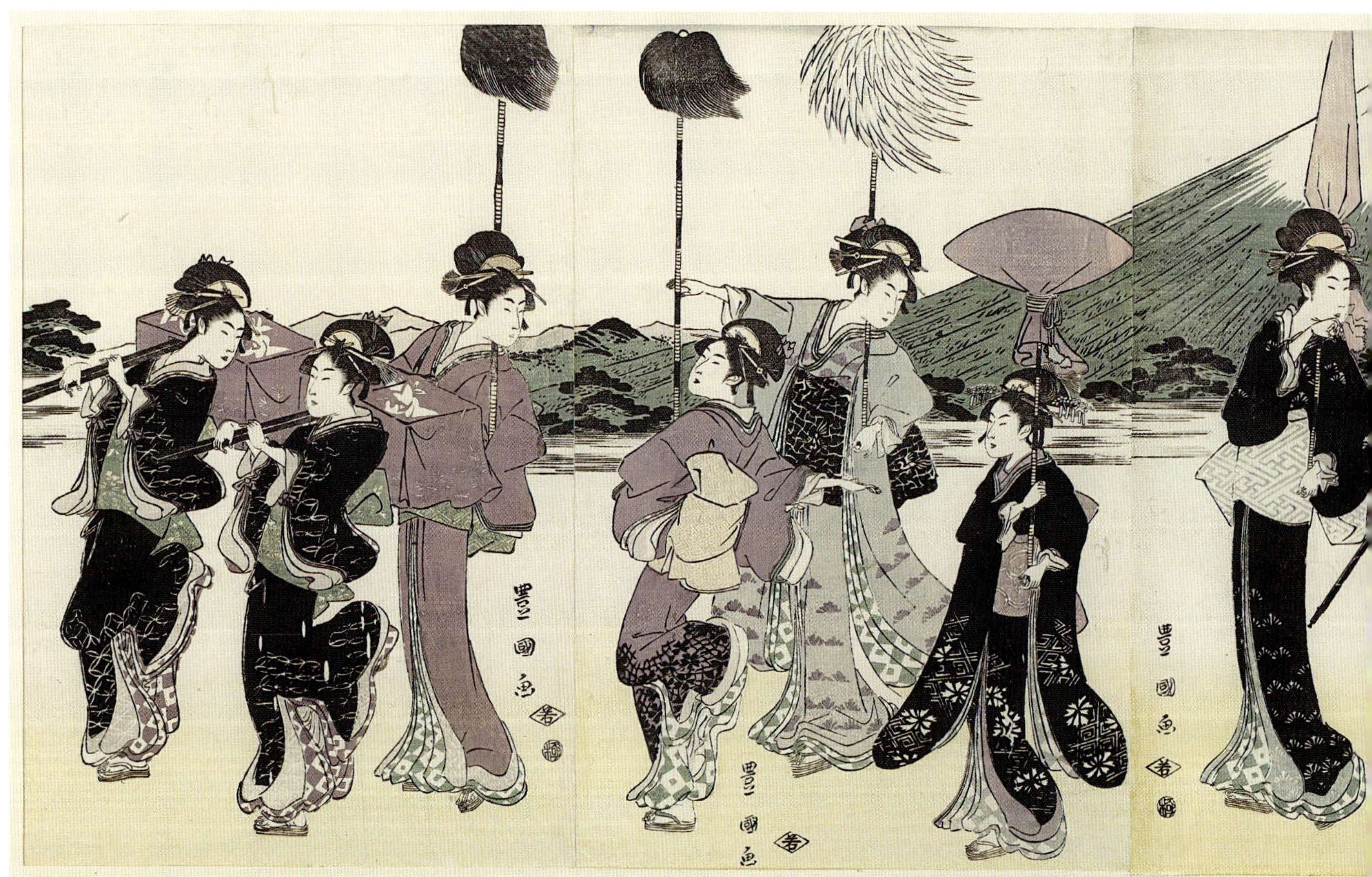

During the Edo period, the Tokugawa shogunate implemented a system that required *daimyo* (land-owning warlords) to alternate their residence between their domain and the capital city of Edo (present-day Tokyo). This policy aimed to maintain control over the samurai class and prevent them from amassing too much individual power. Processions to the capital consisting of *daimyo* and their households, known as *daimyo gyoretsu* or *sankin-kōtai,* were grand, ceremonial displays that could include hundreds or even thousands of retainers, servants, and porters, who would travel along the major roads connecting their domains to Edo. The processions were highly organized and followed strict protocols, with participants dressed in formal attire and carrying various weapons, such as spears and swords, to symbolize the *daimyo*'s military might.

This panoramic multi-panel print depicts a group of primarily young courtesans as if they were participating in such a procession. This playful subversion of gender roles and social

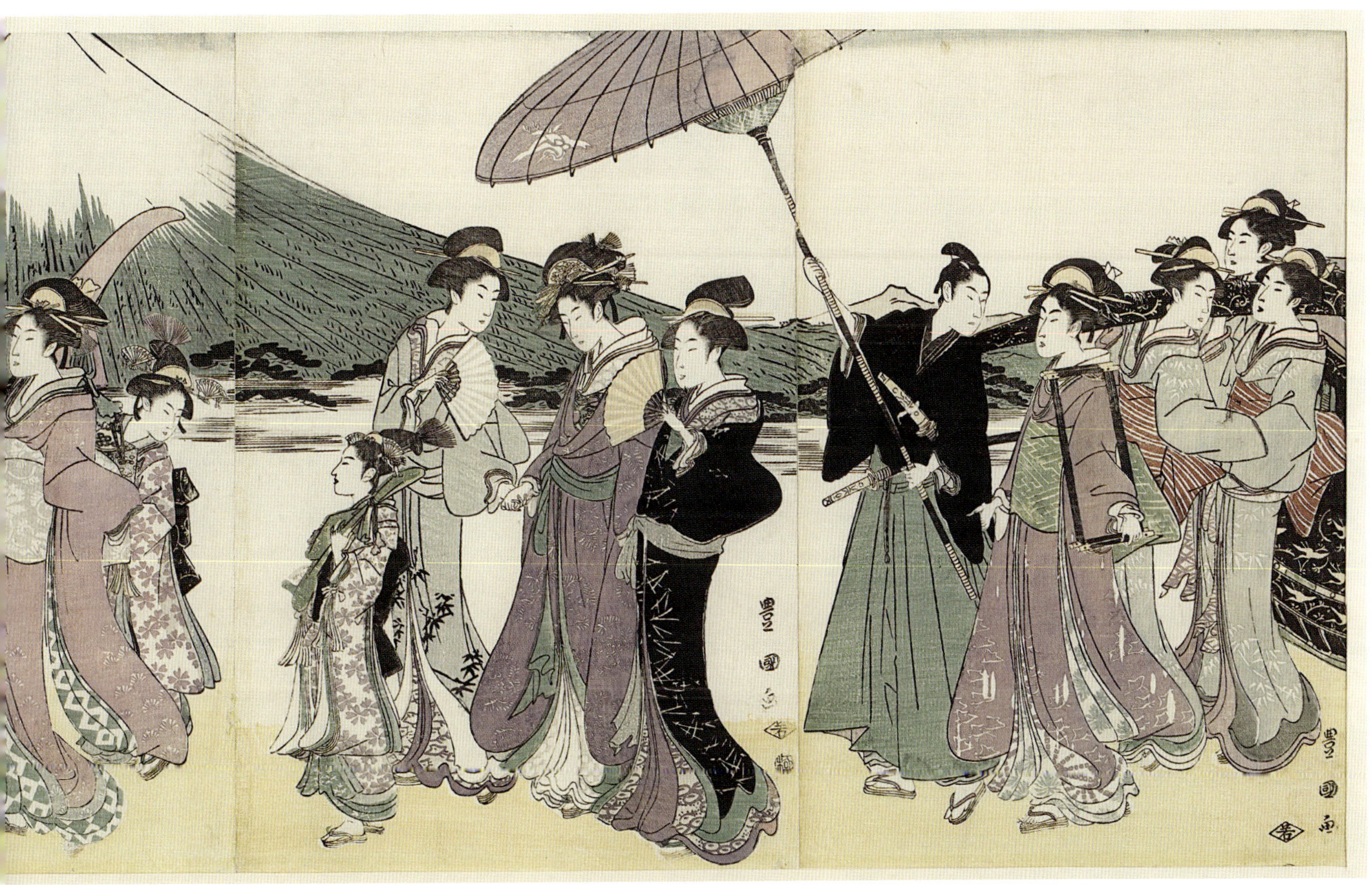

norms makes this print a *mitate-e*—a genre of Japanese art that employs visual metaphors, allusions, and parodies to playfully comment on or critique contemporary society. In particular, by portraying figures associated with the floating world in an activity associated with the social elite, the artist may have been poking fun at the rigid social hierarchies and gender roles of Edo-period Japan while also showcasing the wit and creativity that were highly valued in *ukiyo-e* and other forms of popular art at the time.

The use of the *murasaki-e*, characterized by the dominant use of purple in an otherwise limited color palette, further adds to the visual impact and distinctiveness of this artwork. Moreover, the extensive use of purple in women's garments and surroundings creates a sense of luxury, elegance, and perhaps even irony, considering that this shade was reserved for the upper classes.

KITAGAWA UTAMARO I

(early 1750s–1806)

Woman Holding a Round Fan, ca. 1793

Publisher: Tsutaya Jūzaburō
Woodblock print: ink, color, and mica on paper
Aiban: 35.1 × 23.8 cm (13¹³⁄₁₆ × 9⅜ in.)
John Chandler Bancroft Collection, 1901.278

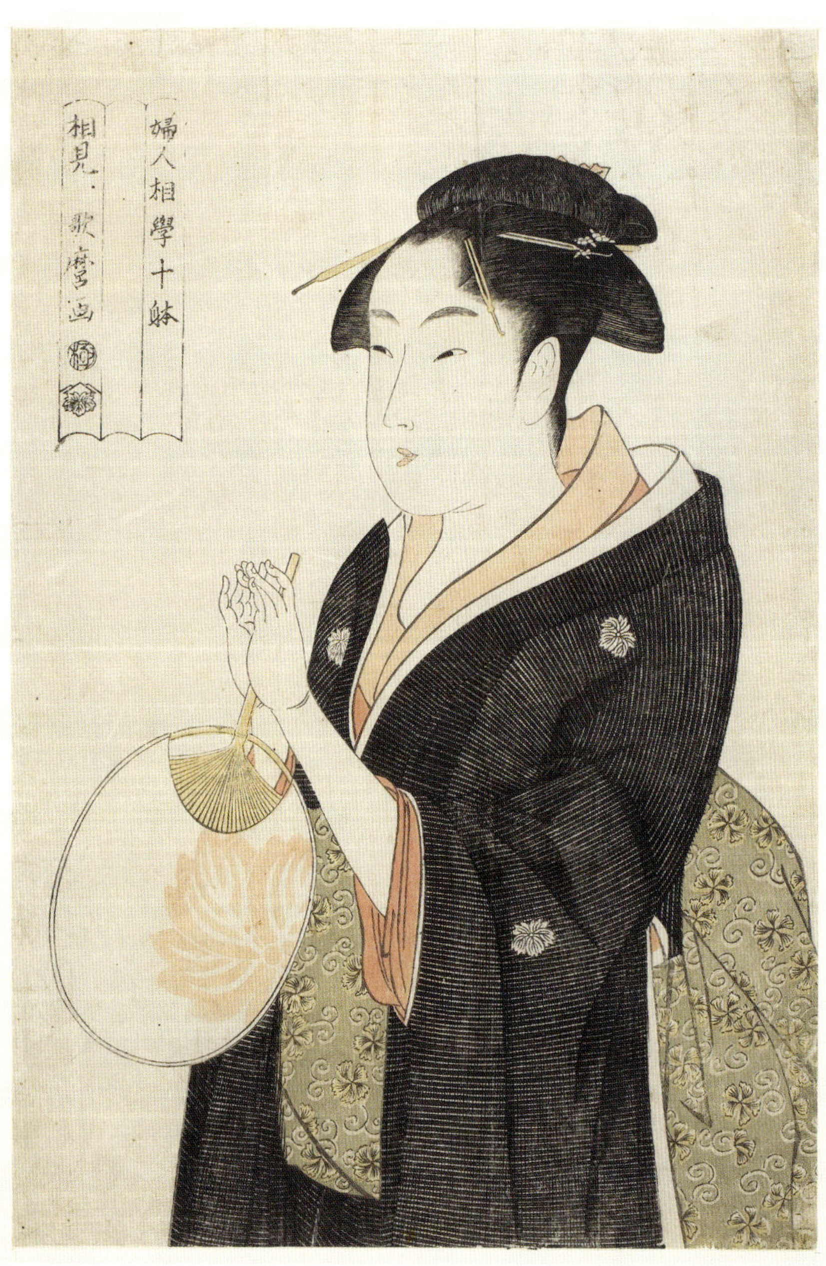

Kitagawa Utamaro's captivating portrait of Ohisa, a waitress from the Takashima-ya teahouse, epitomizes the alluring yet restrained *iki* ("stylish") aesthetic cherished by the affluent townsfolk of the Edo period. The half-length portrait depicts Ohisa elegantly facing left, holding an *uchiwa* (round fan) adorned with the distinctive ivy leaf emblem of the Takashima-ya. This motif is subtly echoed on the shoulders and sleeves of her translucent kimono, demonstrating Utamaro's meticulous attention to detail and his ability to convey the essence of his subject through delicate visual cues. Utamaro further enhances the design by employing the *surikira* technique, a process that involves incorporating mica into the printing ink to create a shimmering, iridescent background. This effect is achieved by diluting mineral paints with water and gelatin, which serve as a binder, and then applying the mixture onto the woodblock to produce nuanced background coloring. The result is a mesmerizing interplay of light and texture that adds depth and dimensionality to the portrait.

TŌSHŪSAI SHARAKU

(active 1794–95)

Actor Ōtani Tokuji I as the Manservant Sōdesuke, ca. 1800

Publisher: Tsutaya Jūzaburō
Woodblock print: ink and color on paper
Vertical *ōban*: 38.7 × 25.4 cm (15¼ × 10 in.)
Museum Purchase, 1930.14

Though he was only active as an *ukiyo-e* artist from May 1794 to February 1795, Sharaku made an indelible mark on the trajectory of the genre. He is credited with 140 designs, primarily bust-length portraits (*ōkubi-e*) of kabuki actors, that were distinguished by their strikingly vivid expressions and evocative body language. While initially controversial due to their unconventional and often unflattering depictions, Sharaku's unique approach to portraying his subjects has since garnered comparisons to renowned portraitists from around the world such as Rembrandt.

Around 1800 Sharaku produced a notable series of mica-background portraits highlighting actors from the play *Hana ayame Bunroku Soga,* which was performed in 1794 at the Miyako Theater in Edo. This play is based on the twelfth-century story of the Ishii brothers' quest for vengeance following their father's murder. The print featured here captures Ōtani Tokuji I as Sōdesuke, a manservant who assists the brothers, his determination captured through his tight-lipped expression and hopeful eyes.

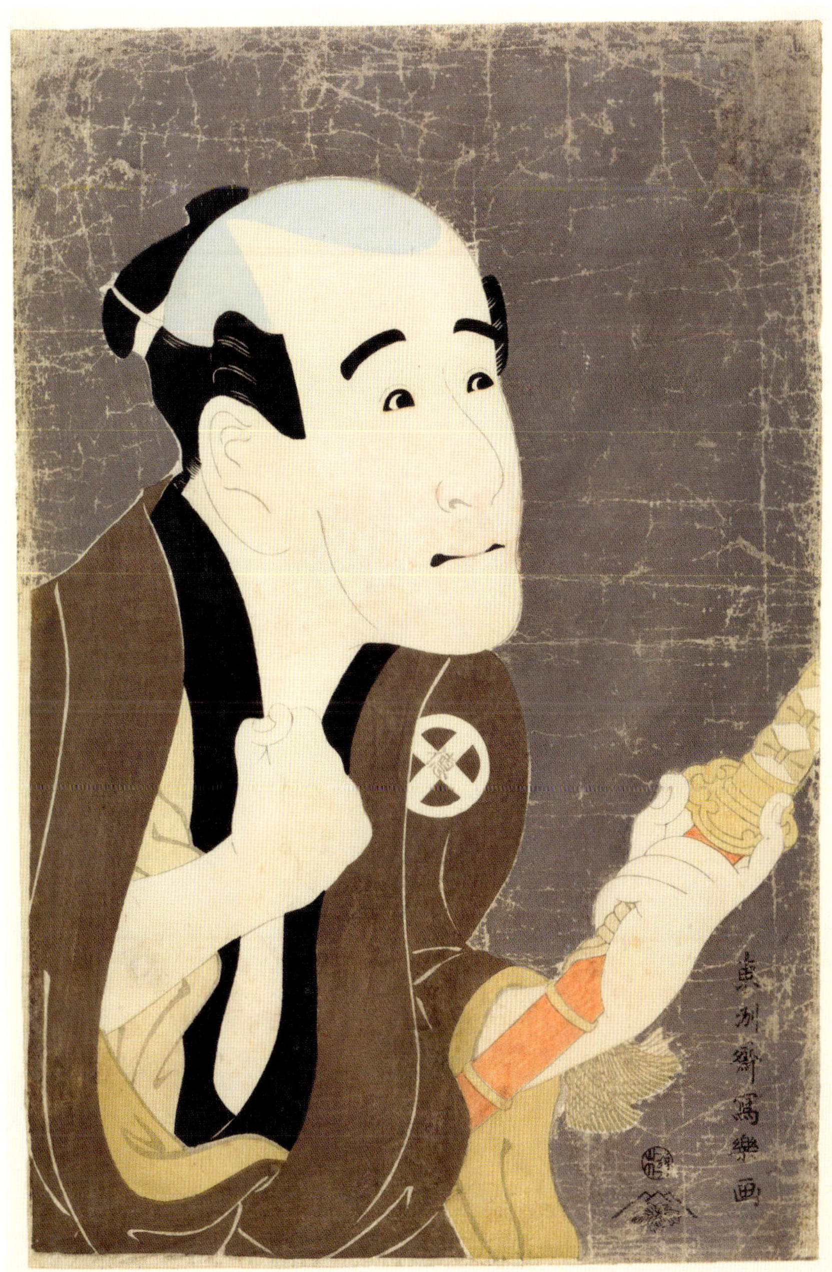

KITAGAWA UTAMARO I

(early 1750s–1806)

Picture of the Pleasures of the Taiko and His Five Wives at Rakuto, 1804

Publisher: Kagaya
Woodblock print: ink and color on paper
36.9 × 75.5 cm (14½ × 29¾ in.)
John Chandler Bancroft Collection, 1901.120

This triptych shows the cherry-blossom viewing party held by the warlord Toyotomi Hideyoshi (1537–1598) at Daigo Temple in Kyoto in 1598. While it appears to be a scene of innocent enjoyment, its subject was intended as a brazen challenge to the ruling Tokugawa family officials of Edo. Hideyoshi had been a primary political opponent of the Tokugawa immediately before the Edo period; images of his face had been banned in 1802. This print appeared around two years later and thus represented a bold stand against the Edo government and its restrictive practices. For his defiance of the law, the artist Utamaro was placed under house arrest in 1804 and spent fifty days in hand chains. This, combined with the death of his friend and publisher Tatsuya in 1797, initiated a downward spiral in Utamaro's physical and mental health, and seems to have affected the quality of his later work.

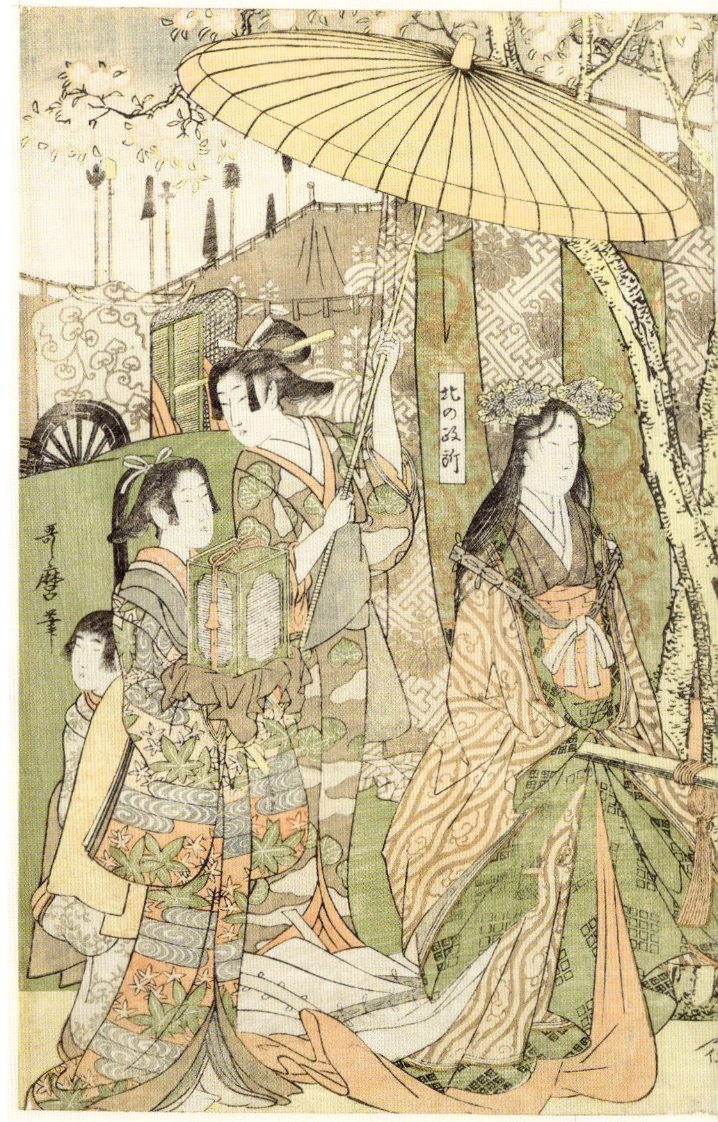

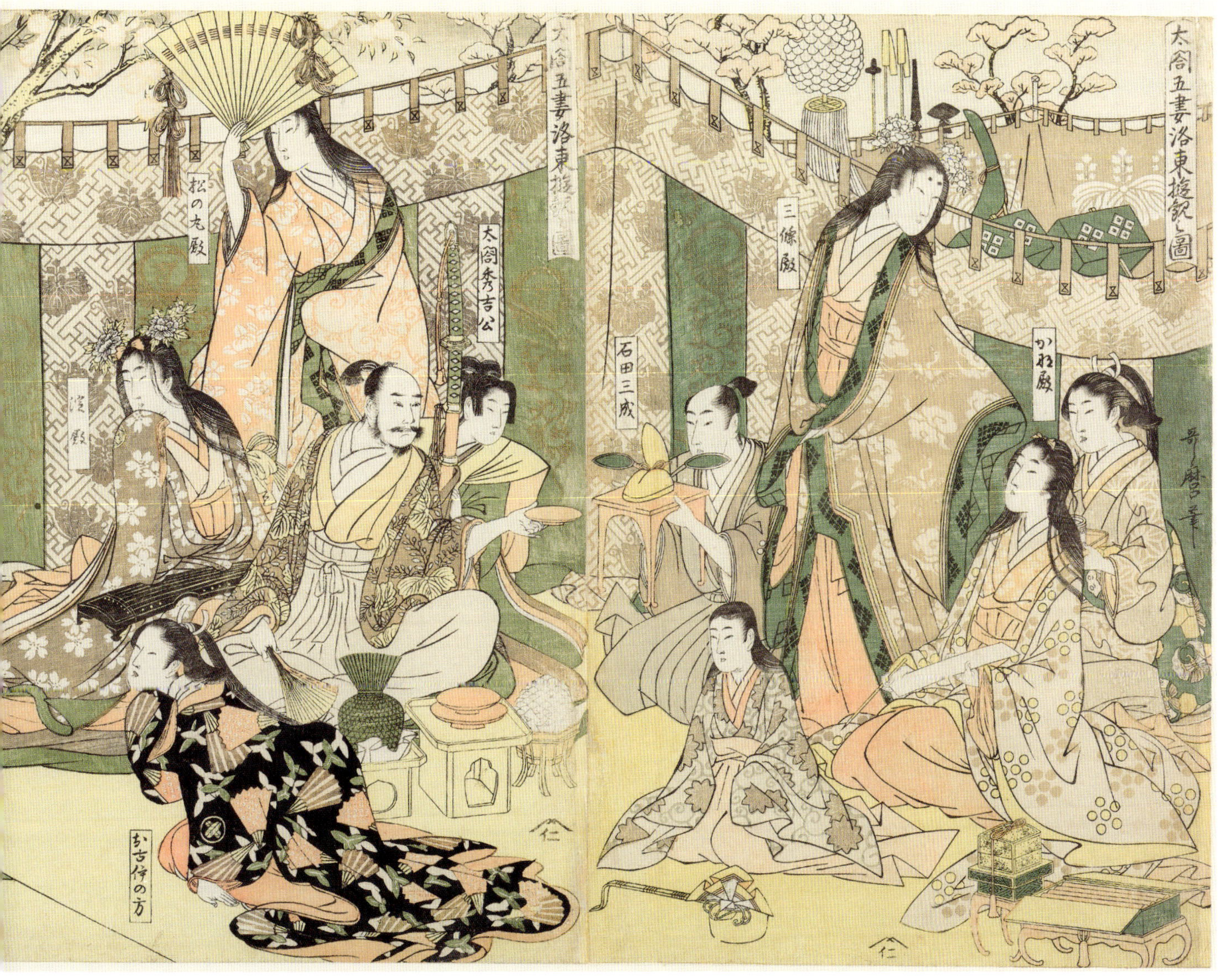

太閤五妻洛東遊観之圖
松の丸殿
太閤秀吉公
淀殿
太閤五妻洛東遊観圖
お吉伊の方
三條殿
石田三成
かね殿
歌麿筆

UTAGAWA TOYOKUNI I

(1769–1825)

***Actor Iwai Hanshirō V as a Calligraphy Student*,** from the series "Iwai Hanshirō Performing the Dance of Seven Changes", 1806

Publisher: Tsuruya Kinsuke
Woodblock print: ink and color on paper
37.5 × 24.8 cm (14¾ × 9¾ in.)
John Chandler Bancroft Collection, 1901.59.2487

***Actor Iwai Hanshirō V as a Blind Man*,** from the series "Iwai Hanshirō Performing the Dance of Seven Changes", 1806

Publisher: Tsuruya Kinsuke
Woodblock print: ink and color on paper
37.5 × 24.8 cm (14¾ × 9¾ in.)
John Chandler Bancroft Collection, 1901.789

***Actor Iwai Hanshirō V as a Court Lady*,** from the series "Iwai Hanshirō Performing the Dance of Seven Changes", 1806

Publisher: Tsuruya Kinsuke
Woodblock print: ink and color on paper
37.5 × 24.8 cm (14¾ × 9¾ in.)
John Chandler Bancroft Collection, 1901.59.2488

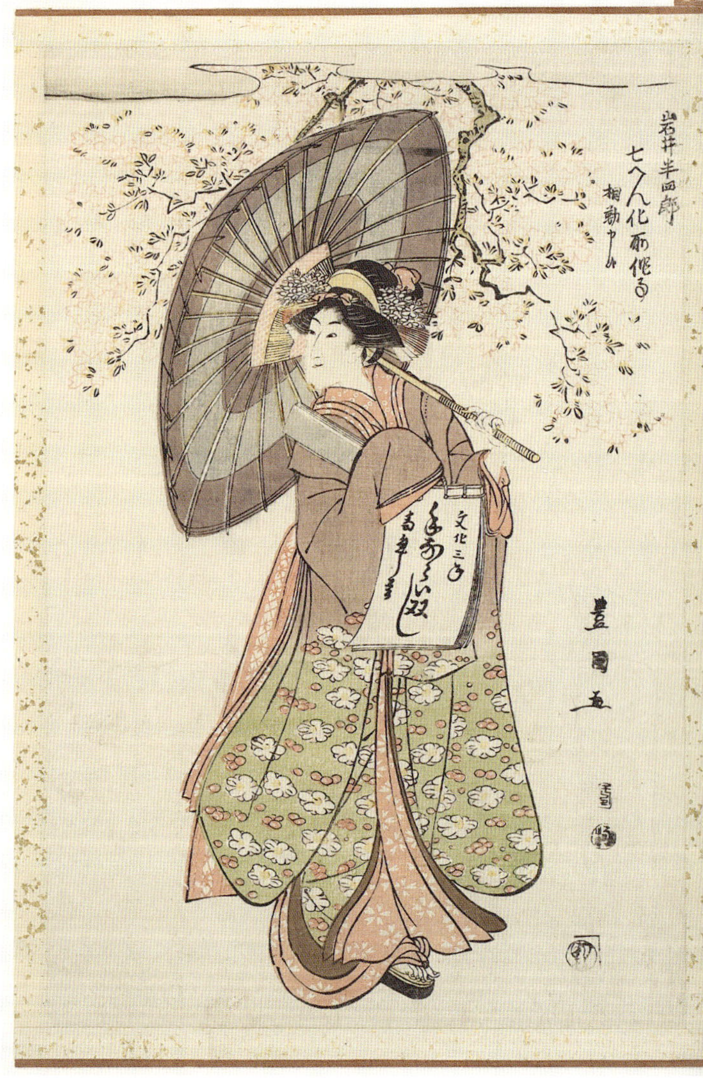

Utagawa Toyokuni I, known as the "face likeness master" in his lifetime, frequently employed thinner lines to achieve more recognizable depictions of his subjects, particularly celebrity actors. By doing so, he pioneered a shift in the design and function of *yakusha-e*.

The prints pictured here represent three stages of a *hayagawari*, or "quick-change dance." In the dance, a single kabuki actor—here, Iwai Hanshirō V (1776–1847)—goes through a series of quick costume changes during a performance. This theatrical trick, known as *keren*, entailed a variety of techniques such as removing upper layers of clothing, altering makeup, covering the shaved portions of their hair to assume a female role, or having stage assistants supply additional accessories. Viewers could continue to recognize Hanshirō despite these

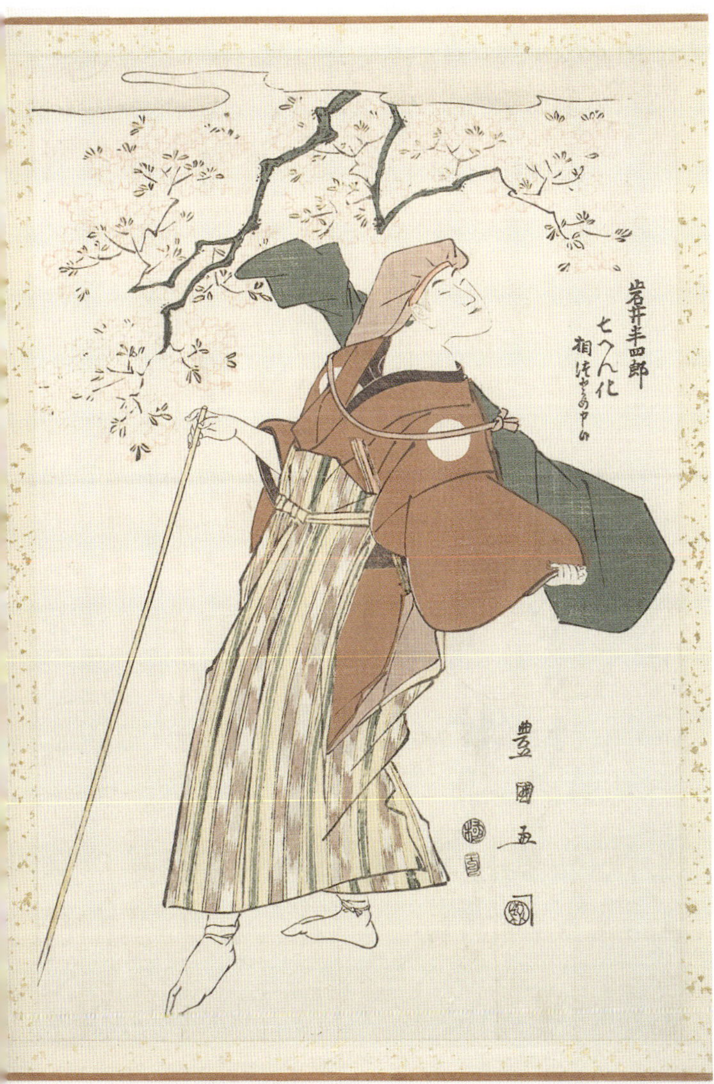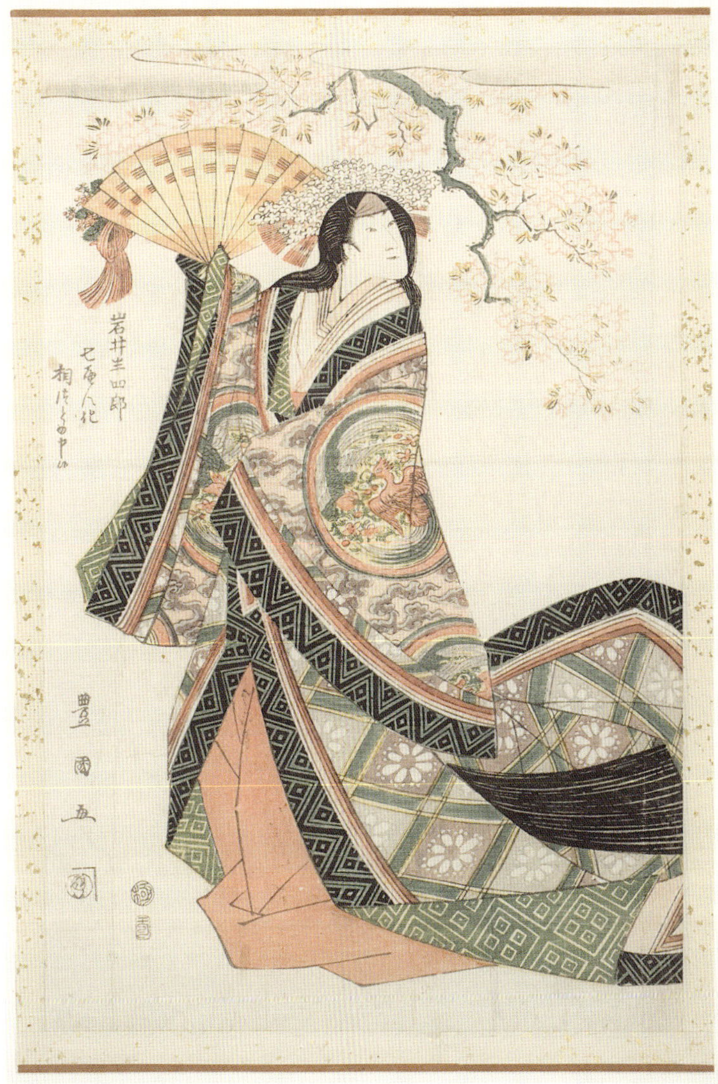

changes, though, due to his distinctive features: an oval face, long straight nose, and signature impish smile. The prints also demonstrate his ability to embody the identity of the different characters he portrayed, such as a blind man who is feeling the space ahead of him with his feet, or a woman dressed as a Heian-period courtier with her regal posture and haughty expression.

KUBO SHUNMAN

(1757–1820)

Eastern Bullfinches, ca. 1800

Poet: Sentoan Hanamitsu
Woodblock print: ink and color on paper
20.3 × 18.1 cm (8 × 7⅛ in.)
John Chandler Bancroft Collection, 1901.59.1949

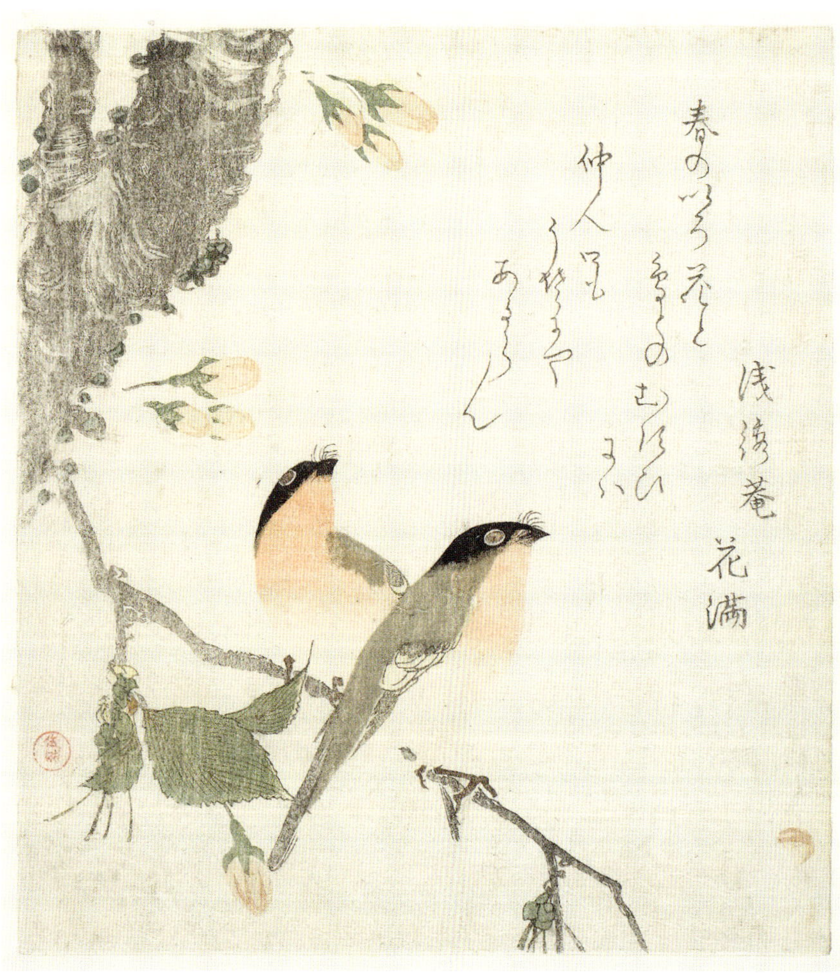

Kubo Shunman is best known for his lush pictures of the natural world, particularly birds, flowers, and butterflies. In this exquisite *surimono*, a type of print often privately commissioned by literary circles, he masterfully combines intricate artwork with an accompanying *kyoka* ("crazy verse") poem by Sentoan Hanamitsu:

> The colors of spring,
> In the union of flowers and birds—
> Could even a matchmaker's words
> Be false?

Shunman's choice of subject here is appropriate considering the poem's emphasis on springtime imagery while also functioning as a clever visual pun. In the context of the poem "uso" means "lie" but is also a homonym for "bullfinch," the bird depicted in the print

Shunman's distinctive style is evident in his "boneless printing" technique, which forgoes clear outlines in favor of subtle bokashi ink gradations. This combined with blind printing (embossment using an uninked woodblock) adds depth and dimensionality to his forms.

ISODA KORYŪSAI
(1735–1790)

The Chinese Dog, ca. 1777

Woodblock print: ink and color on paper
27.6 × 21 cm (10⅞ × 8¼ in.)
John Chandler Bancroft Collection, 1901.398

During the Edo period, Western and Chinese dogs were imported via Nagasaki as fashionable pets for the wealthy. This small Pekinese is tempted by a bowl of treats left on the floor by its owner, who has apparently disrobed before going to bathe or change. Although this *surimono* bears no text beyond the name of the artist, the contents of the bowl suggest that it was commissioned for the New Year as such sweets were typically eaten during the holiday. Given the subject of this print, it is probable that it was made in a Year of the Dog in the Chinese calendar, putting its likely production date in 1777.

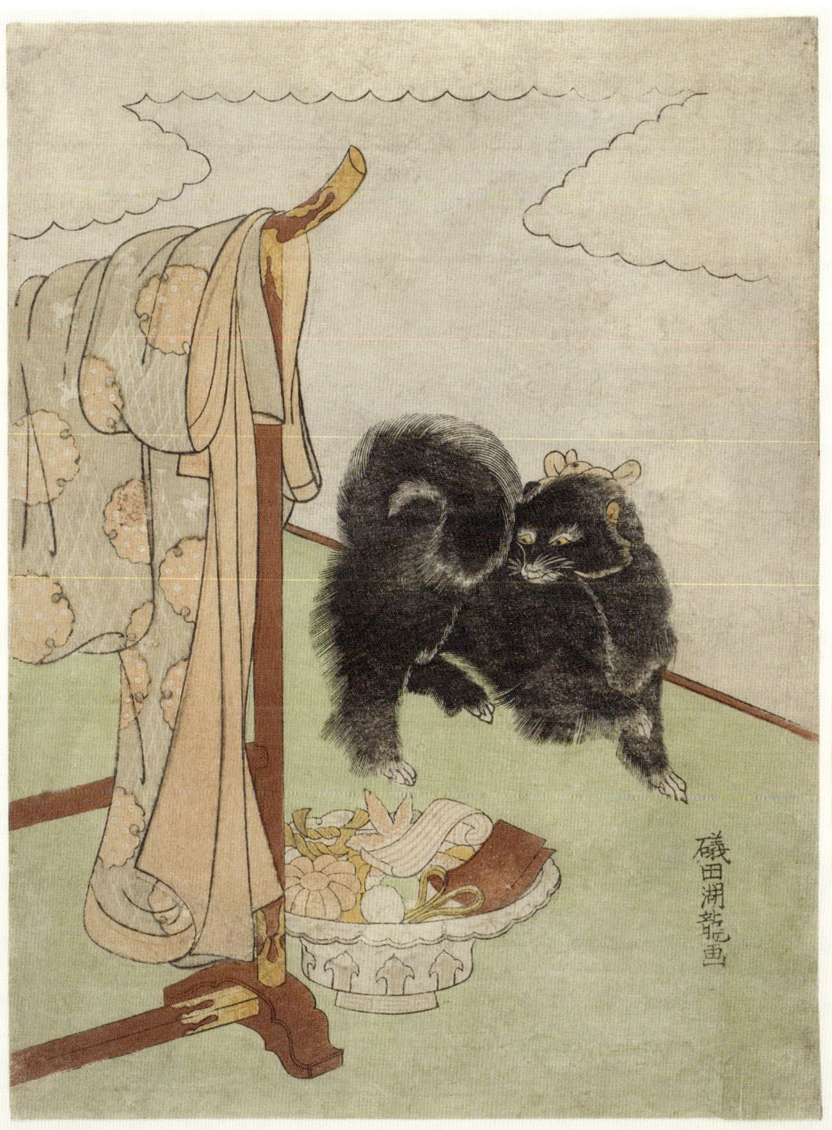

KATSUSHIKA HOKUSAI

(1760–1849)

The Salt Maiden Matsukaze, 1830

Woodblock print: ink, color, and metallic pigments on paper
48.2 × 55.2 cm (19 × 21¾ in.)
John Chandler Bancroft Collection, 1901.1196

This privately printed work commemorates a performance
of the Noh play *Matsukaze*, performed at the Komparu Noh
Theater in Kyoto by pupils and friends of actor Yoshimura
Isaburo (1780–?) as a tribute to him on his fiftieth birthday on
March 24, 1830. The extensive text lists the names of every
person who participated in or contributed to the production,
highlighting the collaborative nature of the event and the
respect held for Yoshimura within the theater community.

The featured figure is the play's titular character, a
"salt maiden" (a poetic name for a woman who uses brine
to manufacture salt) standing on the shores of Suma Bay
beside a pine tree. Hanging on its boughs is the coat of
her faithless lover Yukihira, who abandoned her and never
returned. The image captures a poignant moment in the play,
as Matsukaze contemplates her lost love and the symbol of
his broken promise. The combination of the detailed text and
the evocative illustration creates a compelling record of this
special performance and the significance of Noh theater in
Japanese culture.

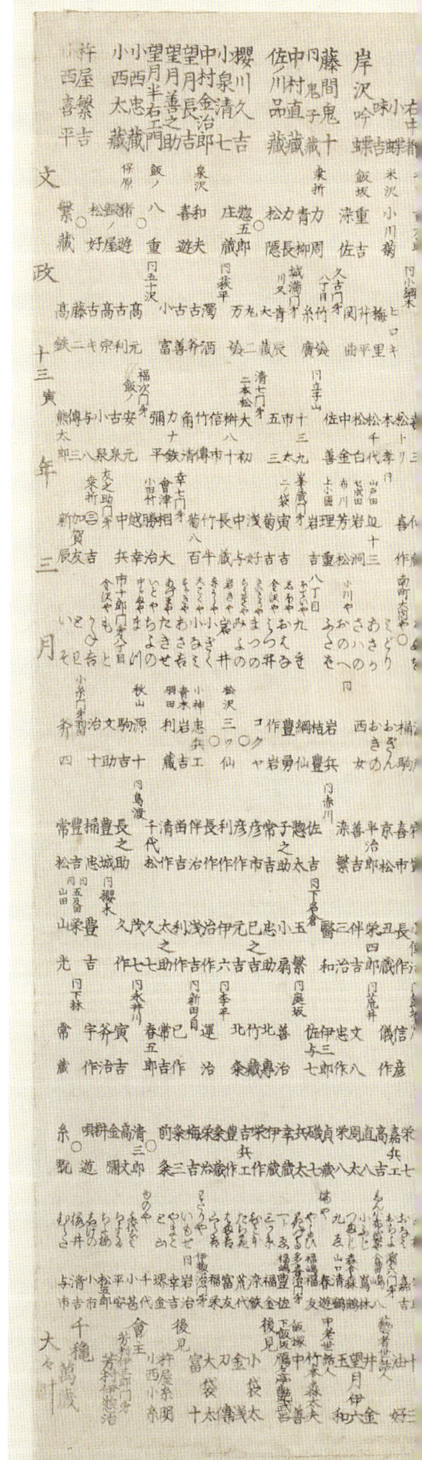

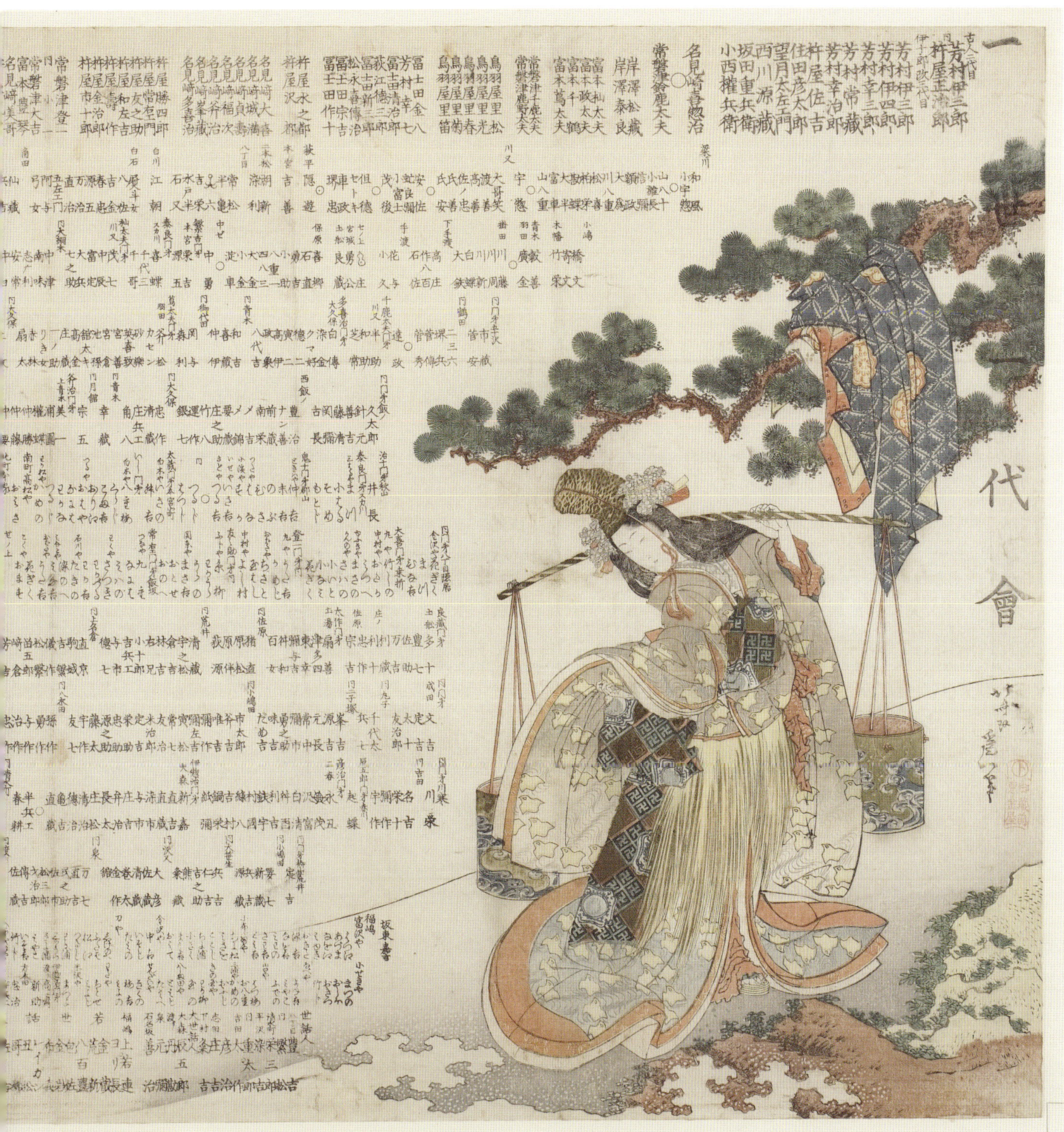

一
一代會

UTAGAWA TOYOKUNI I

(1769–1825)

Ladies-in-Waiting with Male Entertainers, early 19th century

Publisher: Yamamotoya Kyubei
Woodblock print: ink and color on paper
37.8 × 76.1 cm (14⅞ × 29¹⁵⁄₁₆ in.)
John Chandler Bancroft Collection, 1901.1002

At first glance, the group in this triptych appears to be composed entirely of women. However, several of the figures are young male entertainers called *wakushū*. Like their female counterparts in the pleasure quarters, they wear long-sleeved kimonos called *furisode*, but in this case some of them can be identified by the way their hair is styled to cover shaved forelocks, a distinctively male fashion. They, in addition to the shamisen player on the right and the two standing figures, seem to have been hired by three ladies-in-waiting from a samurai household to entertain them for the evening. They sit before a brazier, chatting and playing music.

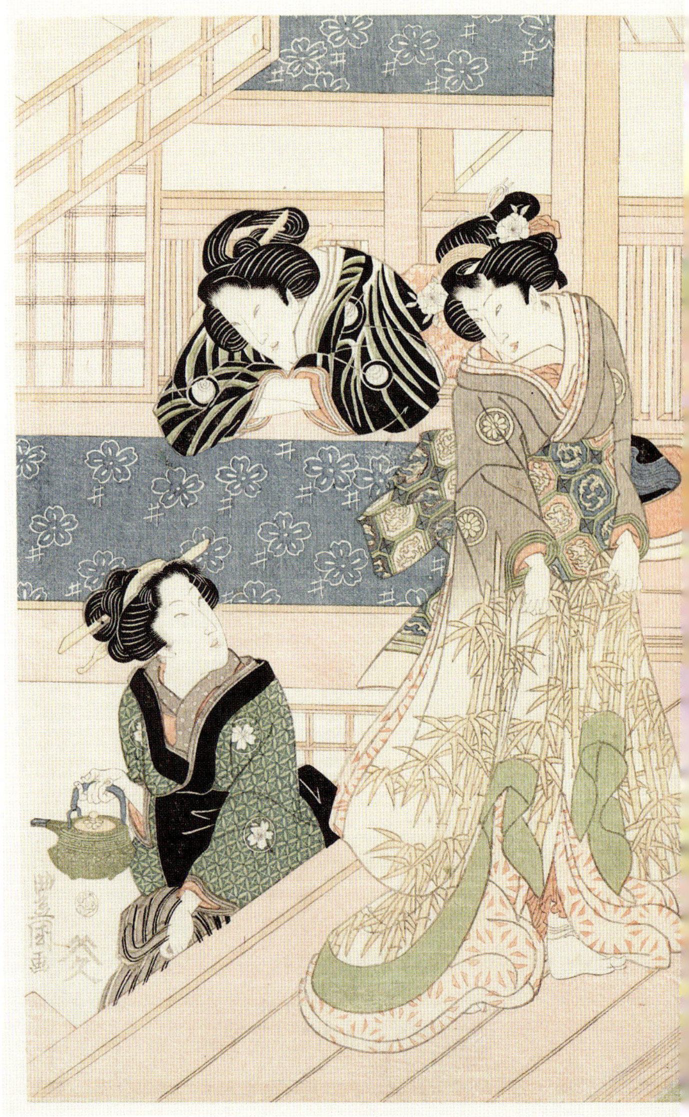

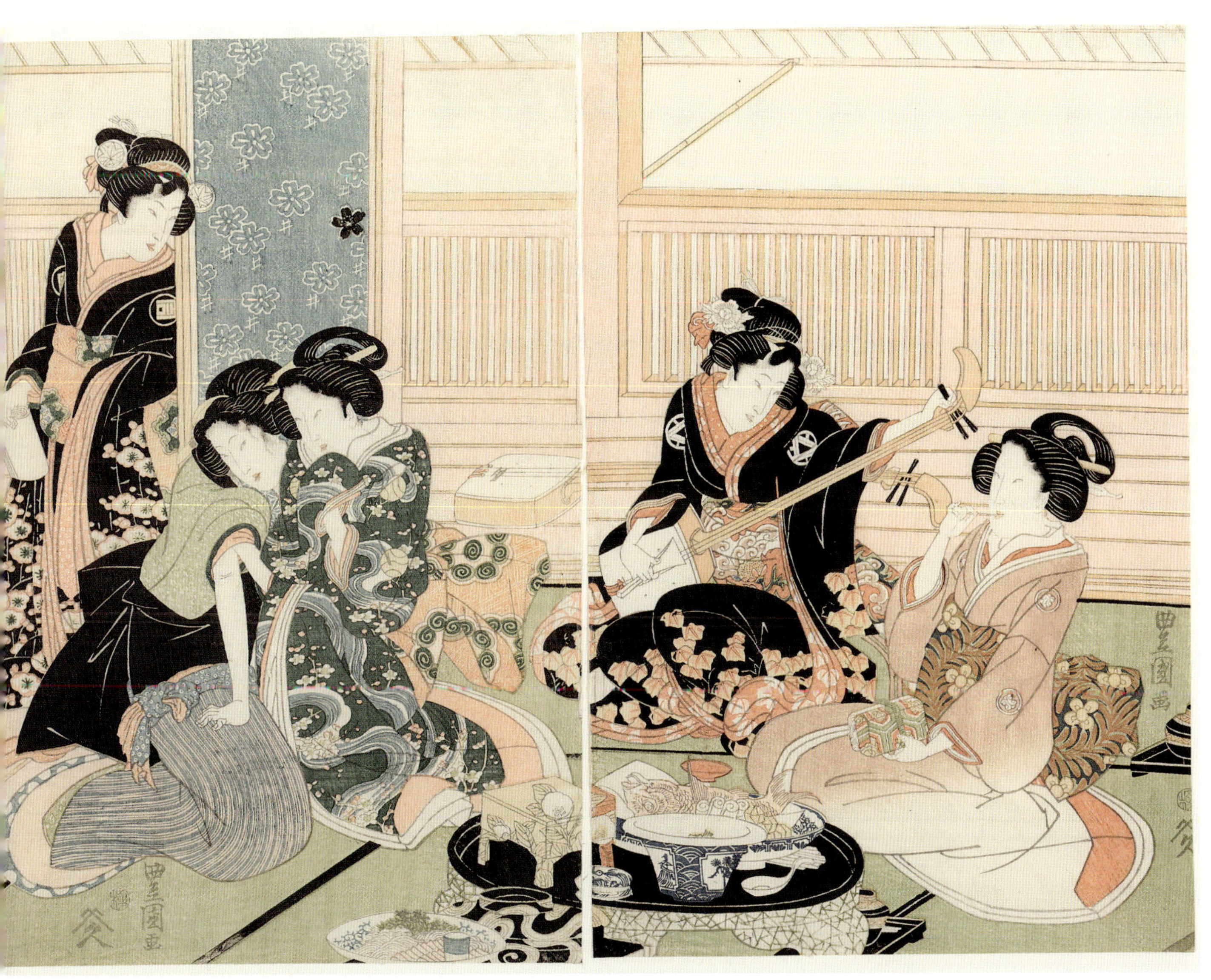

KATSUKAWA SHUNSEN (SHUNKŌ II)

(1762–ca. 1830)

Evening Glow at Ryōgoku Bridge, **from the series "Eight Views of Edo in Triptychs",** 1813

Publisher: Izumiya Ichibei
Woodblock print: ink and color on paper
Vertical *ōban* triptych: 36.3 × 73.6 cm (14⁵⁄₁₆ × 29 in.)
John Chandler Bancroft Collection, 1901.134

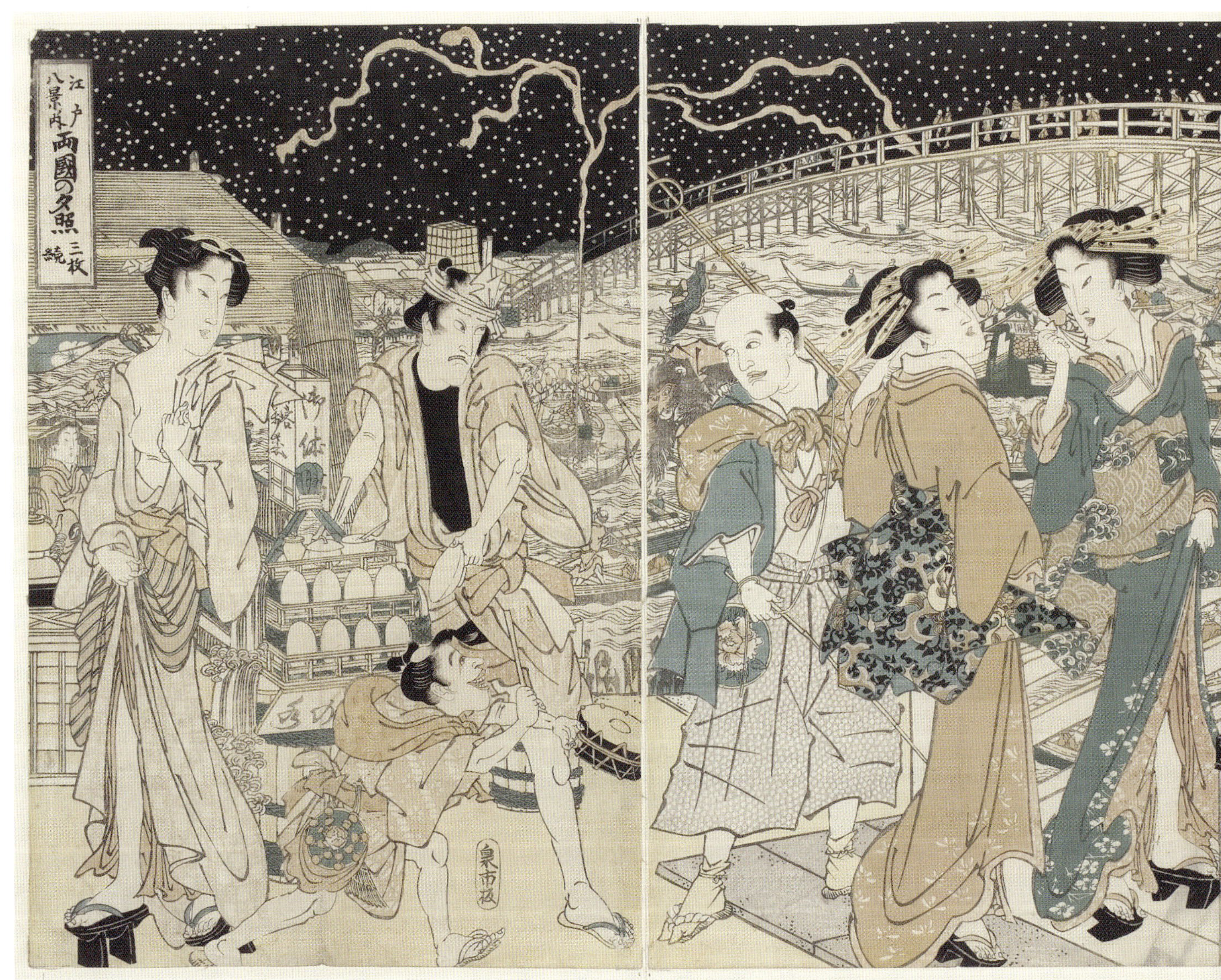

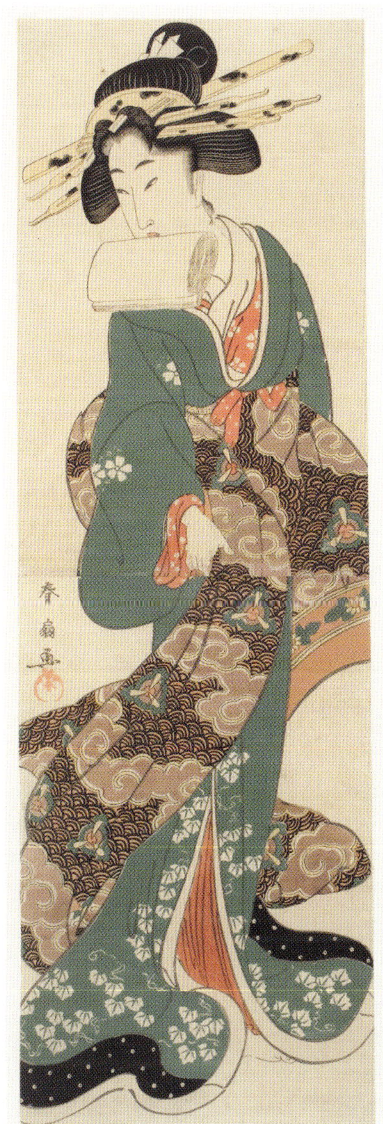

***Geisha Tying Her Sash while Holding a Roll of
Tissues between Her Teeth,*** ca. 1815–20

Woodblock print: ink and color on paper
Vertical diptych: 73.6 × 24.5 cm (29 × 9⅝ in.)
John Chandler Bancroft Collection, 1901.261

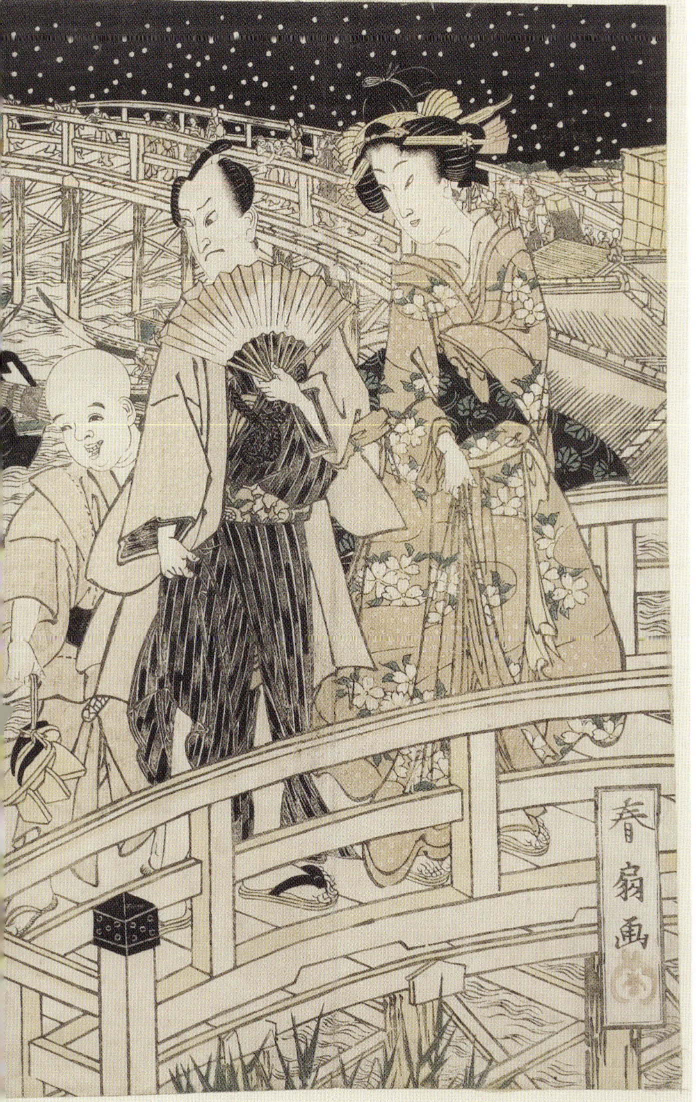

As a hub of commerce and transportation, Ryōgoku Bridge
was one of the most recognizable landmarks on the Sumida
River in Edo. In late May, the annual Kawabiraki Festival marked
the river's opening to recreational boating and, by extension,
the beginning of the summer season in the city. It remained a
popular place to spend evenings through August; large crowds
of people from all walks of life gathered there to lounge in
covered *yakatabune* (pleasure boats), shop at local stalls, and
watch the "evening glow" or fireworks.

In Shunsen's urban landscapes such as this, one can often
find figures from his other works. The fashionable beauty seen
in the vertical diptych pictured to the right shows remarkable
similarity in pose and costume to the beauty on the bridge.

UTAGAWA KUNISADA I

(1786–1865)

The Popular Type, **from the series "Thirty-two Physiognomies in the Modern World",** ca. 1822–23

Publisher: Nishinomiya Shinroku
Woodblock print: ink and color on paper
37.1 × 25.1 cm (14⅝ × 9⅞ in.)
John Chandler Bancroft Collection, 1901.59.2528

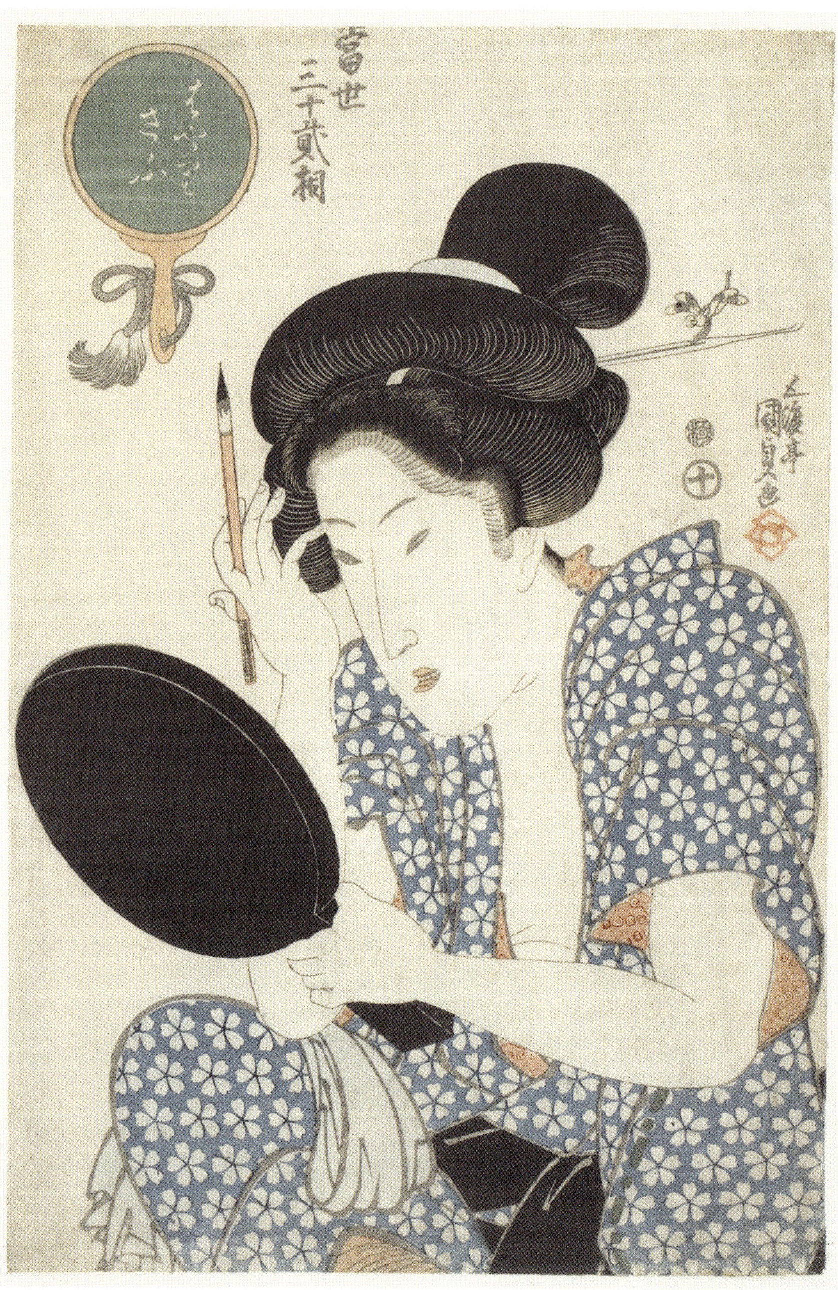

Kunisada's series "Thirty-two Physiognomies in the Modern World" offers a parody of the thirty-two physical attributes of the Buddha by categorizing the different "types" of women considered attractive at the time, often showing them in a flurry of activity as they try to appear effortlessly beautiful. The little mirror above each woman notes her type. They reference those used by physiognomists to examine their clients' faces and openly invite the viewer to evaluate her appearance.

The "popular type" seen here holds a cosmetic brush as she uses her little finger to smooth her right eyebrow, enhancing its shape and color with black pigment. The ornament on her hairpin references the popular association between the men who frequented the Yoshiwara and dragonflies; the insects were believed to fly north, and this was the direction of the pleasure quarters in relation to the center of Edo.

TOTOYA HOKKEI

(1780–1850)

A Shinto Ceremony at Mekari in the Province of Nagato, from the series "Famous Places in the Provinces", ca. 1834–35

Publishers: Nishimuraya Yohachi (Eijudō) and Nakamuraya Katsugorō
Woodblock print: ink and color on paper
7.8 × 37.1 cm (3⅛ × 14⅝ in.)
John Chandler Bancroft Collection, 1901.700

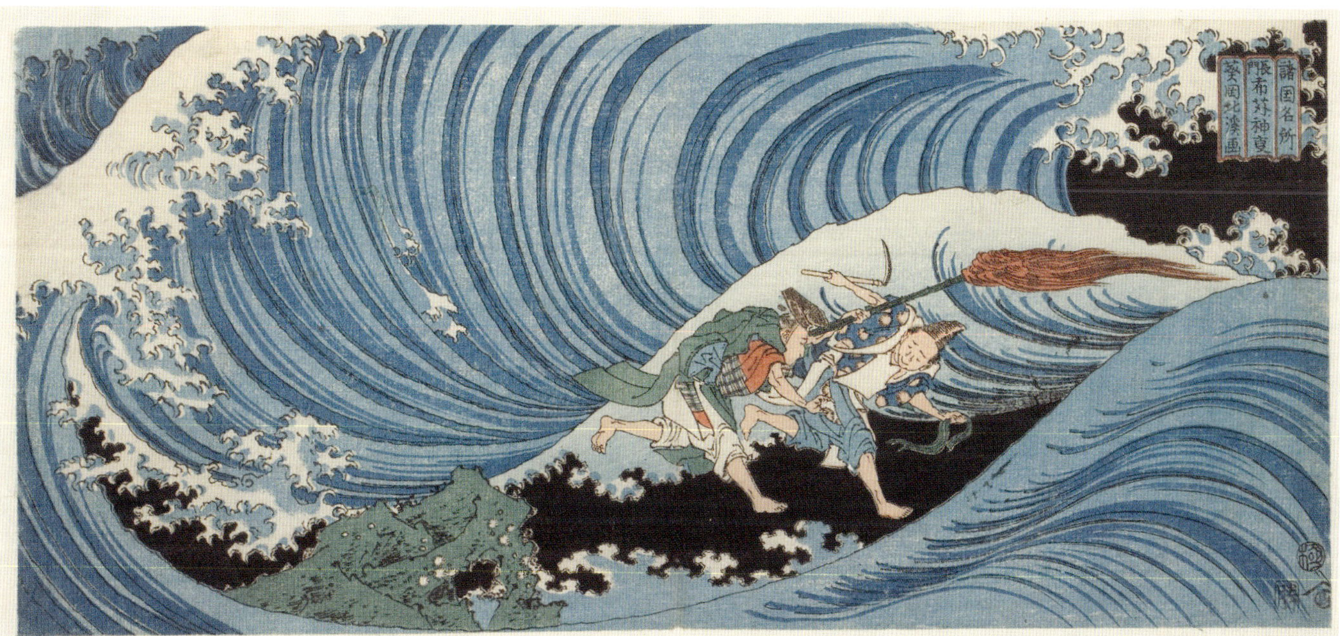

This print portrays a time-honored New Year's ritual held at Mekari Shrine in Japan. During this event, participants gather at low tide to harvest *wakame* seaweed from the ocean, which symbolizes wealth and good fortune for the coming year. The collected seaweed is then presented on the shrine's altar as an offering to secure luck and prosperity. The ceremony is led by two Shinto priests dressed in traditional attire, who are guided to the sea by another priest carrying a three-meter-long torch. The design was inspired by a book illustrated by the renowned artist Katsushika Hokusai, Hokkei's teacher.

UTAGAWA KUNISADA I

(1786–1865)

Memorial Portrait of Hiroshige, 1858

Publisher: Sakanaya Eikichi
Woodblock print: ink and color on paper
36.2 × 24.8 cm (14¼ × 9¾ in.)
John Chandler Bancroft Collection, 1901.569

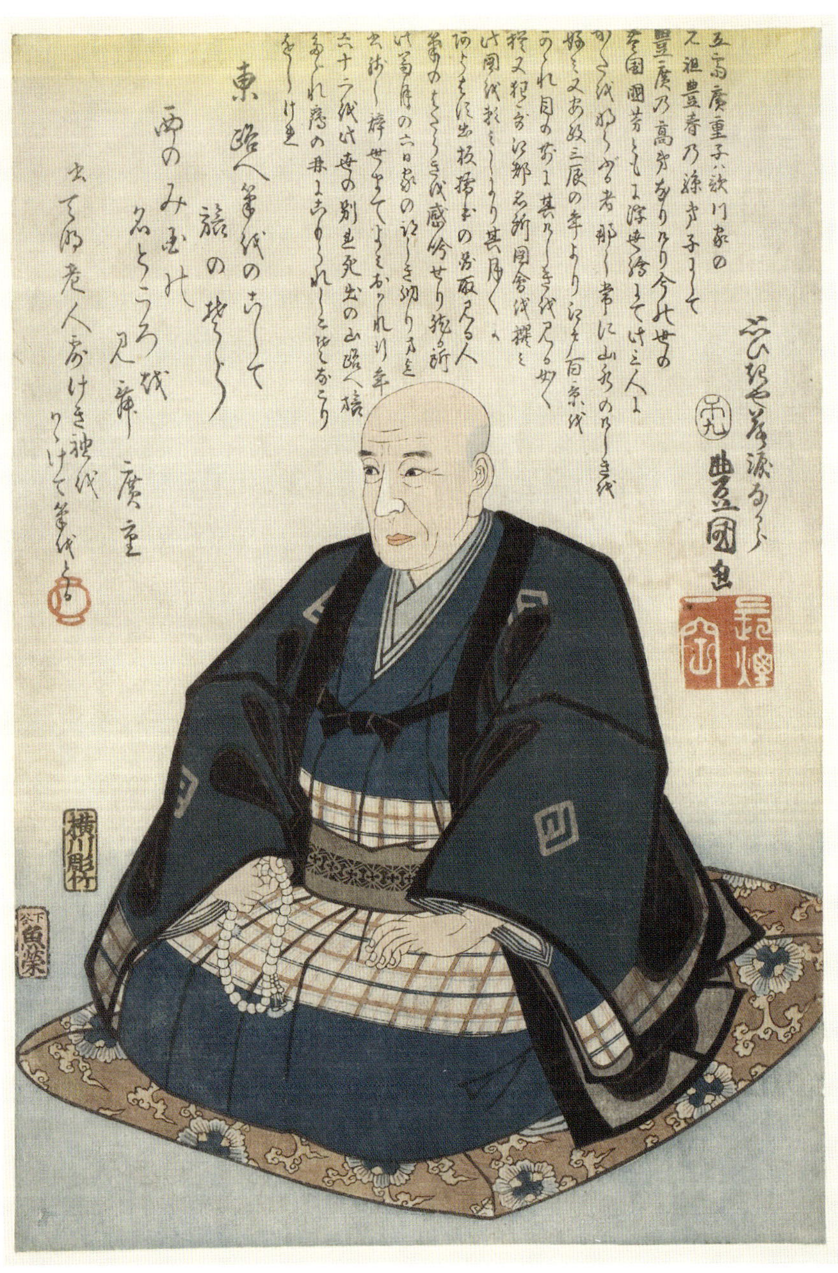

This image pays homage to the great Utagawa Hiroshige (1797–1858), who was a friend and respected peer of Kunisada I. Made just months after Hiroshige's death, it depicts him as he was at the end of his life, a Buddhist monk living in austerity. Kunisada's portrayal is made even more poignant knowing that the relationship between the two designers spanned several decades. Both trained in the Utagawa school; they were recognized as leaders in their areas of expertise—landscape and actors/beauties respectively—and occasionally collaborated. The accompanying text in this print provides a succinct overview of Hiroshige's notable achievements and life, enriched by a poem he penned in his final days that captures his personal reflections on art and spirituality at the end of his life: "I am leaving my brush in the Eastern skies / So to see the famous places of Western Paradise."

KIKUGAWA EIZAN

(1787–1867)

Women in Front of the Iwaki Matsuya Department Store, early 1800s

Woodblock print: ink and color on paper
36.8 × 25.1 cm (14½ × 9⅞ in.)
John Chandler Bancroft Collection, 1901.59.2623

Due in part to the reputation of the
Yoshiwara in popular culture, images of
abstracted beauties, or *bijin*, often were
used as vehicles for popular fashions in
print, demonstrating to consumers how
one could layer kimono, experiment with
combinations of colors or patterns, or
arrange hair. Here, a group of women, one
accompanied by a child, stand before
the renowned Iwaki Matsuya department
store, which opened in the Edo period
and continues to be celebrated for its
exquisite silks and fashionable textiles
today. Their elaborate garments reflect
the flamboyant direction that fashion
took in the 1820s and '30s.

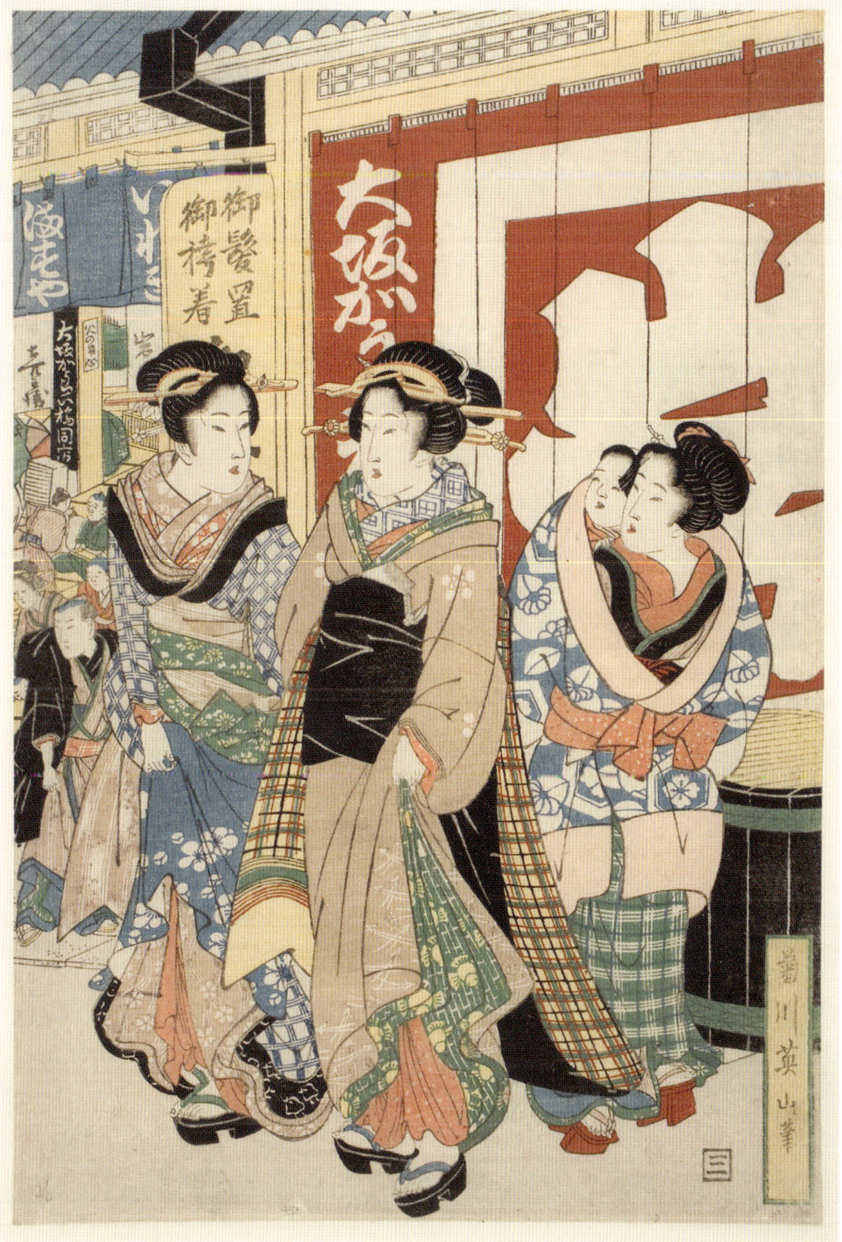

KESAI EISEN

(1790–1848)

Modern Figures at Dawn on a Snowy Day, 1830s

Publisher: Sanoya Kihei (Kikakudō)
Woodblock print: ink and color on paper
Ōban triptych: 36 × 75.5 cm (14³⁄₁₆ × 29¾ in.)
John Chandler Bancroft Collection, 1901.146

Kesai Eisen was known for his energetic and innovative interpretations of classic *ukiyo-e* genres such as *bijin* ("beautiful women"), landscapes, and Western-perspective pictures (*uki-e*). In this print, Eisen's experience depicting these subjects is evident. The three elegantly dressed women are portrayed promenading along the shore of Edo Bay to witness the first sunrise of the year, a traditional New Year's custom known as *hatsuhinode*. This practice was believed to bring good fortune and prosperity for the coming year, and it provided an opportunity for people to dress in their finest attire and celebrate the occasion with friends and family.

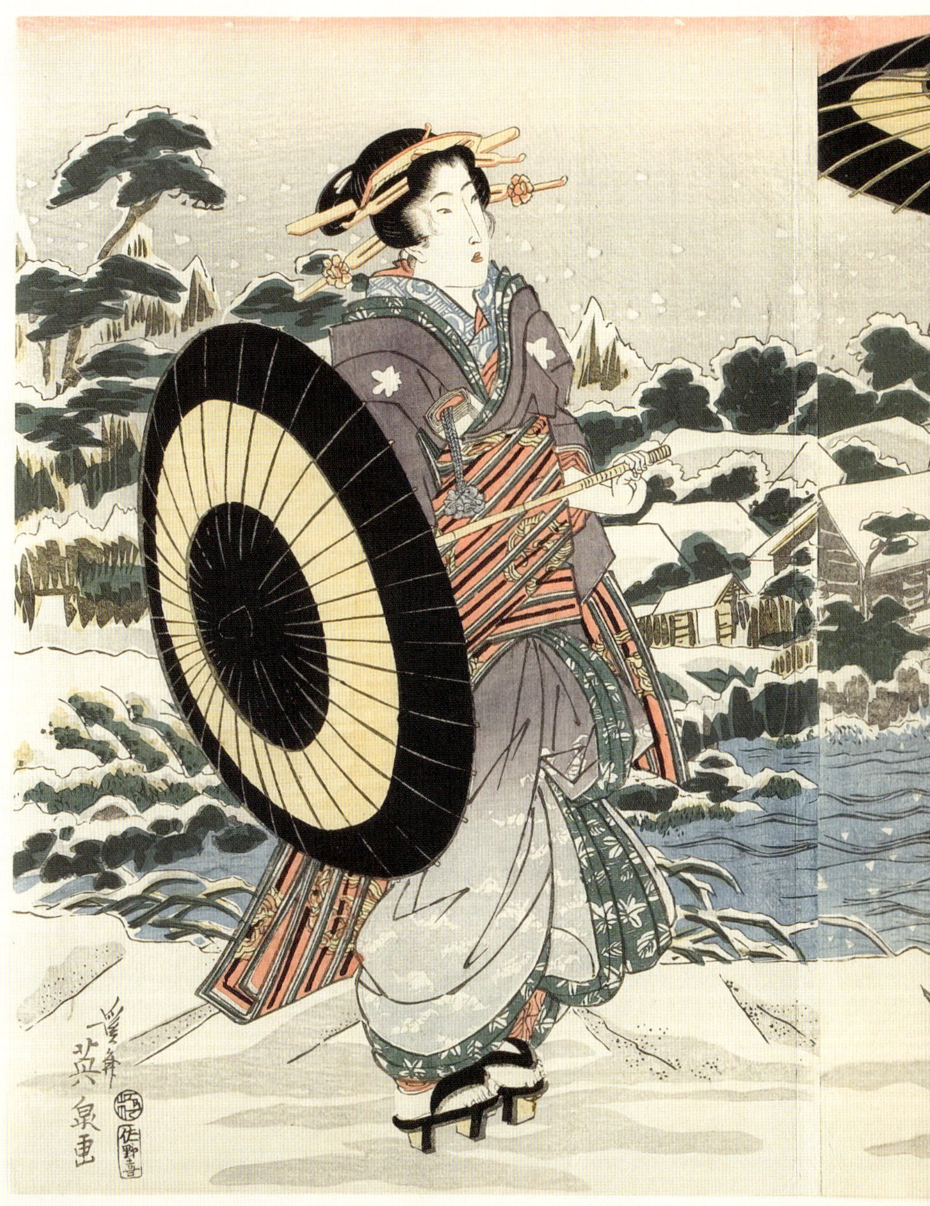

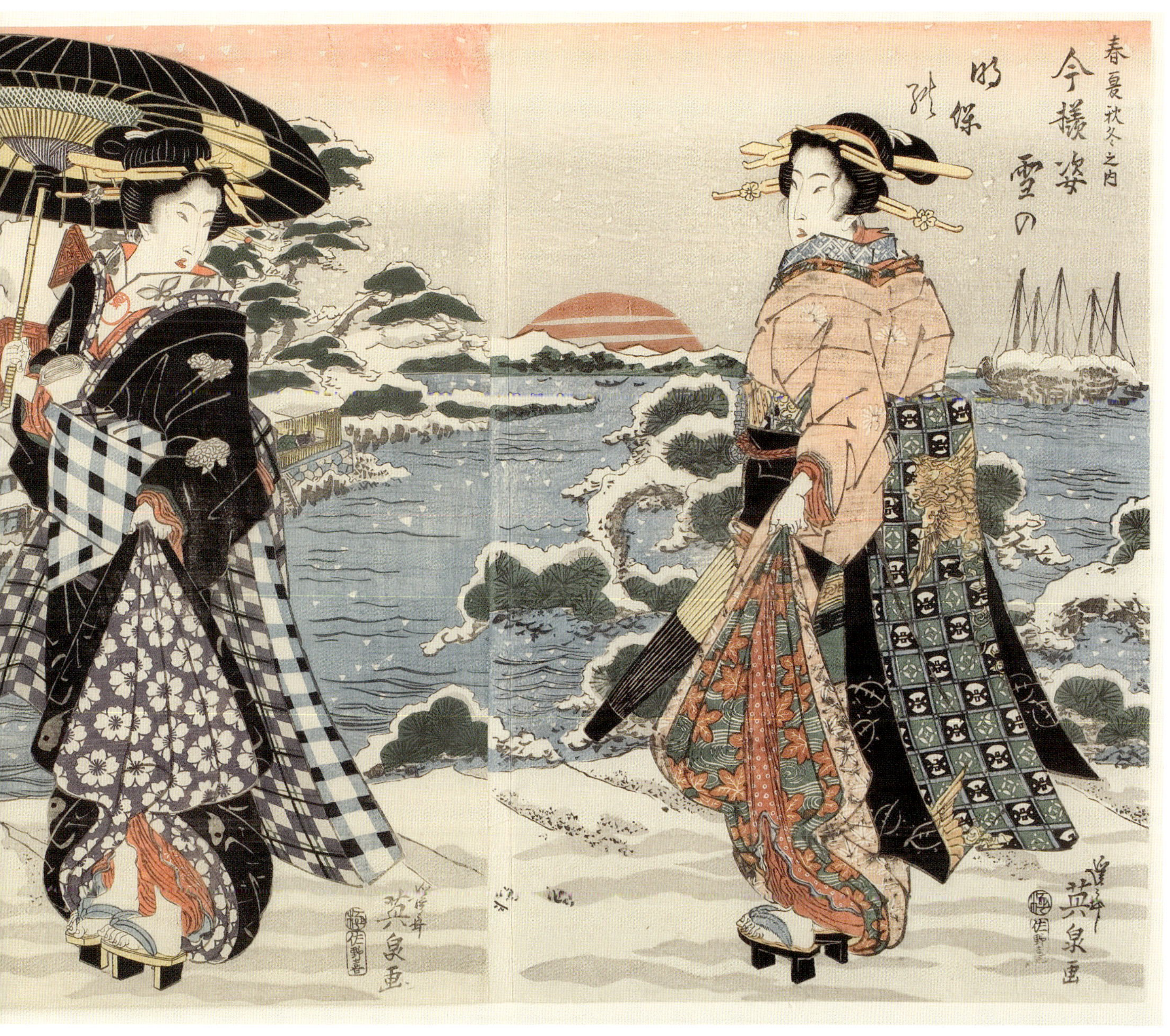
春夏秋冬之内
今様姿
雪の
明保
英泉画
英泉画

KATSUSHIKA HOKUSAI

(1760–1849)

Laughing Demoness, from the series "One Hundred Ghost Tales", ca. 1831–32

Publisher: Tsuruya Kiemon (Senkakudô)
Woodblock print: ink and color on paper
18.7 × 6.3 cm (7⅜ × 10⅜ in.)
Museum Purchase, 1901.742

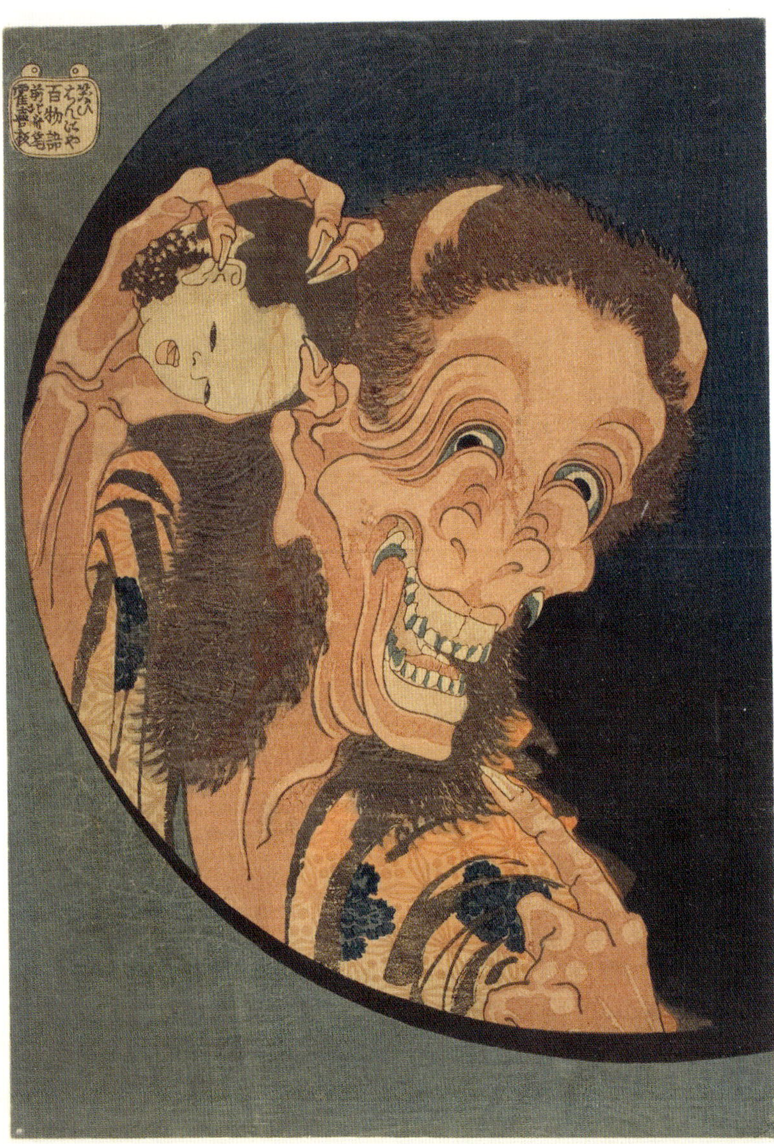

Hokusai designed this acclaimed series at the end of his career. Here, he depicts a _hannya_, a violent horned demon believed to appear when a woman was overcome by jealousy or rejection. In order to heighten the macabre overtones of the subject, Hokusai cleverly synthesized the lurid red skin and contorted expression associated with _hannya_-character masks from Noh theater with the filthy hair and clothes of another supernatural, infant-eating crone known as a _yamauba_.

This print is an exemplar of the _yūrei-zu_ genre of Japanese prints, characterized by portrayals of the paranormal or haunting interpretations of traditional folklore, which were enthusiastically consumed by urban audiences throughout the nineteenth century.

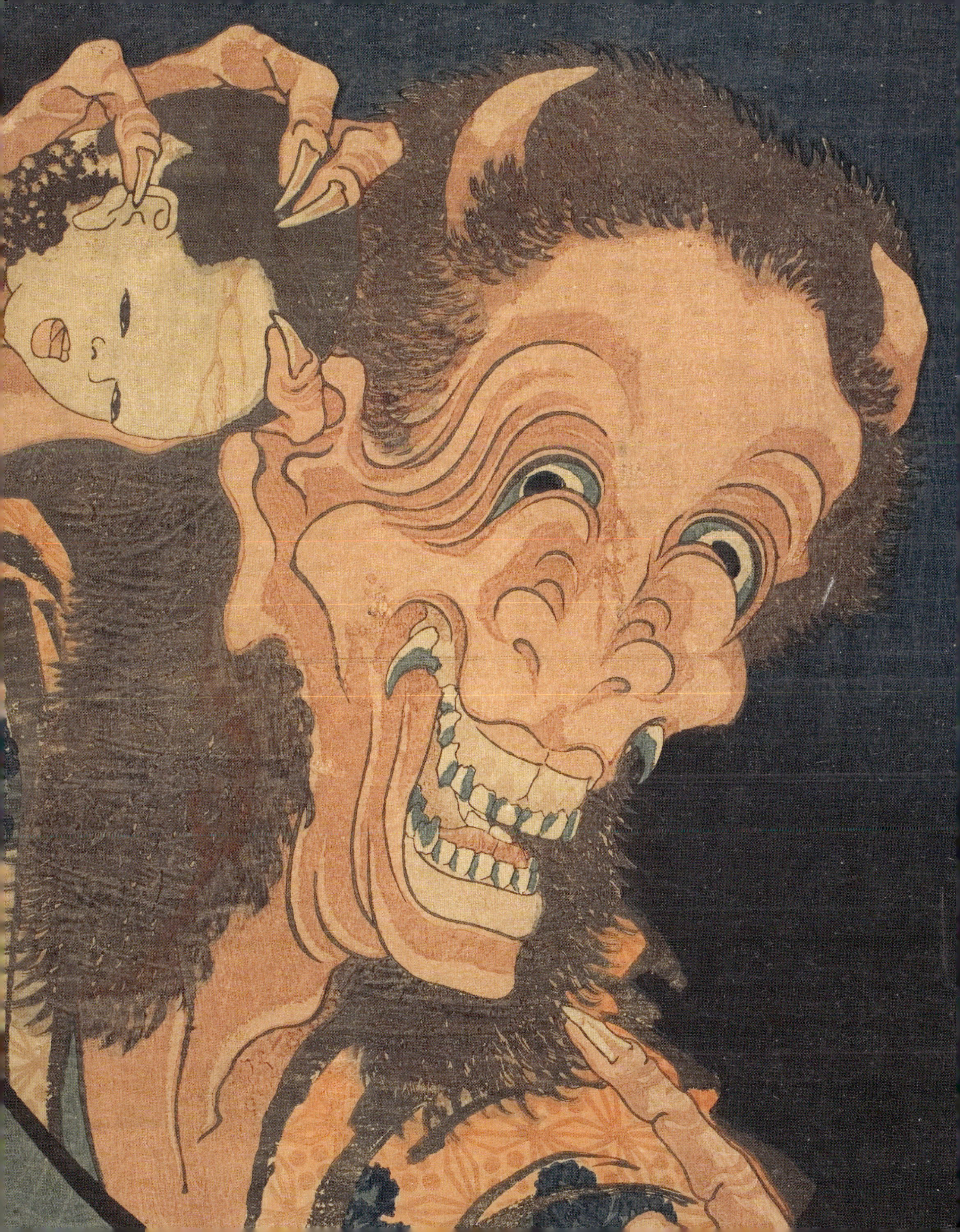

KATSUSHIKA HOKUSAI

(1760–1849)

A Hawk in Flight, ca. 1840

Woodblock print: ink and color on paper
Sheet: 22.3 × 29.5 cm (8¾ × 11⅝ in.)
John Chandler Bancroft Collection, 1901.59.3075

Uchiwa-e prints were made from color woodblocks and produced in the distinctive rounded shape related to their function. They were often cut out, and mounted on flat, wooden frames with handles and sold as fashionable and affordable fans. Very few of these prints have survived because they were used and thus deteriorated over time or were discarded. In this print portraying a goshawk as it begins its ascent above the cloud line in a brilliant blue sky, Hokusai creates a sense of dynamic movement in a very restricted space. This print is exceedingly rare, as only a few impressions of it survive in the world.

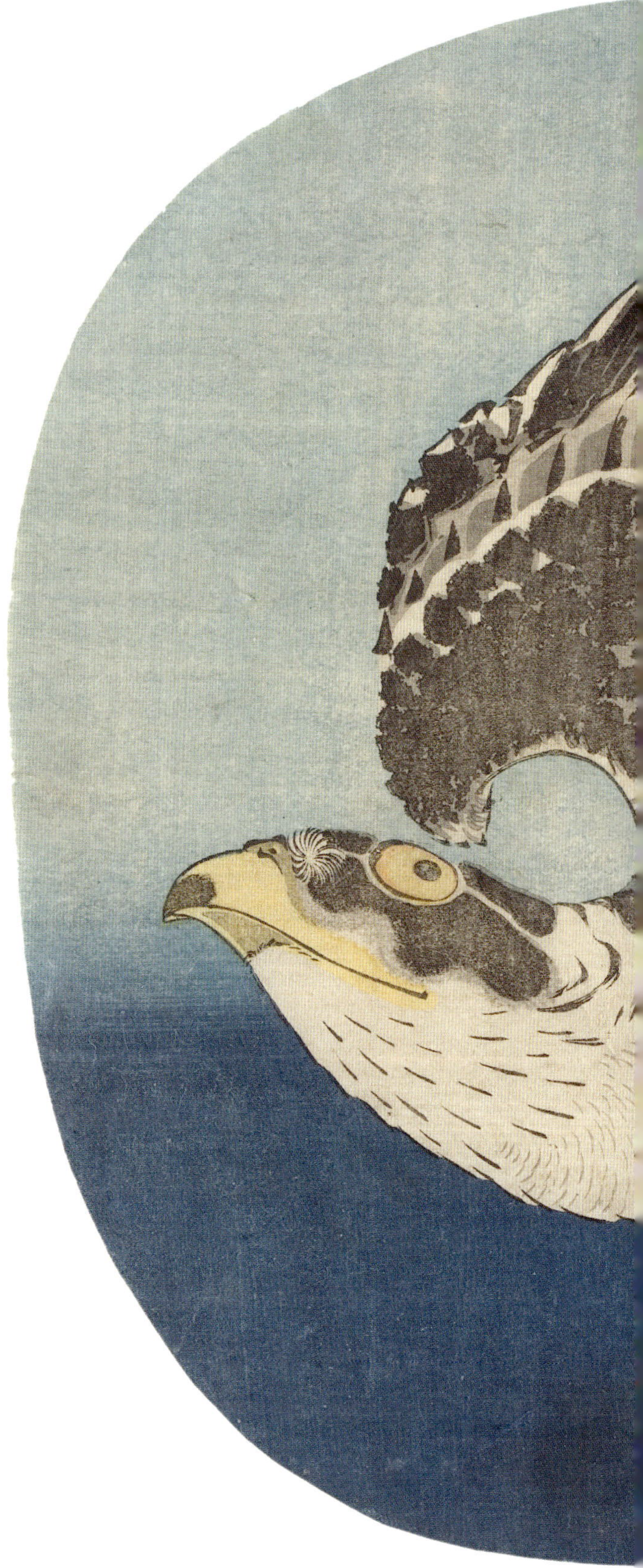

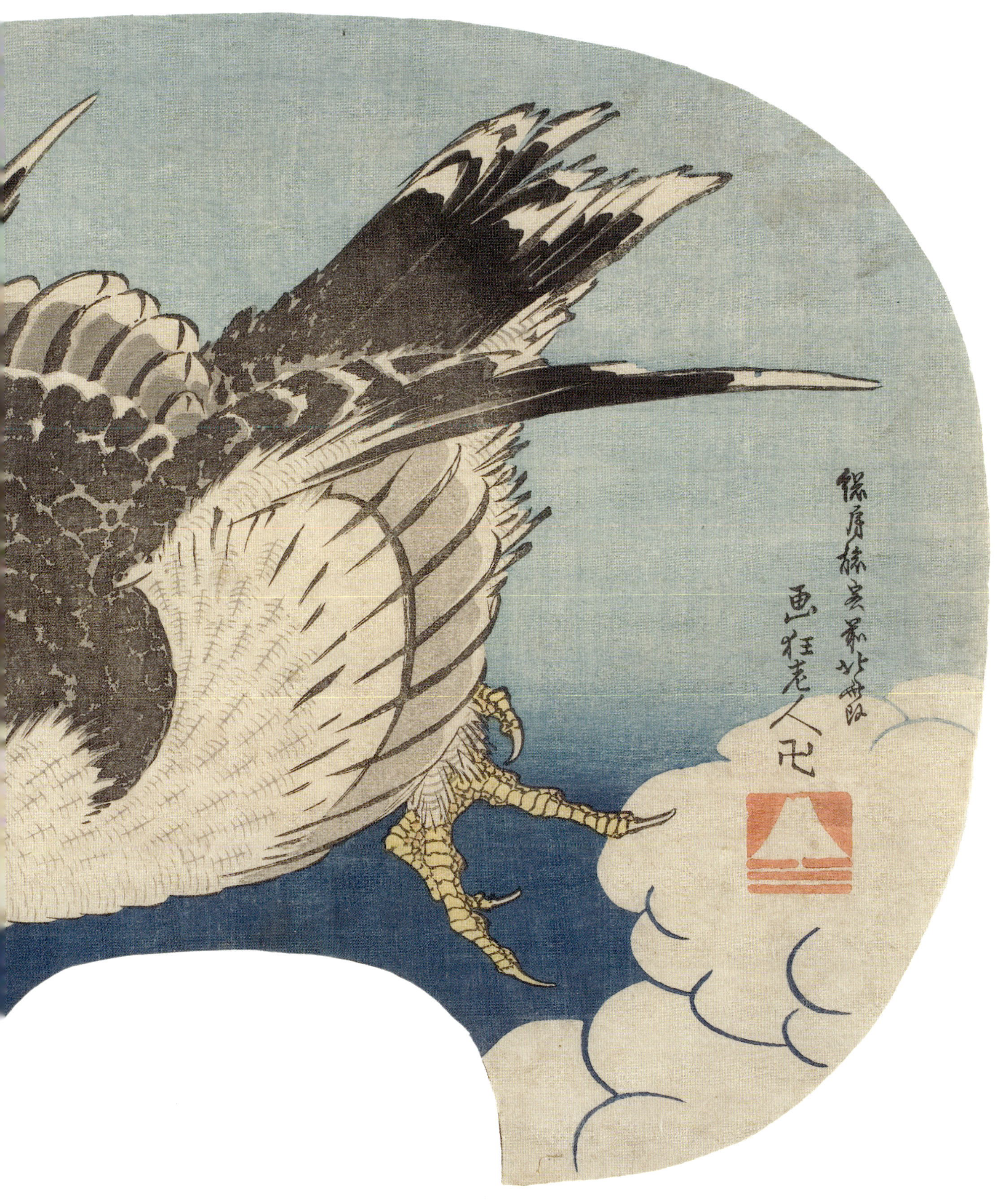
前北斎為一筆
画狂老人卍

KATSUSHIKA HOKUSAI

(1760–1849)

Three plates from the series "Thirty-six Views of Mount Fuji", ca. 1831

a) *South Wind, Clear Sky or Red Fuji*

Publisher: Nishimura Yohachi
Woodblock print: ink and color on paper
25.1 × 35.5 cm (9⅞ × 14 in.)
John Chandler Bancroft Collection, 1901.784

b) *Under the Wave off Kanagawa*

Publisher: Nishimura Yohachi
Woodblock print: ink and color on paper
24.5 × 36.5 cm (9⅝ × 14⅜ in.)
John Chandler Bancroft Collection, 1918.9

c) *Fuji from Gotenyama, at Shinagawa on the Tōkaidō*

Publisher: Nishimura Yohachi
Woodblock print: ink and color on paper
24.5 × 36.8 cm (9⅝ × 14½ in.)
John Chandler Bancroft Collection, 1901.760

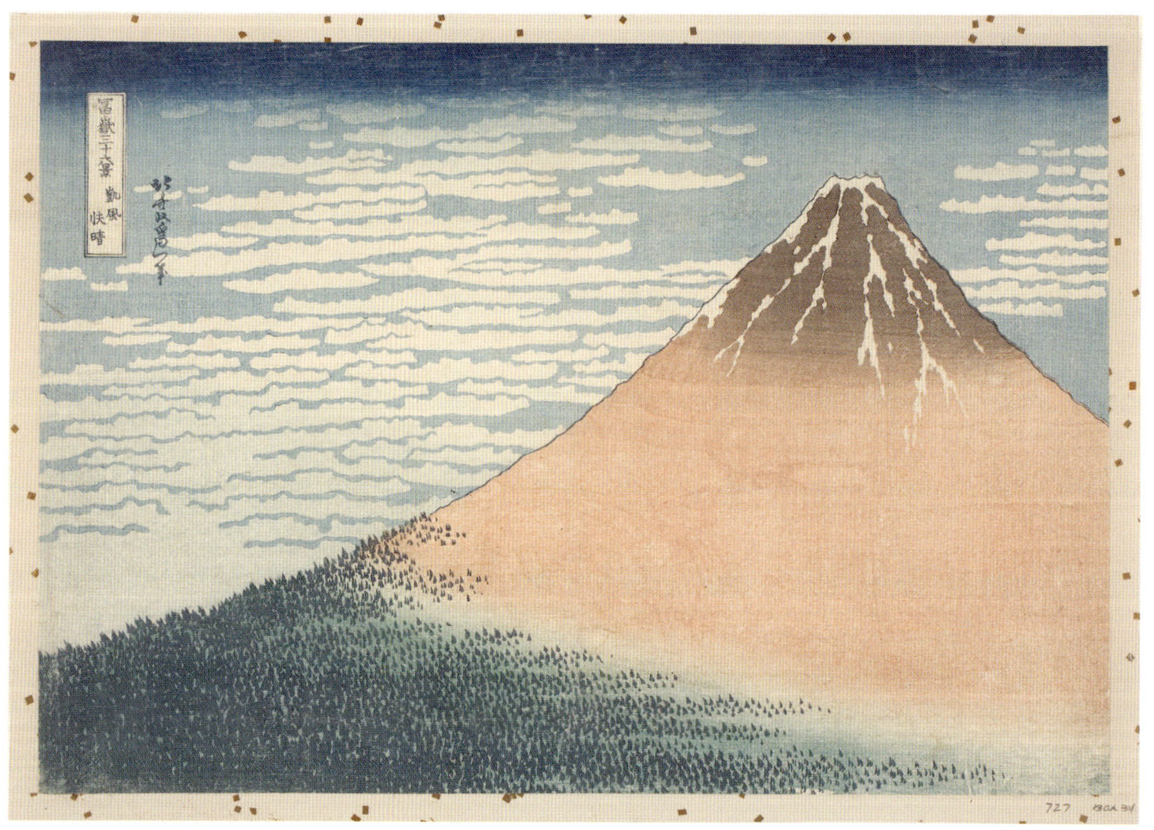

a

In this iconic series, Hokusai celebrates Mount Fuji, the focal point of the landscape around Edo, showing it from different angles and under a variety of atmospheric conditions. In some cases, the peak appears like a tiny dot on the horizon while in others it dominates the composition. Although the prints include red, green, and yellow hues, this series was initially marketed as a set of *aizuri* pictures, as they were all printed primarily in imported Prussian blue.

South Wind, Clear Sky captures the moment at dawn when warm sunlight hits the mountain's face so that it briefly emanates a rosy glow. It is also among the most simplistic and abstract in the series, as the face of the mountain and the clouds are not rendered with naturalistic spatial recession or surface texture. Because the ink gradation was added manually, each imprint of this design is different. The two "eyes"—circular gaps on the center of the mountain slope created by the grain of the woodblock—mark this print as an early impression.

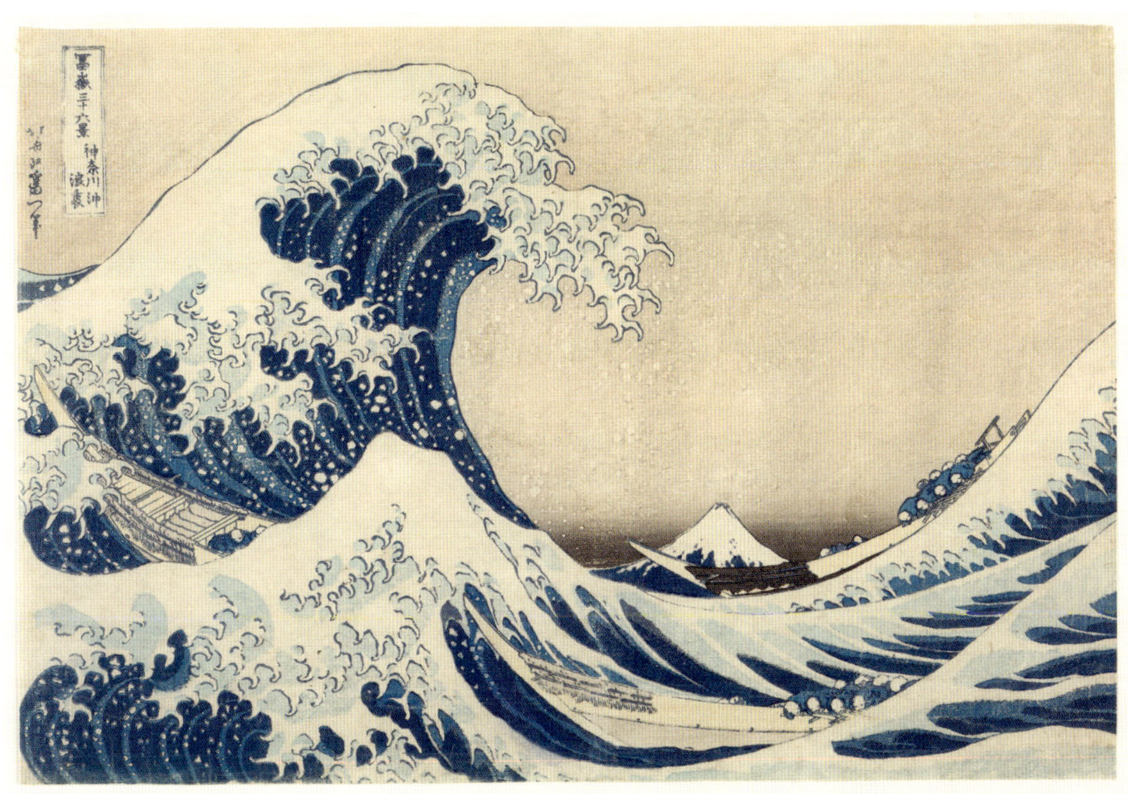

b

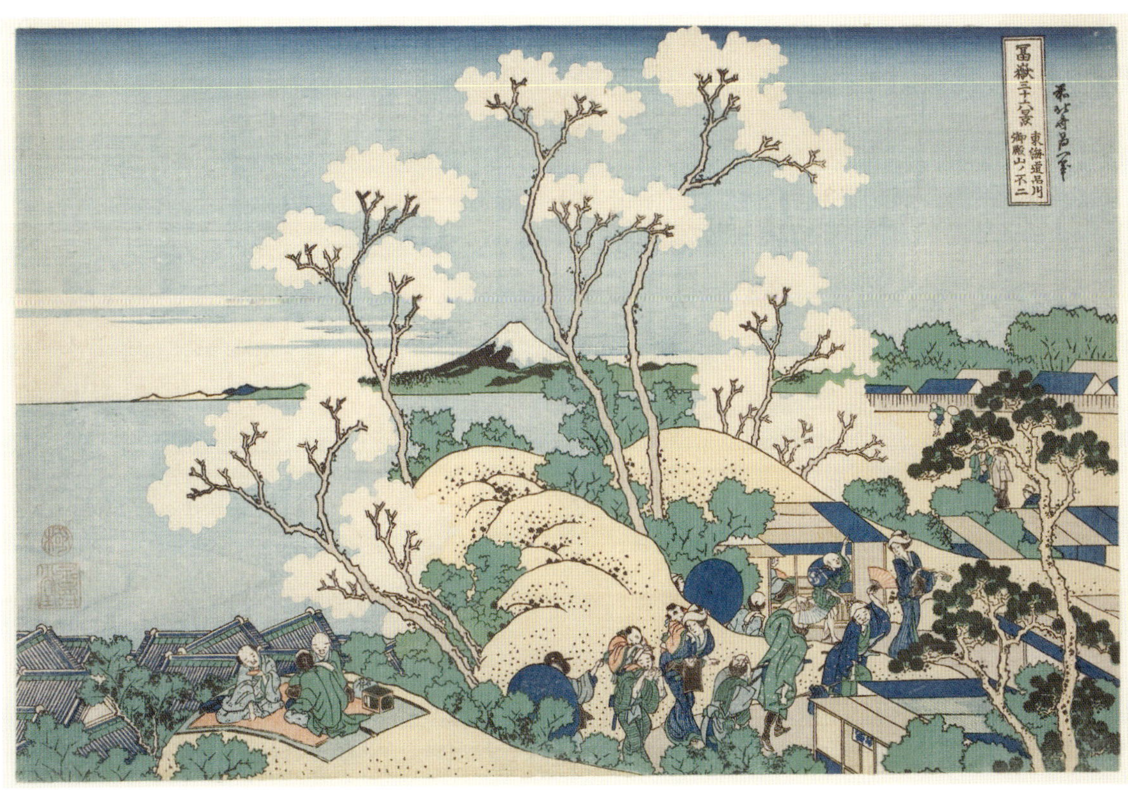

c

KATSUSHIKA HOKUSAI

(1760–1849)

The Falls at Aoigaoka in the Eastern Capital, from the series "A Tour of Waterfalls in Various Provinces", ca. 1832

Publisher: Nishimuraya Yohachi (Eijudō)
Woodblock print: ink and color on paper
Vertical *ō-ōban*: 37.9 × 25.4 cm (14¹⁵⁄₁₆ × 10 in.)
John Chandler Bancroft Collection, 1901.735

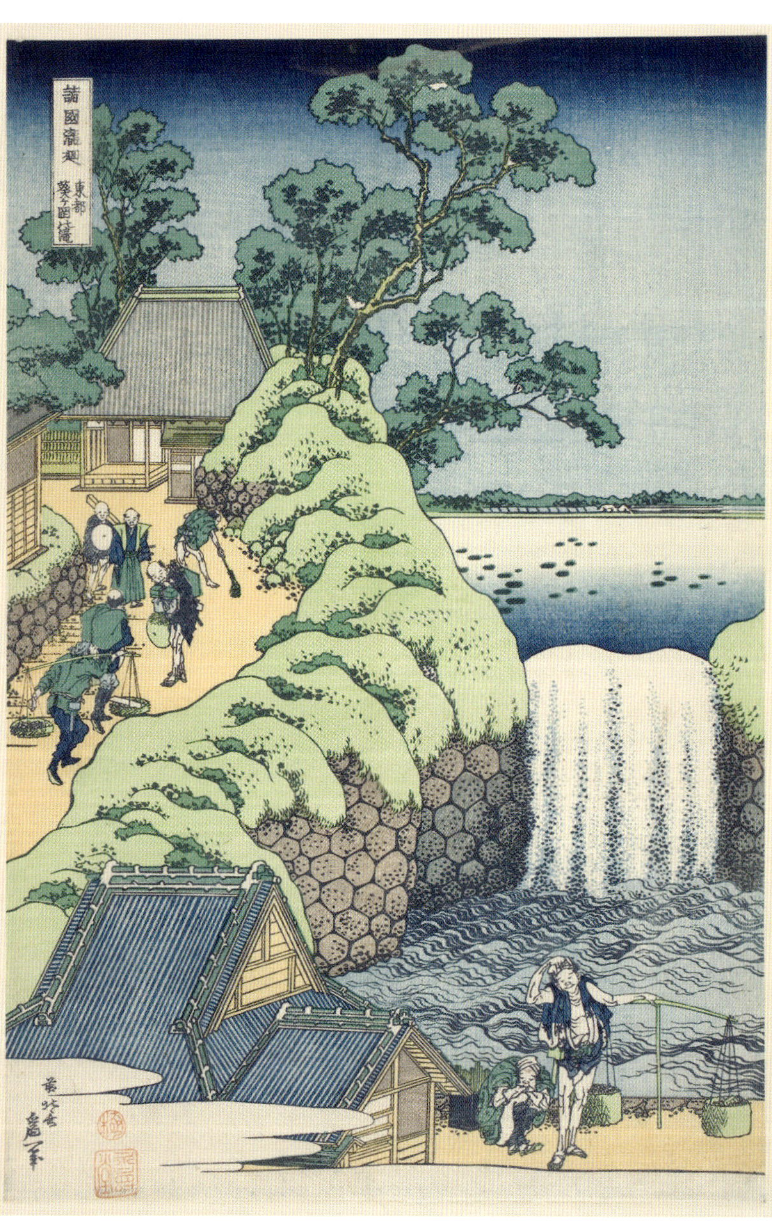

Although prints from Hokusai's series "A Tour of Waterfalls in Various Provinces" (ca. 1832) could arguably be considered a part of the *meisho* "famous places" genre, they defy easy categorization with their historical allusions, mythological subject matter, and religious overtones. The series gives unique insight into Hokusai's spirituality and how it impacted his approach to depicting the natural world. A practitioner of Nichiren Buddhism—a sect that celebrates the intrinsic spiritual potential of all living beings—and Shinto—the native, animistic belief system in Japan—he often chose to portray waterfalls like this one that were located beside major pilgrimage destinations such as shrines or temples to underscore their comparable roles as sites for contemplation of the divine. The water cascades are rendered in vibrant Prussian blue and almost always dwarf any figures or structures in the composition, contrasting the transience of human experience with the expansive, almost monolithic power of nature.

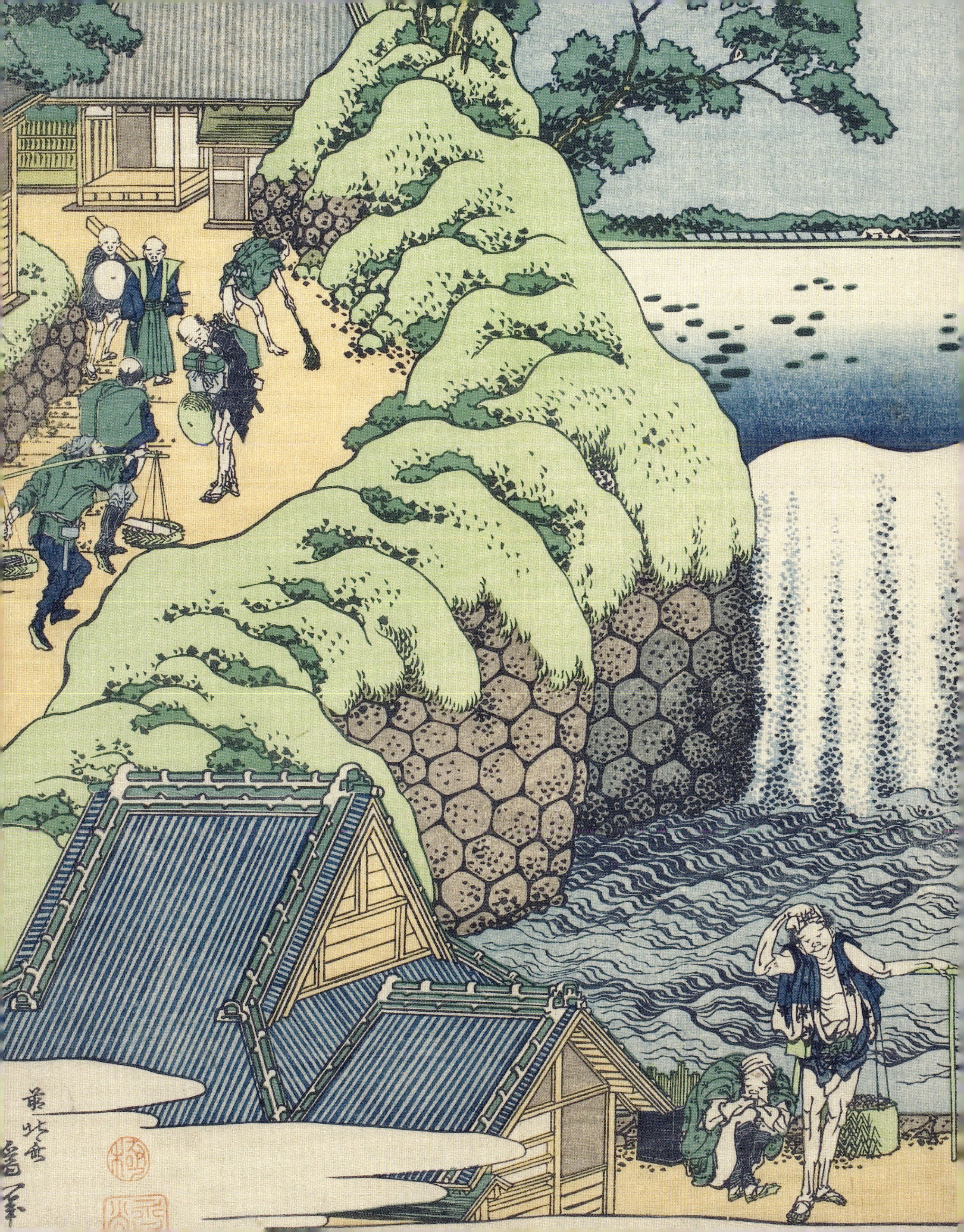

UTAGAWA HIROSHIGE

(1797–1858)

Kanbara: Evening Snow, from the series "Fifty-three Stations of the Tōkaidō", 1833–34

Publisher: Hoeido
Woodblock print: ink and color on paper
Horizontal *ōban*: 22.5 × 35.2 cm (8⅞ × 13⅞ in.)
John Chandler Bancroft Collection, 1901.1053

The series "Fifty-three Stations of the Tōkaidō" comprises views along the "Eastern Sea Road," connecting Edo, Kyoto, and Osaka. By Hiroshige's time, it had transitioned from a hazardous but utilitarian route to a refurbished recreational one for travelers seeking sightseeing, pilgrimage, and adventure. The highly variable landscape, full of famous sites, ensured the Tōkaidō's special presence in Edo-period (1603–1868) visual culture. Hiroshige portrayed it many times, but this series—the first to depict each station—launched his celebrity and was admired for its balanced compositions and imaginative perspectives.

Kambara: Evening Snow captures the pristine stillness of a village blanketed in snow in Shizuoka prefecture. It is likely an imagined scene, as the region rarely saw such heavy snowfall. However, the familiar name served as a vehicle for Hiroshige's portrayal of wintry quietude. The absence of a discernable light source allows the white landscape to emerge from planes of negative space that seem to emit their own glow, expanding on the inherently graphic qualities of woodblock prints in unprecedented ways.

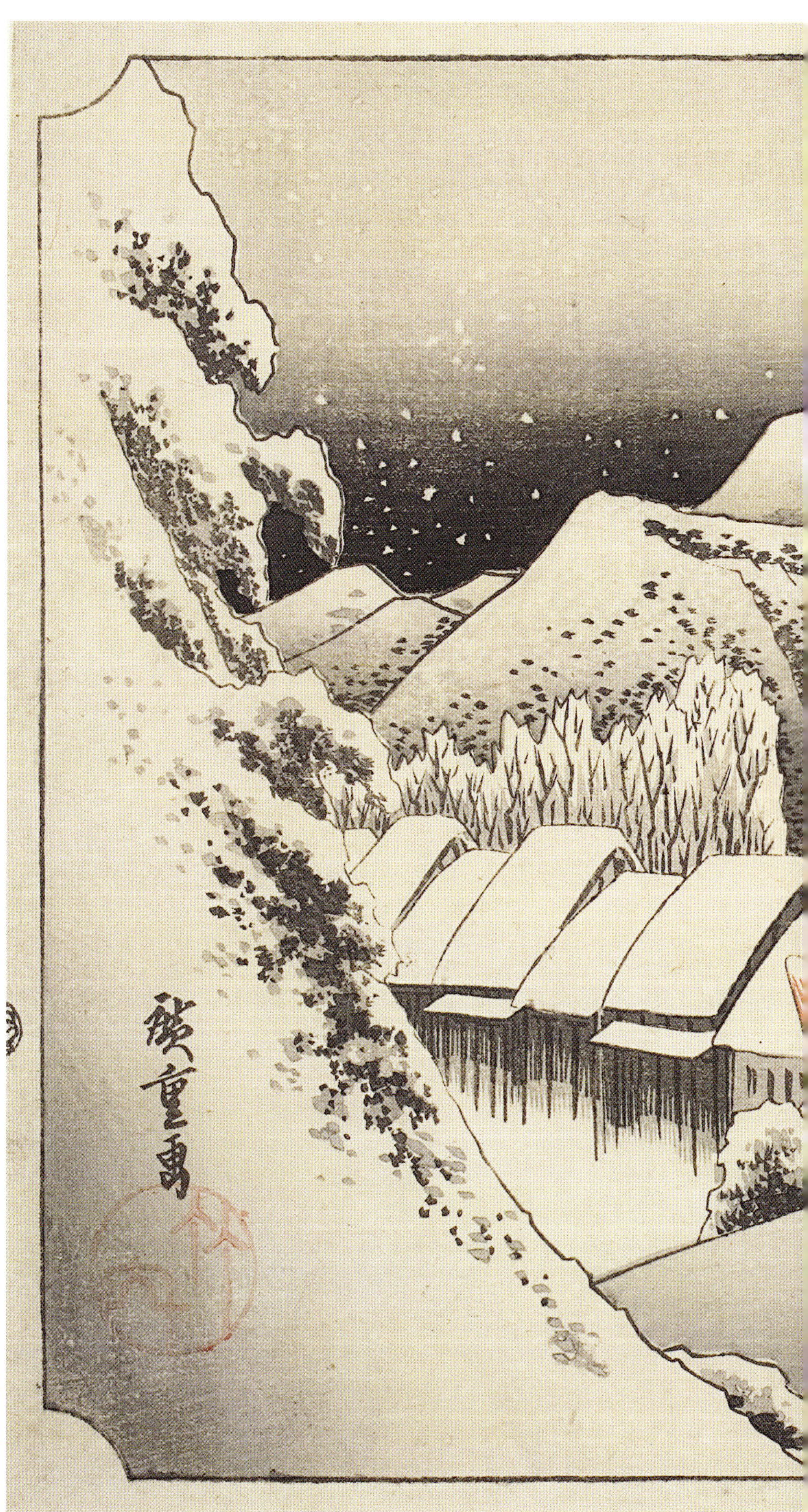

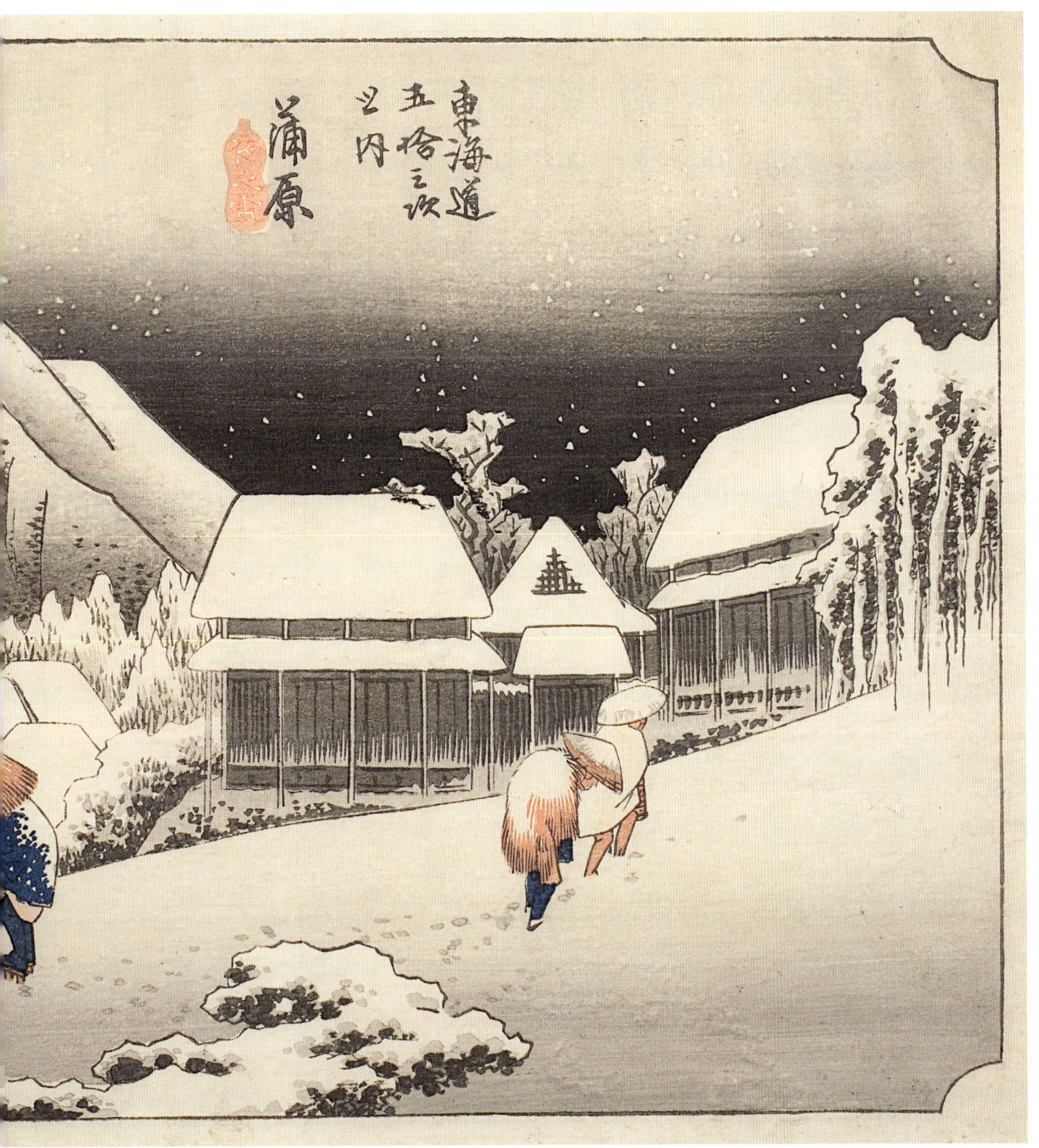
東海道
五拾三次
之内
蒲原
夜之雪

UTAGAWA SADAHIDE

(1807–1873)

Mushi-e, ca. 1850

Publisher: Tsujiokaya Bunsuke
Woodblock print: ink and color on paper
37.1 × 74.2 cm (14⅝ × 29³⁄₁₆ in.)
John Chandler Bancroft Collection, 1901.153

The study of natural history gained popularity in Japan during the Edo period, partly due to the influx of Dutch scientific materials and illustrations. Japanese scholars and artists, fascinated by these imported materials, began to incorporate more scientifically accurate depictions of flora and fauna into published materials, leading to the emergence of _ukiyo-e_ genres such as _mushi-e_: artworks like the one seen here that feature detailed illustrations of various insects, reptiles, and small creatures, often arranged in a grid or categorical format.

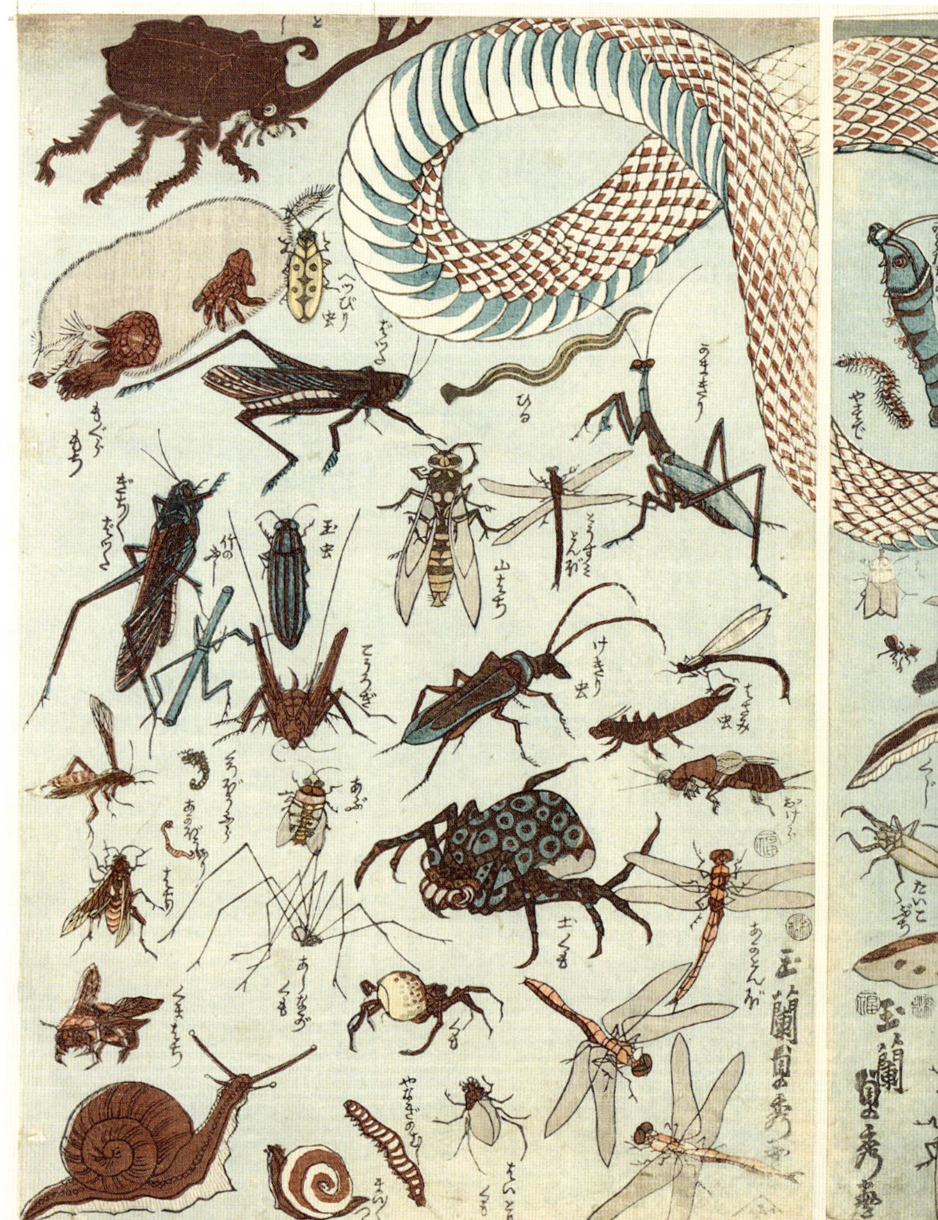

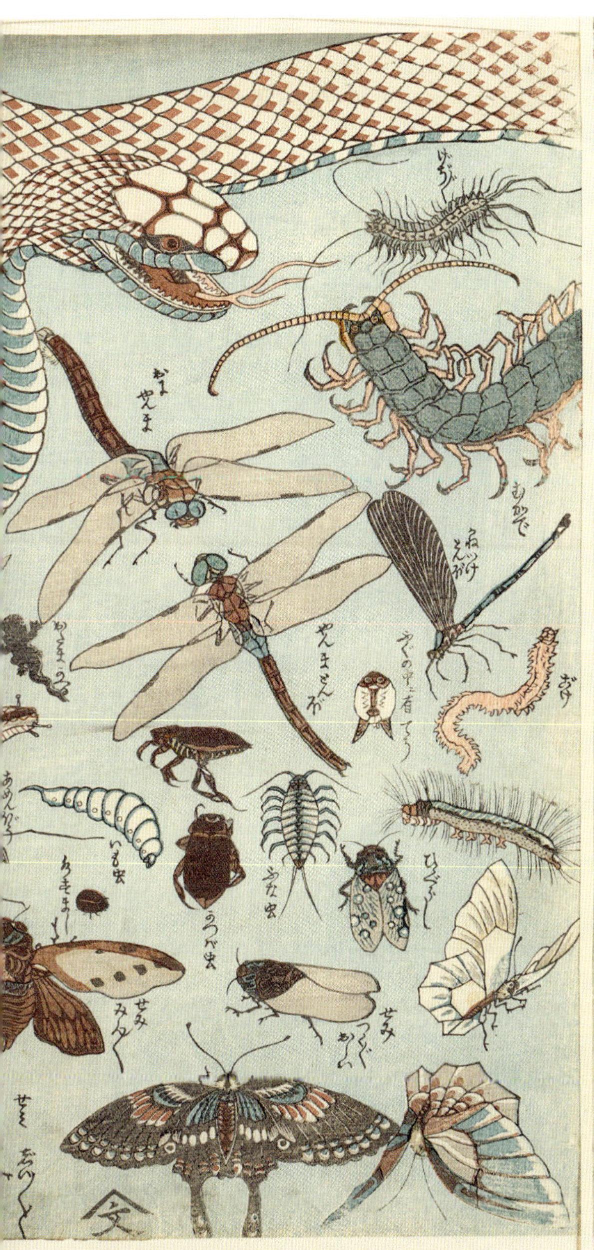
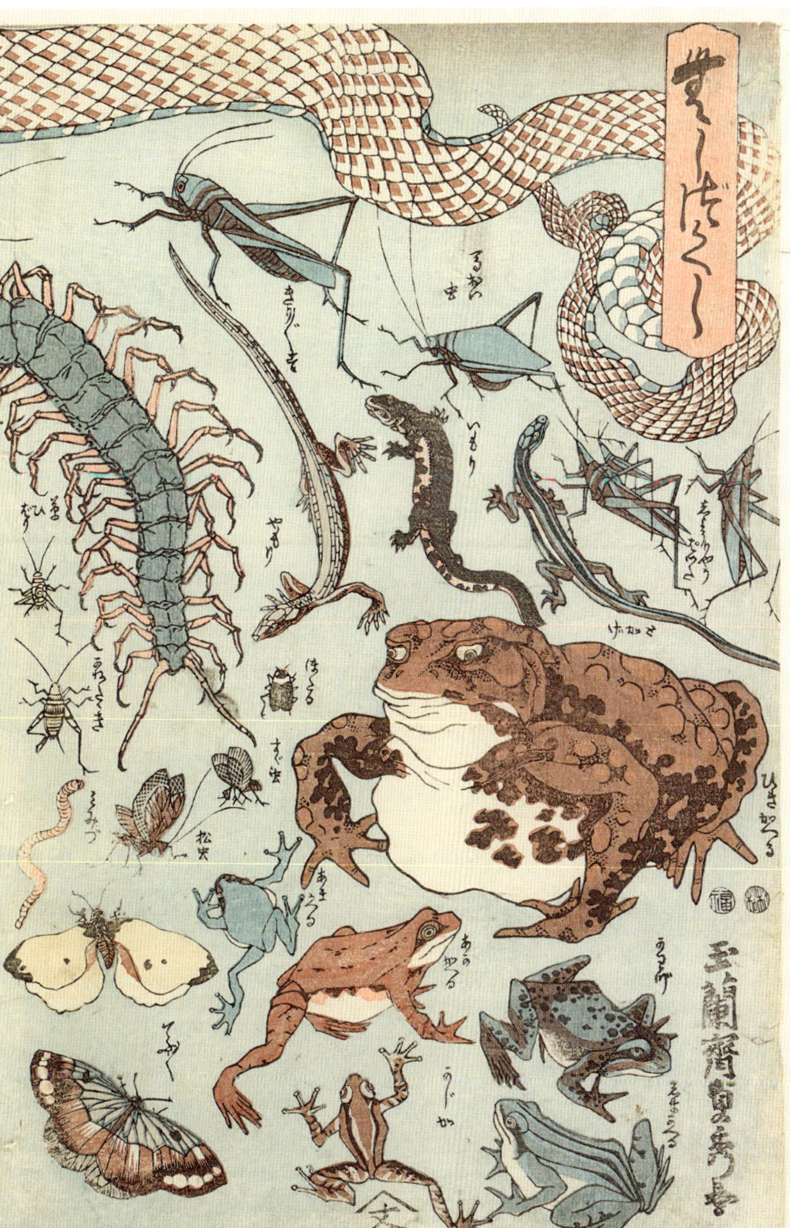

UTAGAWA KUNIYOSHI

(1797–1861)

The Tatsuta River in Autumn, from the series "The One Hundred Poems by One Hundred Poets", ca. 1840

Publisher: Ehiko
Woodblock print: ink and color on paper
34.9 × 23.5 cm (13¾ × 9¼ in.)
John Chandler Bancroft Collection, 1901.646

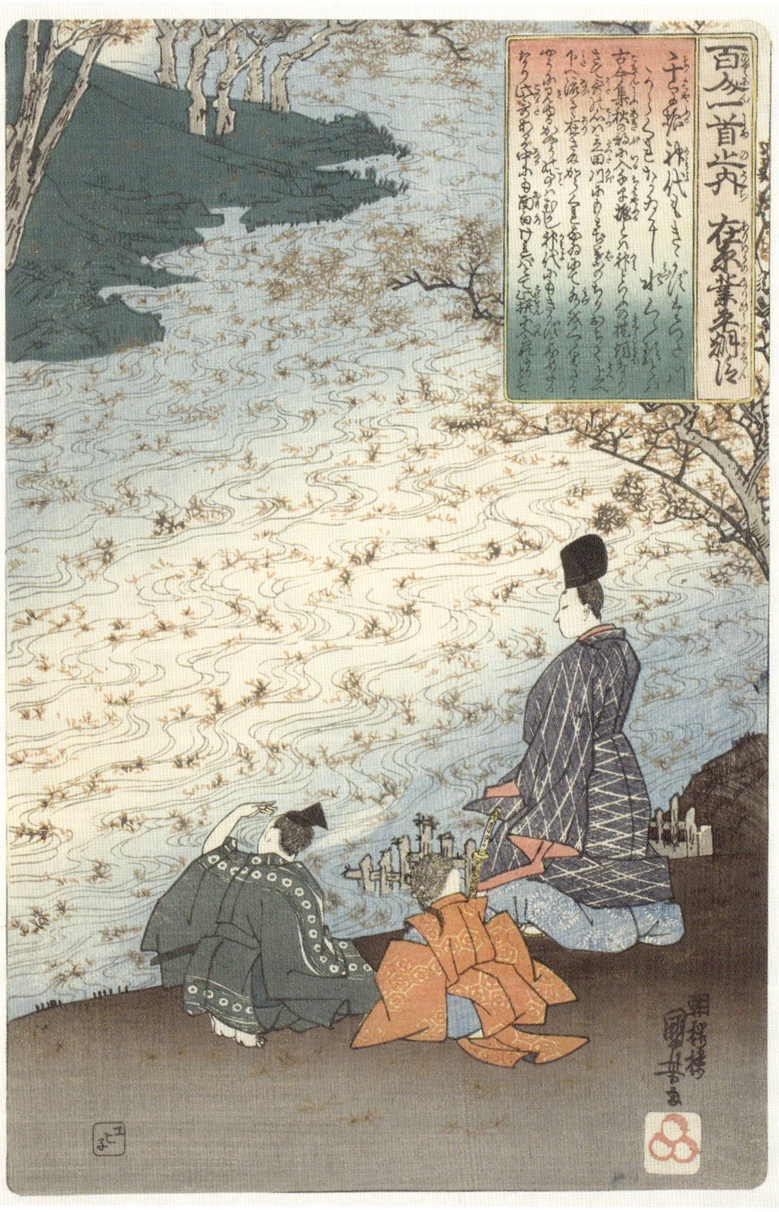

The Tatsuta River, which flows through Nara prefecture, has long been a popular destination for those seeking to witness the brilliant red foliage of maple trees lining its banks in the autumn season. For centuries, Japanese poets and artists have found inspiration in the way fallen leaves float across the water, creating mesmerizing swirls of scarlet. Kuniyoshi masterfully captures the essence of this natural phenomenon by employing a unique printing technique. To simulate the reflection of the red foliage on the river's surface, he printed the lines defining the water's current in the same red ink used for the trees.

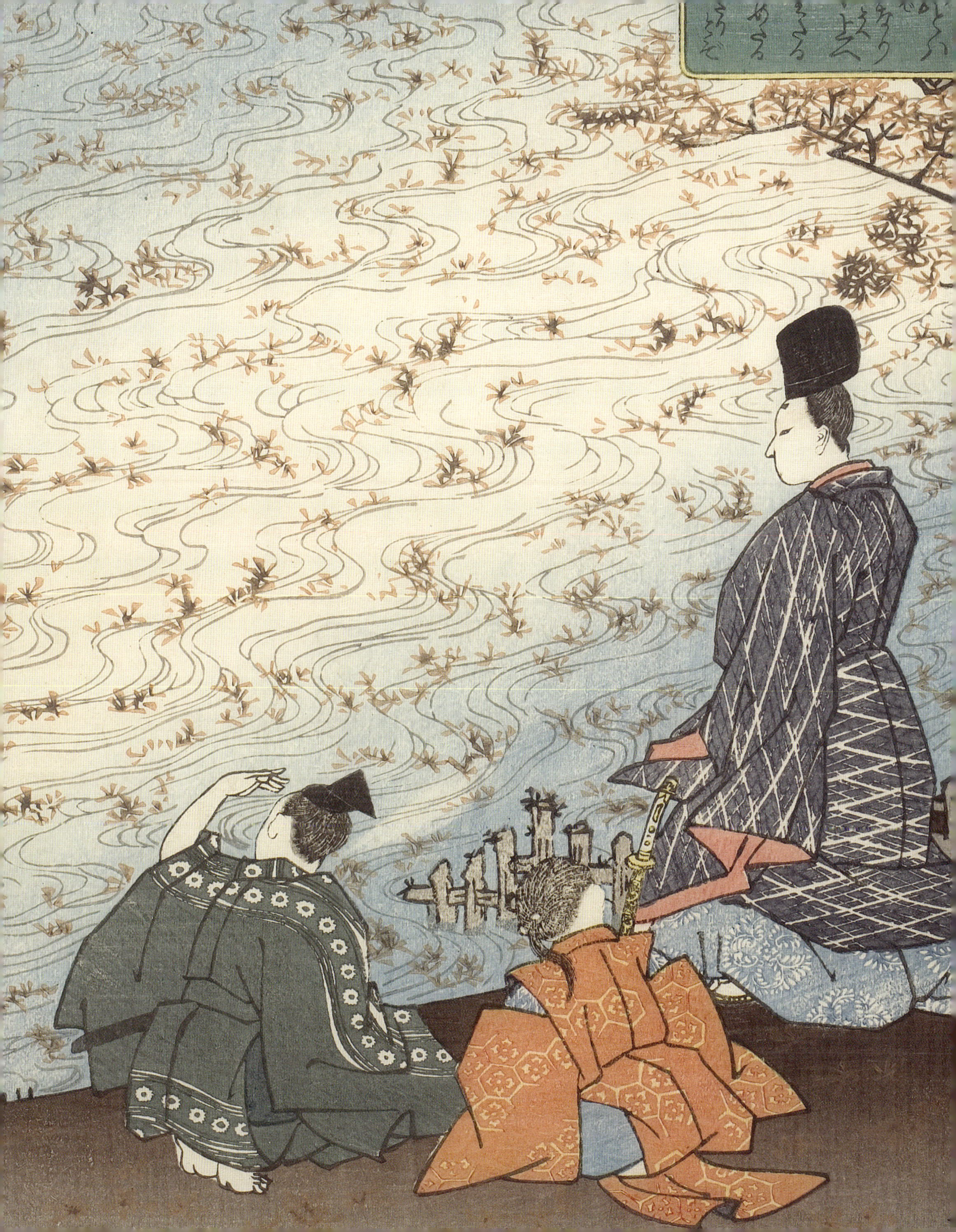

UTAGAWA HIROSHIGE

(1797–1858)

Four plates from the series "One Hundred Famous Views of Edo", 1856–59

a) *Maple Trees at Mama, Tekona Shrine and Linked Bridge*

Publisher: Sakanaya Eikichi
Woodblock print: ink and color on paper
34.9 × 23.5 cm (13¾ × 9¼ in.)
John Chandler Bancroft Collection, 1901.59.1310

b) *Sudden Shower over Shin-Ōhashi Bridge and Atake*

Publisher: Sakanaya Eikichi
Woodblock print: ink and color on paper
34.9 × 23.5 cm (13¾ × 9¼ in.)
John Chandler Bancroft Collection, 1901.59.1275

c) *New Year's Eve Foxfires at the Changing Tree, Ōji*

Publisher: Sakanaya Eikichi
Woodblock print: ink and color on paper
34.9 × 23.5 cm (13¾ × 9¼ in.)
John Chandler Bancroft Collection, 1901.59.1335

d) *Plum Estate at Kameido*

Publisher: Sakanaya Eikichi
Woodblock print: ink and color on paper
34.9 × 23.5 cm (13¾ × 9¼ in.)
John Chandler Bancroft Collection, 1901.59.1244

The series "One Hundred Famous Views of Edo" (1856–59), originally consisting of 118 woodblock prints, represents the pinnacle of Utagawa Hiroshige's artistic achievements, showcasing his innovative style and use of perspective and framing devices. It was deeply admired by the collector John Chandler Bancroft, who included a full set of the series in his seminal bequest of over 3000 *ukiyo-e* prints to the Worcester Art Museum in 1901. Produced largely at the end of Hiroshige's career, these prints were commissioned in the aftermath of a series of natural disasters that struck the capital, including earthquakes and the resulting fires. The series indirectly chronicles and celebrates the process of rebuilding the affected sites, capturing the resilience and spirit of Edo's citizens.

Hiroshige's unique approach to composition and perspective is often attributed to his experience as a firefighter, during which he surveyed the city from observation towers. This vantage point allowed him to experiment with novel ways of depicting the urban landscape, creating dynamic scenes. Although Hiroshige passed away before the series was completed, his remaining designs were faithfully executed by his student, Hiroshige II (1826–1869), ensuring the legacy of the master's vision.

"One Hundred Famous Views of Edo" is divided into four seasons, with each print capturing the essence of a particular time of year. The four prints featured here, one from each group, demonstrate Hiroshige's ability to evoke the atmosphere and beauty of Edo throughout the changing seasons, cementing his position as one of the most influential *ukiyo-e* artists of his time.

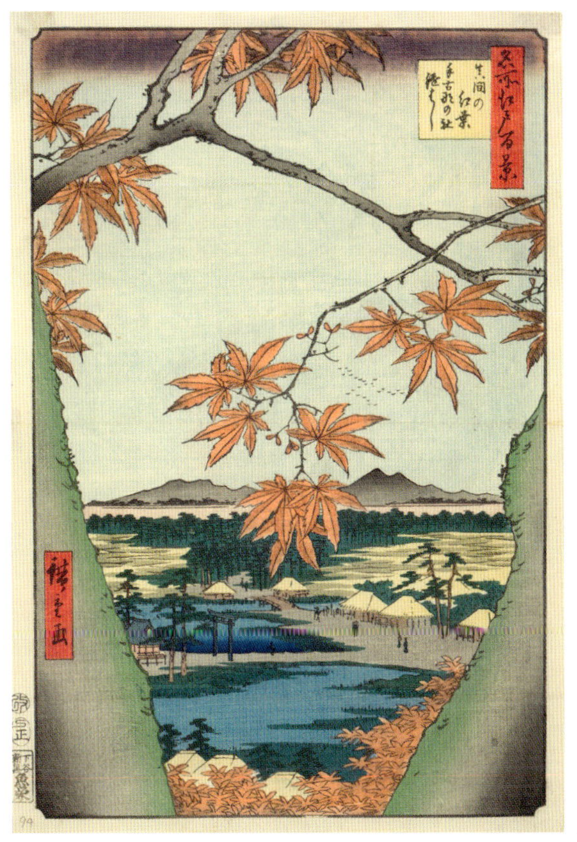

a

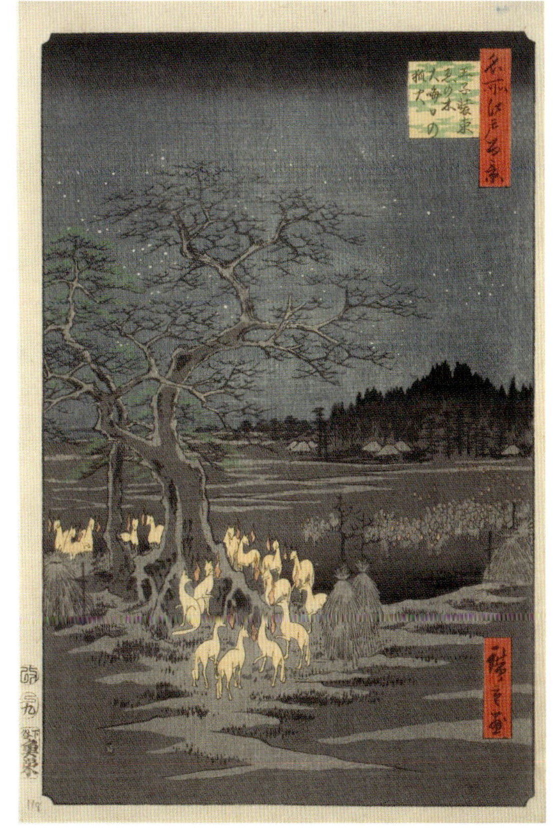

c

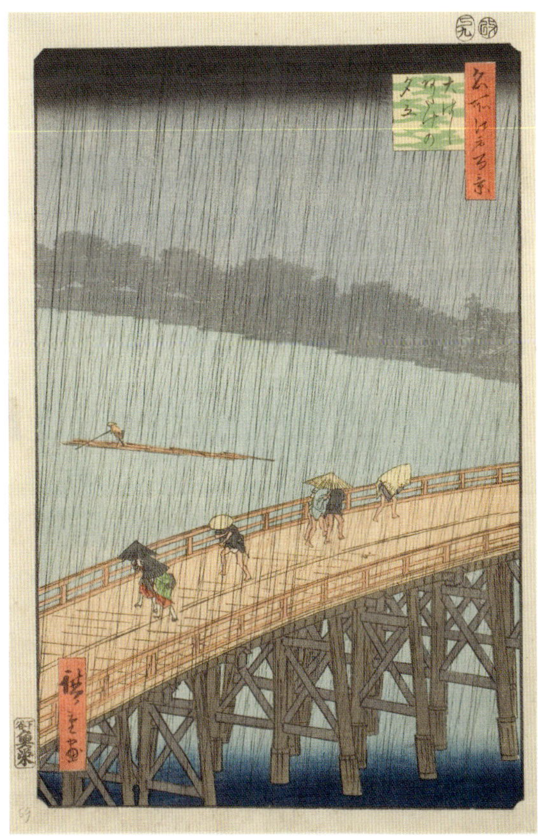

b

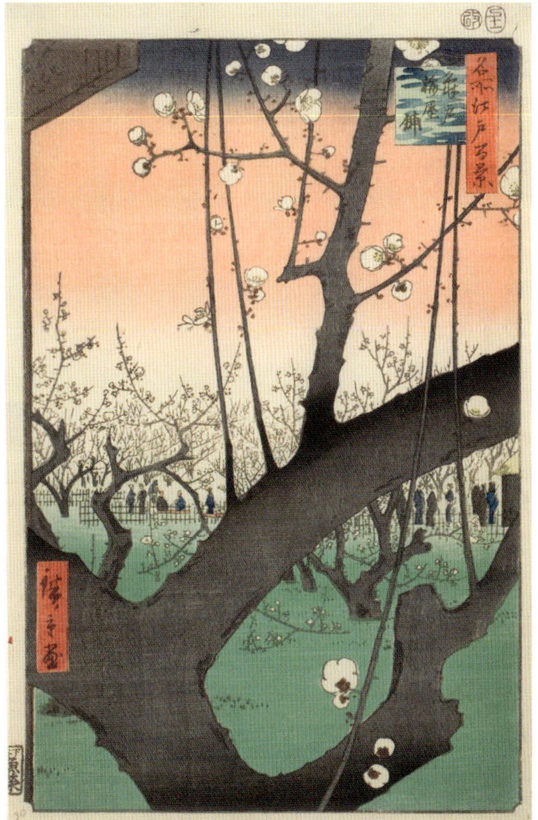

d

UTAGAWA KUNIYOSHI

(1797–1861)

Eleventh Act of the Chushingura: The Loyal Retainers Assemble at Ryōgoku Bridge, 1827–30

Publisher: Kagaya Kichiemon
Woodblock print: ink and color on paper
35.8 × 71.1 cm (14⅛ × 28 in.)
John Chandler Bancroft Collection, 2002.39

Kuniyoshi was renowned for his ability to seamlessly integrate
complex figural arrangements into vivid landscapes, creating
captivating prints that brought the dramatic narratives of kabuki
plays and legendary warrior tales to life. This triptych shows a
climactic moment from the "Treasury of Loyal Retainers" story,
in which forty-seven *rōnin* (samurai who do not have a lord to
serve) gather at Ryōgoku Bridge on the Sumida River in Edo,
preparing to avenge their master's death. They carry lanterns
with the character "chu" meaning "loyalty" or "devotion." They
wear black capes with a white "dog's-tooth" pattern (a common
costuming addition in kabuki plays based on the tale) and carry
weapons used by samurai: two swords as well as bows, halberds,
spears, mallets, ropes, and axes. The leader of these samurai
and protagonist of the story, Oishi Yoshio (1659–1703), can be
seen in the left panel; he wears a green cape decorated with his
double-comma crest over his outfit.

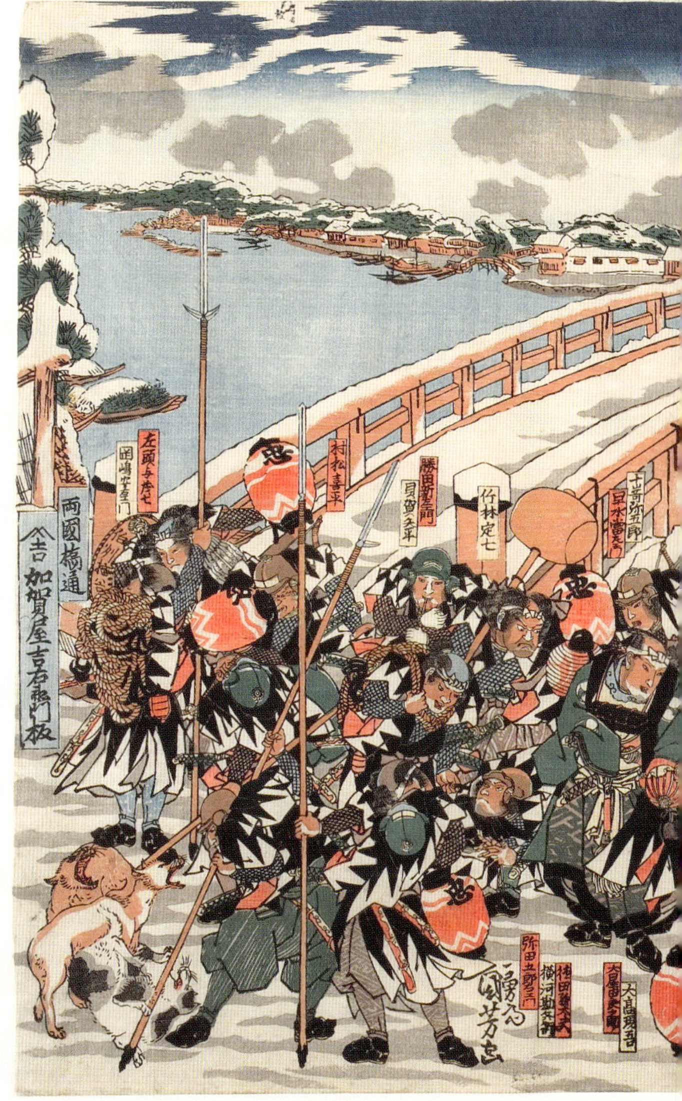

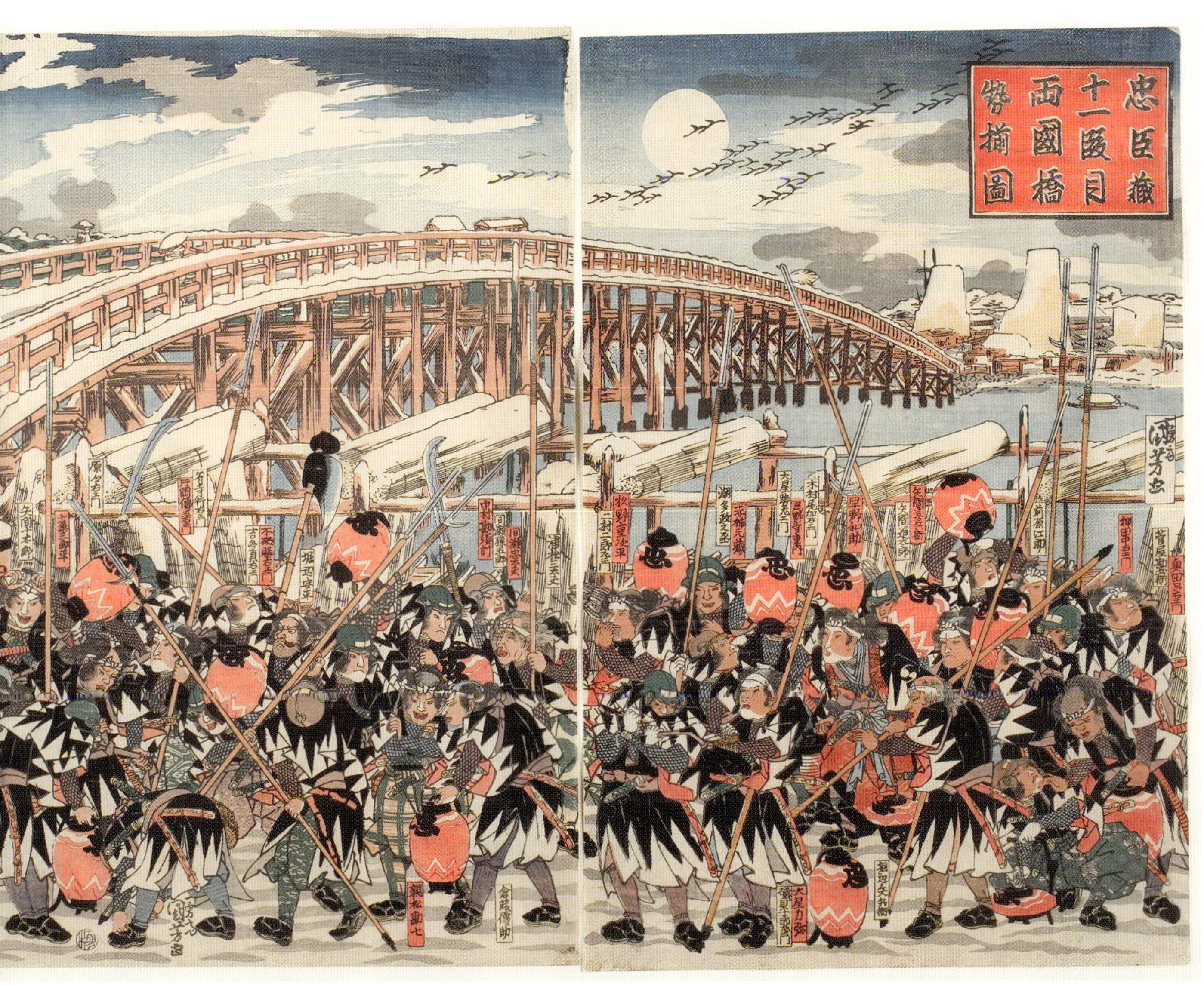

UTAGAWA YOSHIKU

(1833–1904)

Picture of a Great Ship from America: In the Distance, from the series
"Exact Copies of Great Ships of the Five Nations", 1861

Publisher: Maruya Tetsujiro
Woodblock print: ink and color on paper
Ōban triptych: 37.8 × 77.8 cm (14⅞ × 30⅝ in.)
John Chandler Bancroft Collection, 1997.123

On July 8, 1853, Commodore Matthew Perry's American ships
entered the waters of Edo Bay with the intention of opening
Japan's ports to foreign trade. Seeing that the invaders were
prepared to use the mechanized weaponry of their fleet of
so-called "black ships" like the one pictured here, tentative
negotiations resulted in the shogunate lifting bans against
foreigners entering select port cities in the archipelago. These
exchanges, in combination with the growing unrest in Japan and
weakening political structures, ushered in the end of the Edo
period in 1868. In the decades that followed, Japan industrialized
rapidly. The new Meiji emperor dissolved the traditional
Confucian-derived class system and remodeled the constitution
after Western examples.

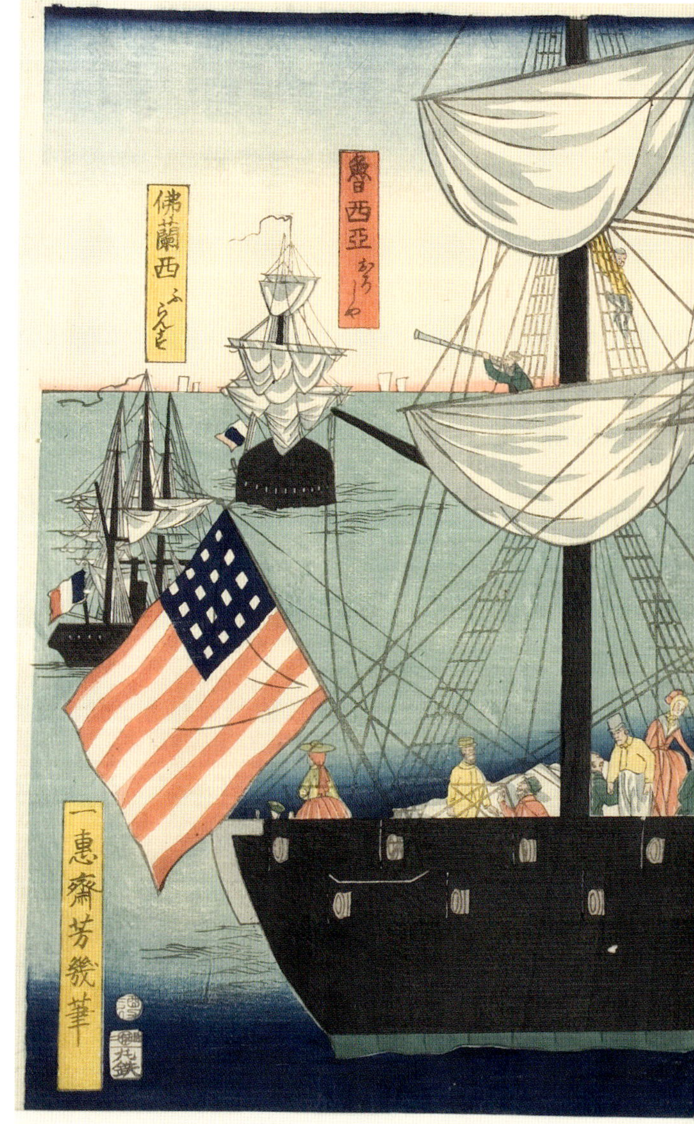

"

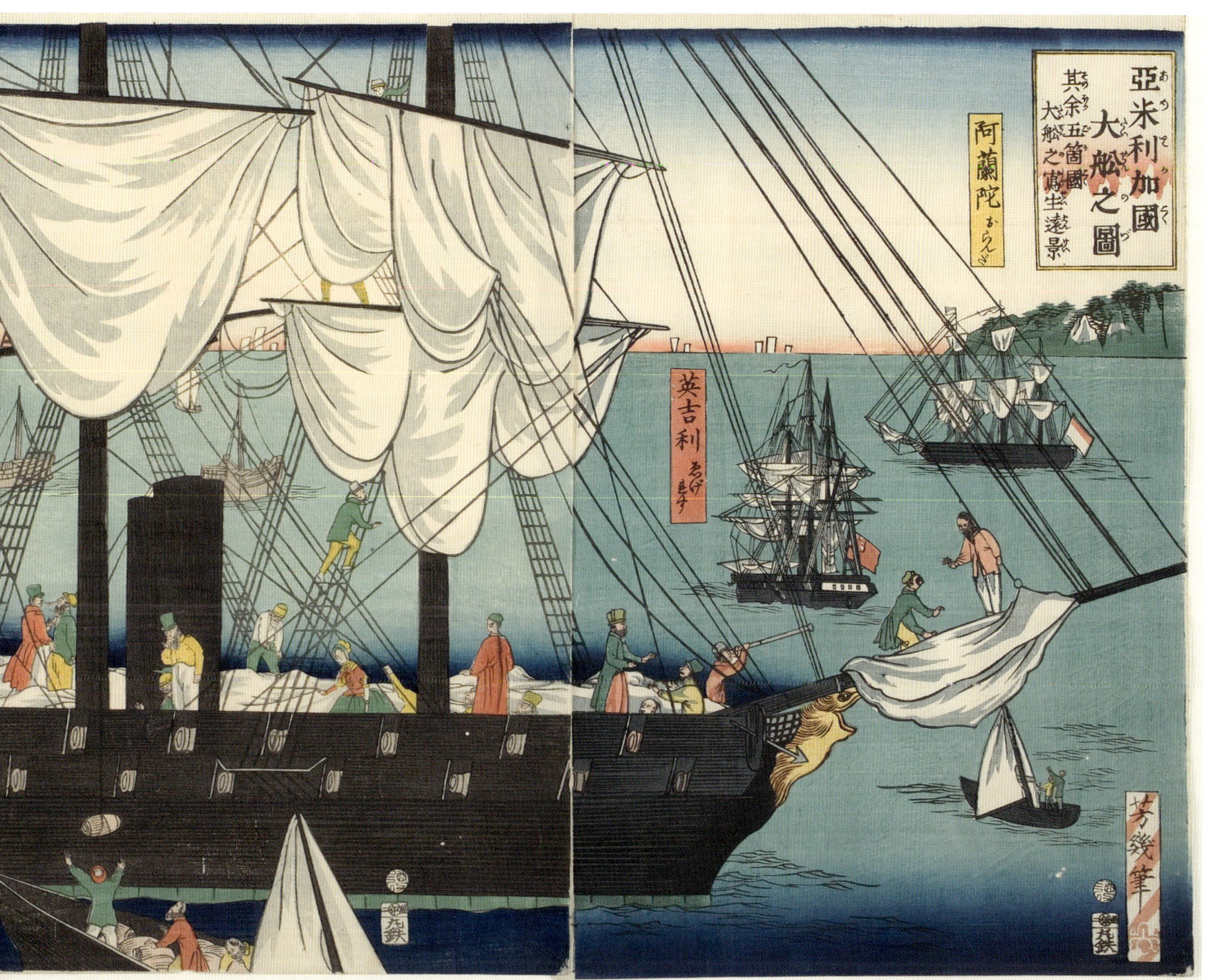
亞米利加國大舩之圖
其余五箇國大舩之寫生遠景
阿蘭陀 おらんだ
英吉利 いぎりす
芳幾筆

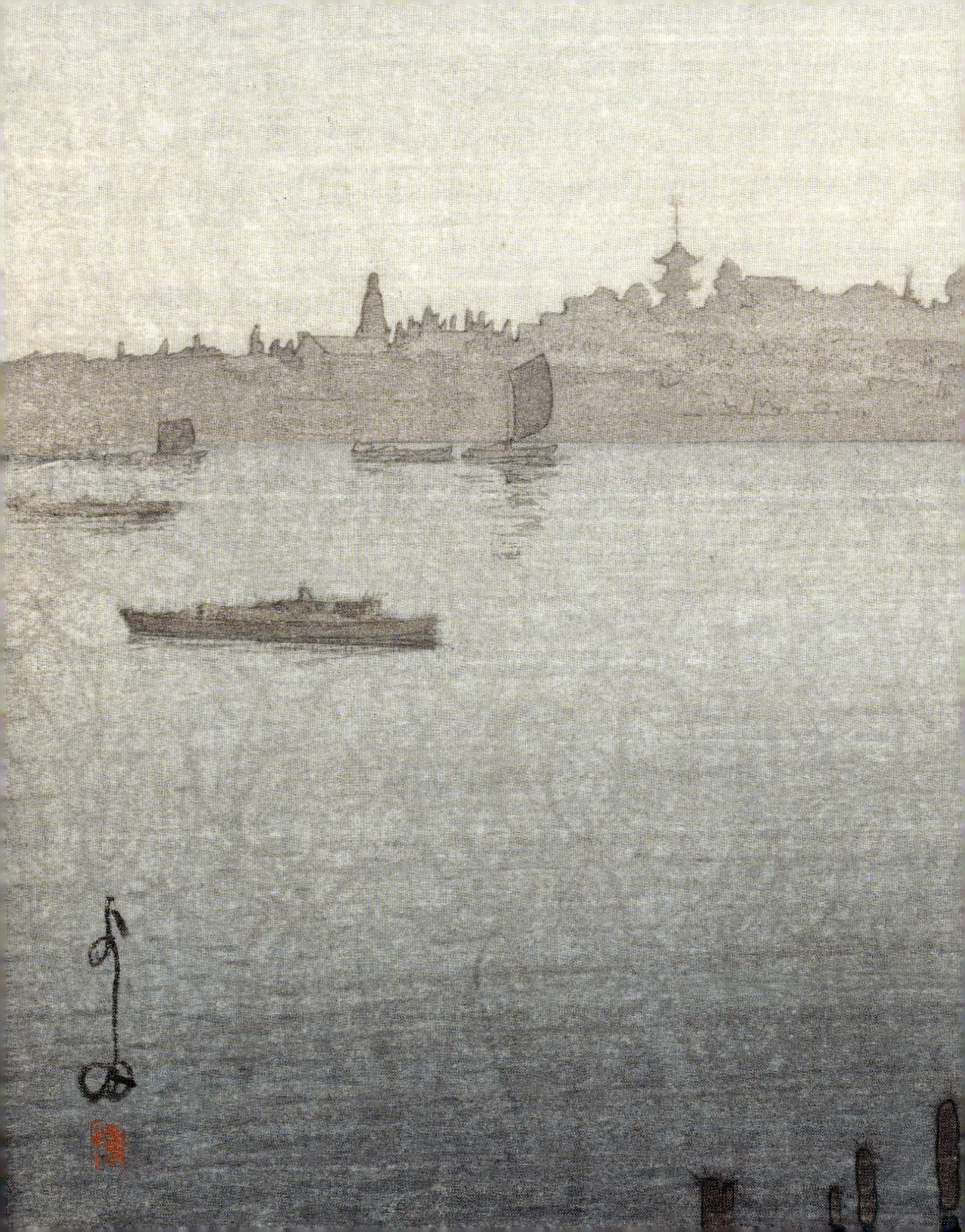

MEIJI AND TAISHŌ PERIODS
1868–1926

TSUKIOKA YOSHITOSHI

(1839–1892)

Based on the Painting "Fujiwara Yasumasa Playing the Flute by Moonlight," Exhibited at the National Painting Exhibition in the Autumn of 1882, February 12, 1883

Publisher: Akiyama Buemon
Woodblock print: ink and color on paper
Vertical ōban triptych: 37.5 × 73.5 cm (14¾ × 28¹⁵⁄₁₆ in.)
Harriet B. Bancroft Fund, 2004.3

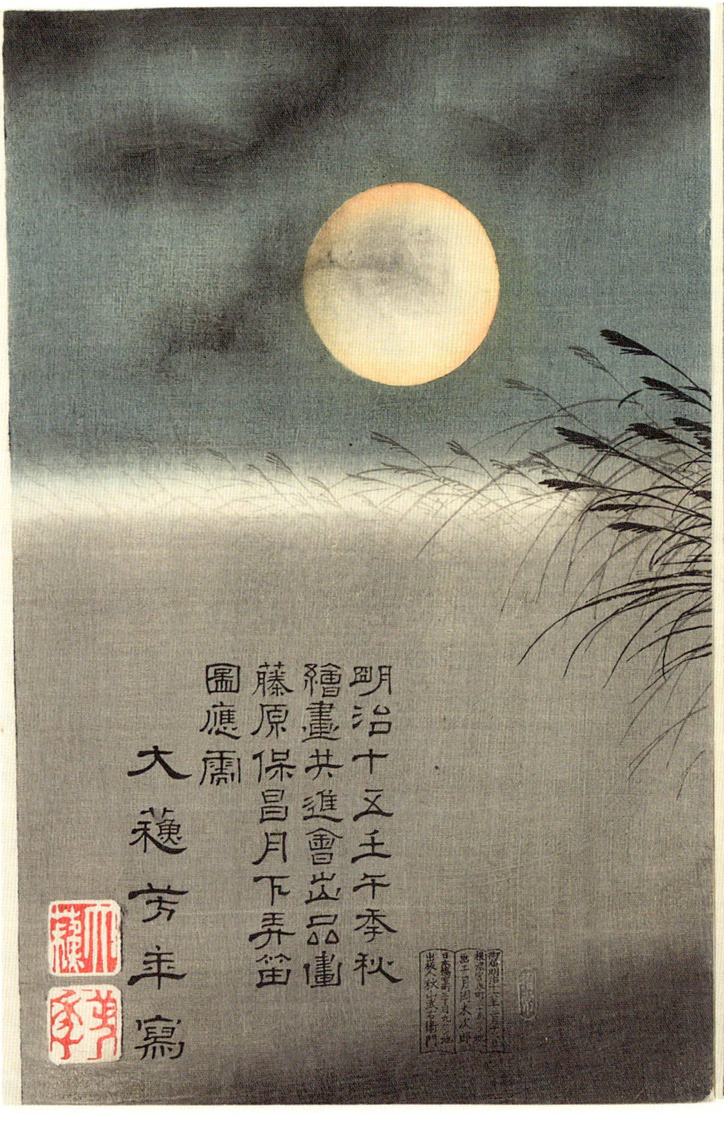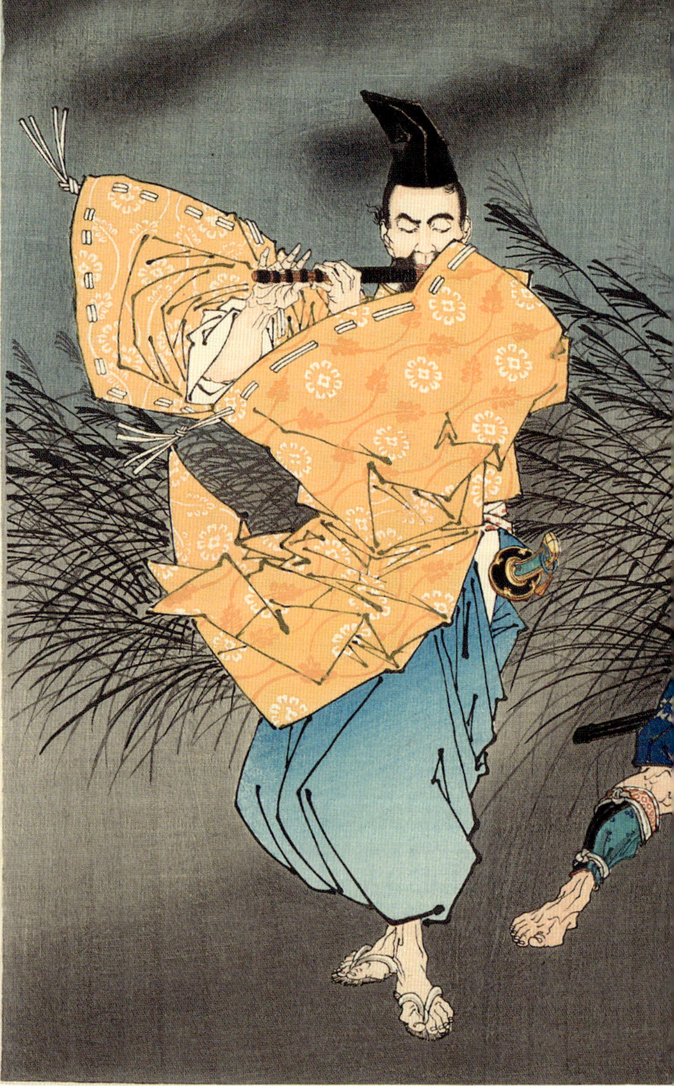

Fujiwara Yasumasa Playing the Flute by Moonlight,
1882

Hanging scroll: ink and color on silk
222.3 × 95.9 cm (87½ × 37¾ in.)
Harriet B. Bancroft Fund, 2004.46

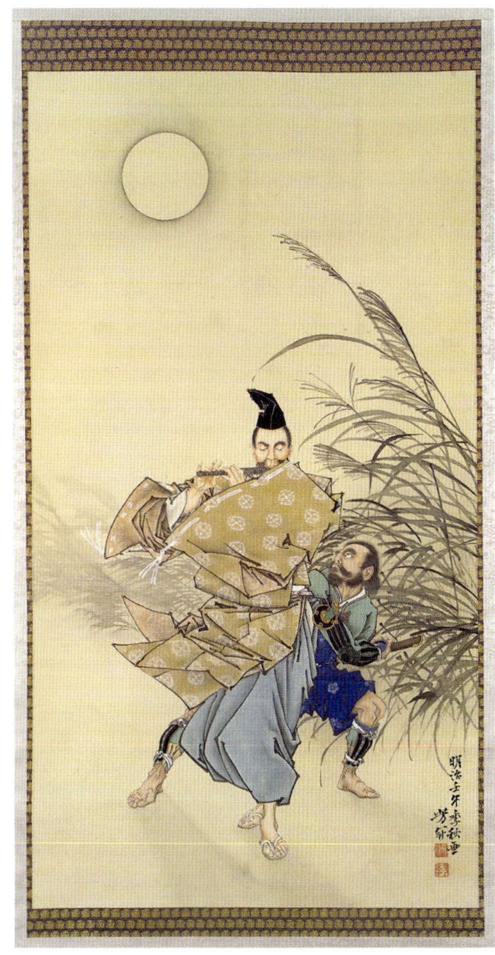

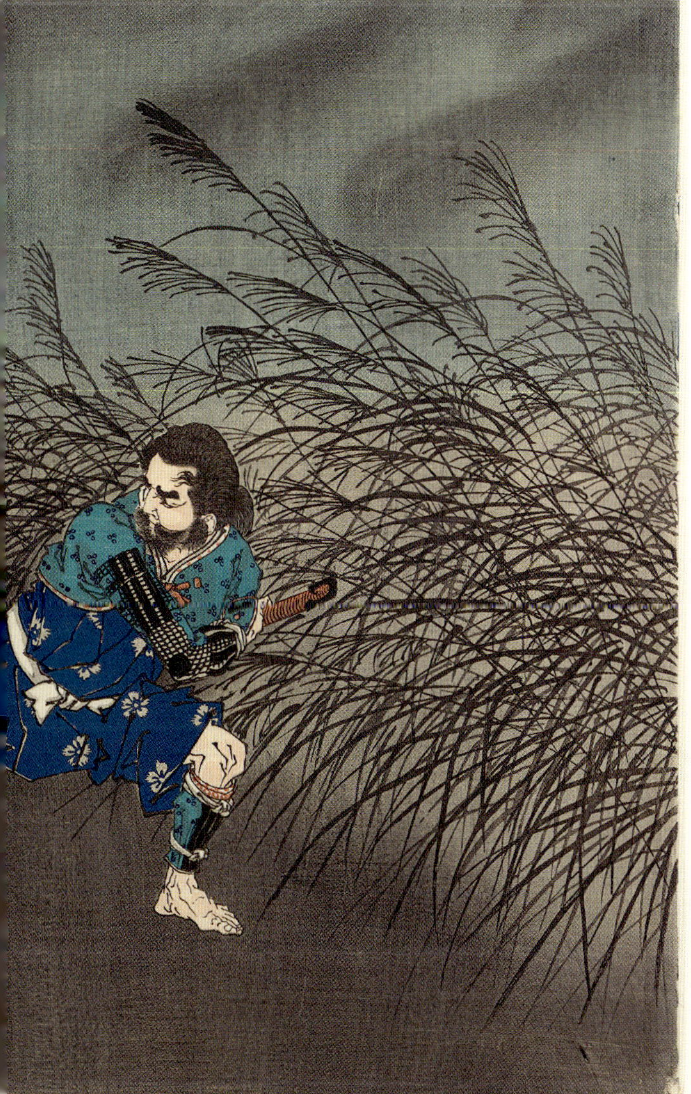

According to legend, Fujiwara Yasumasa, a renowned Heian-period courtier, captivated the notorious bandit Hakamadare Yasusuke with the enchanting melodies of his flute under the moonlit sky. As Yasumasa's music filled the night air, Yasusuke found himself enthralled by its beauty and abandoned his initial plan to rob the courtier.

Less than a year after the debut of the painting *Fujiwara Yasumasa Playing the Flute by Moonlight*, the original composition was expanded into the triptych print seen here. Yoshitoshi skillfully translates the nuance of the original brushwork, adjusting compositional elements such as Yasumasa's clothing, which in the print swings upward in an arc that serves to unify the three panels into a cohesive and harmonious composition. His use of the "gradation without outlines" (*atenashi bokashi*) technique gives it an ethereal quality as well as a kinetic sense of movement. The design was later condensed into a single sheet that belonged to the artist's seminal series "One Hundred Aspects of the Moon" which was published between 1885 and 1892, near the end of his life.

TOYOHARA KUNICHIKA

(1835–1900)

The Kabuki Actors Bandō Kakitsu I as Kongara Kōji, Onoe Kikugorō V as Fudō Monji, Onoe Matsusuke IV as Chūmon Teruzō, and Kataoka Gadō III as Setaka Kiyota, 1883

Woodblock print: ink and color on paper
Vertical *ōban* triptych: 35.6 × 73.4 cm (14 × 28⅞ in.)
Museum purchase through the Alexander H. Bullock Fund and funds by deaccession from the gifts of Judith and Paul A. Falcigno, 2021.16

With over a million inhabitants and largely wooden infrastructures, the city of Edo experienced frequent fires. Firefighters were essential to keeping the city safe, and their daring exploits eventually captivated the city's popular culture. With their tough looks and full-body tattoos, real firefighters were seen as rebellious icons. This print by Kunichika portrays four renowned kabuki actors—Bandō Kakitsu I, Onoe Kikugorō V, Onoe Matsusuke IV, and Kataoka Gadō III—in their roles as firefighters. They are imagined as scaling the treacherous Kachidoki waterfall near Edo, a daunting task through which firefighters could hone their skills and prove their mettle. Although the bright red and purple pigments seen throughout the composition are characteristic of Meiji-era prints, the Prussian blue torrents of the waterfall show the lasting impact of Edo-period artists like Katsushika Hokusai and Utagawa Hiroshige.

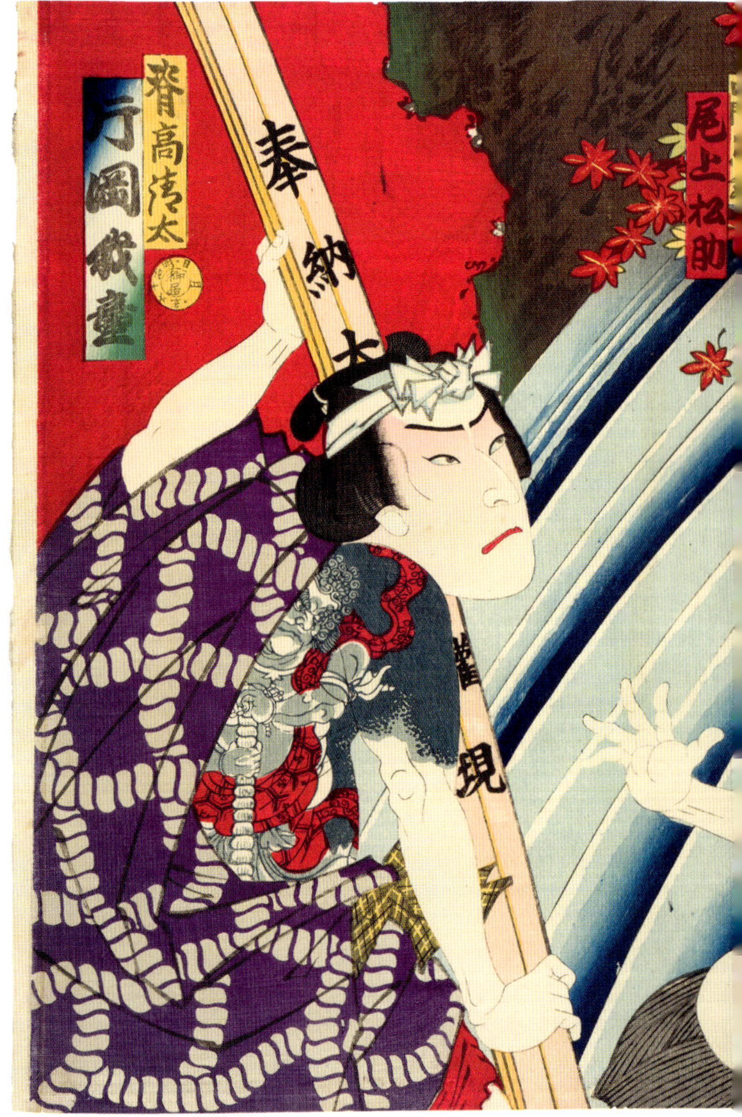

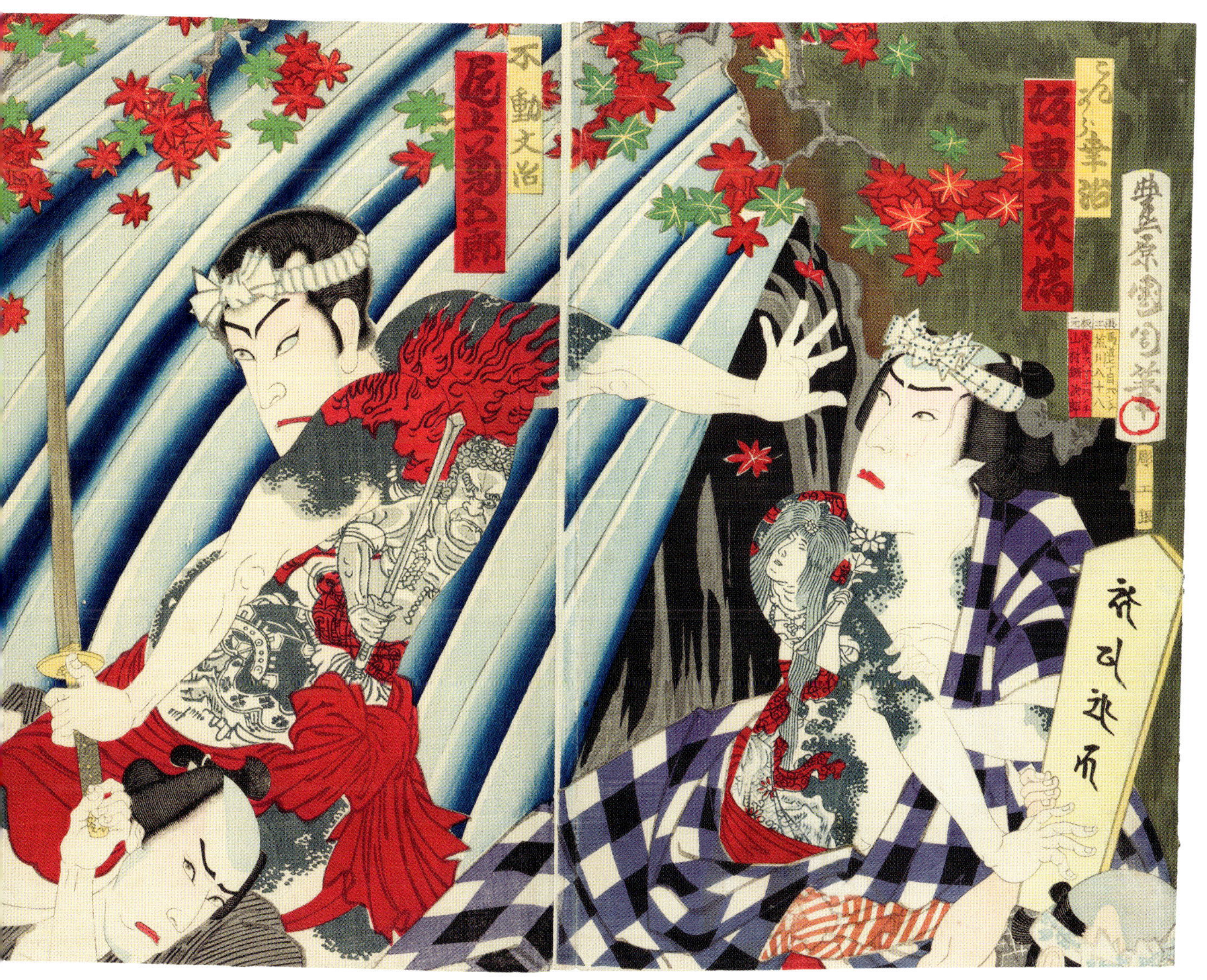
不動文治
尾上菊五郎
坂東家橘
豊原国周筆

ADACHI GINKŌ

(1853–1901)

Kosome Matsumoto, from the series "Renowned Women from Ancient and Modern Times", ca. 1887

Publisher: Matsuki Heikichi (Daikokuya)
Woodblock print: ink and color on paper
Aiban: 35 × 23.8 cm (13¾ × 9⅜ in.)
Asiatic Art Association and Asiatic Art Members' Matching Fund, 1989.156

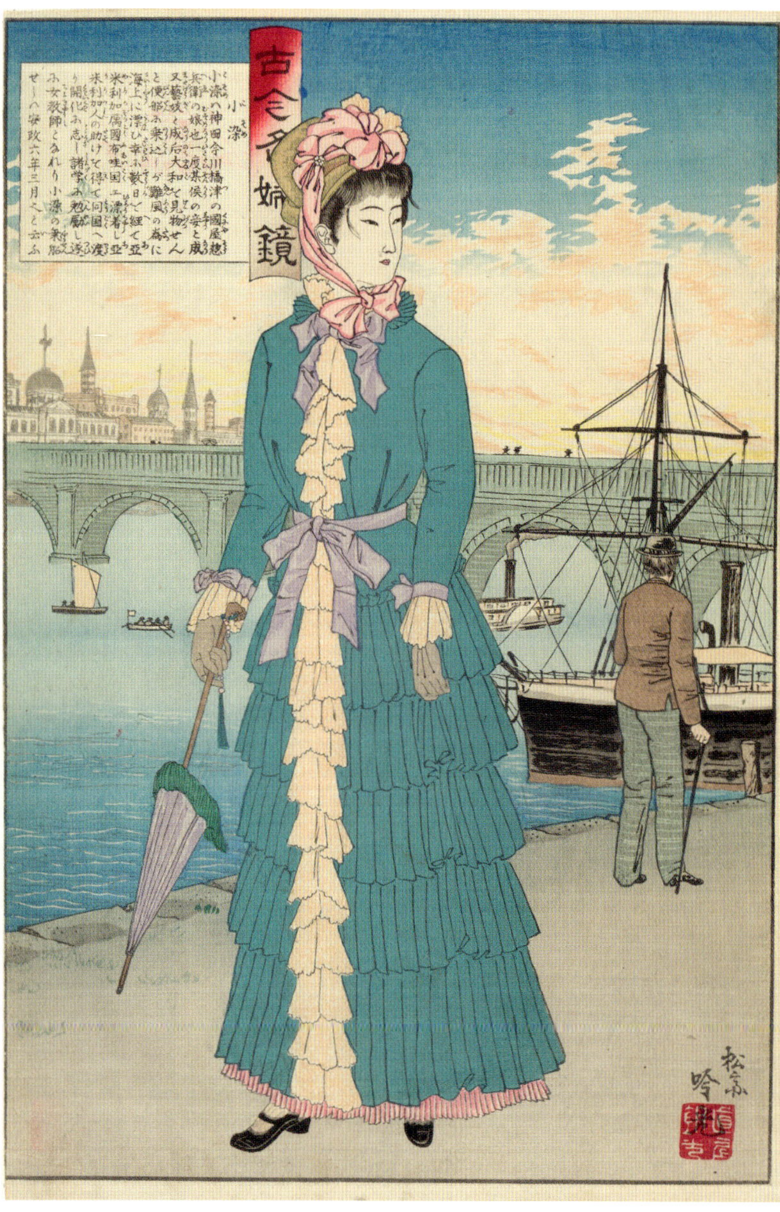

This print featuring a portrait of Kosome Matsumoto is part of a series celebrating renowned women throughout Japan's history. Born into the samurai class in 1827, in 1859 while traveling by ship from Edo (present-day Tokyo) to Kyoto, Matsumoto's vessel was blown off course and she arrived unintentionally in the Kingdom of Hawaii. There, Matsumoto became a teacher at the Waialua Girls' School, where she taught Japanese language and culture to the local population. Her story came to represent the embrace of cultural exchange, and women's roles in furthering modernization during the Meiji period. These sentiments are reflected in Ginkō's choice to portray her in European-style clothing and accessories.

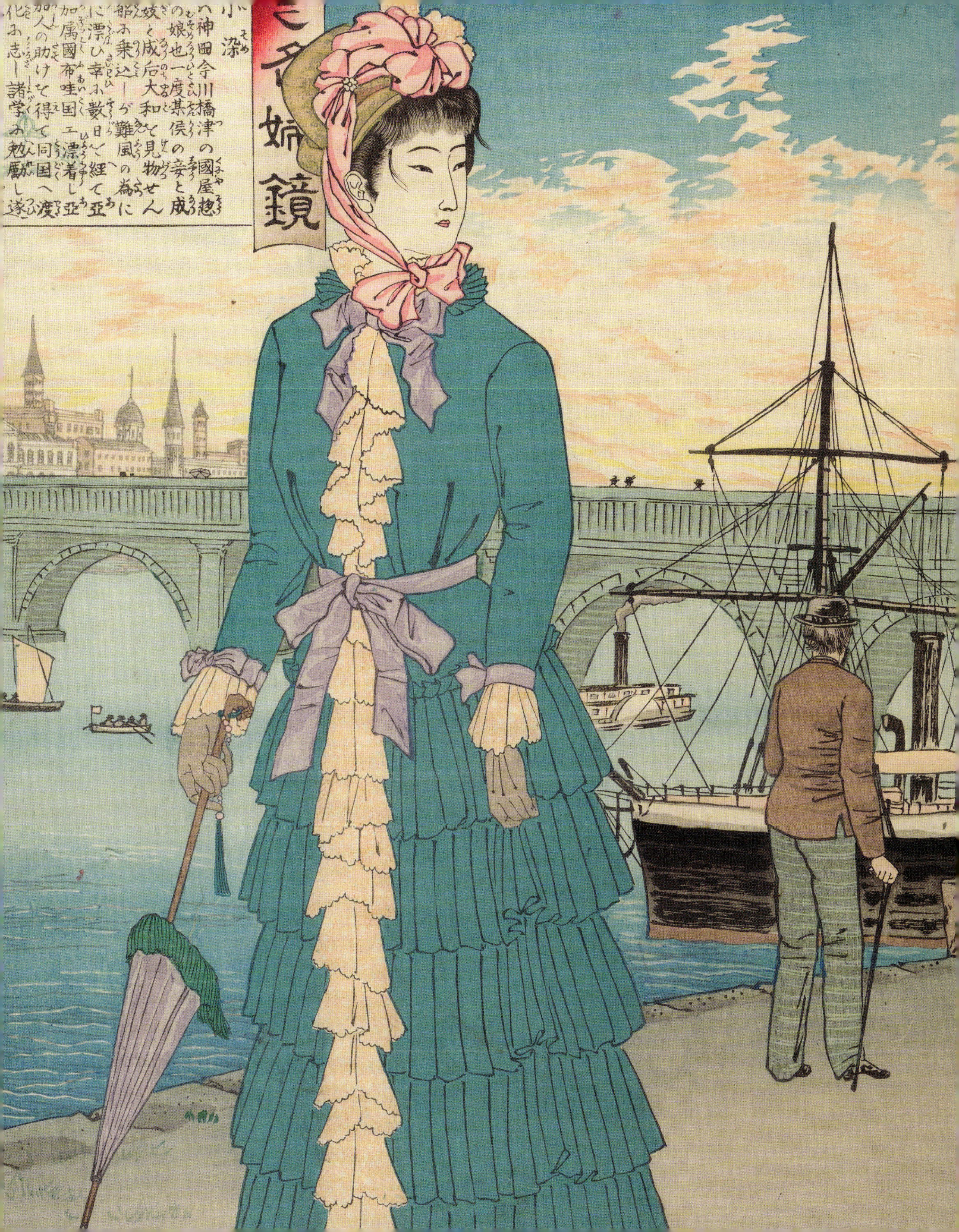
小染
當世姉鏡
神田今川橋津の國屋惣七が娘なり一度某侯の妾と成り其後大和の妓と成り后船に乘込難風に漂ひ幸不散日を經て加属國布哇国に漂着し同国人の助けを得て同国に化に志し諸学を勉励し遂に渡亞

OGATA GEKKŌ

(1859–1920)

Picture of the First Army Advancing on Fengtienfu, 1894 (Meiji 27)

Publisher: Matsuno Yonejirō
Woodblock print: ink and color on paper
27.5 × 76.2 cm (10¹³⁄₁₆ × 30 in.)
Alexander H. Bullock Fund, 1998.105

Despite not having trained as an artist, Gekkō began
developing war prints (*senso-e*) during his experience as a
war correspondent for a Japanese newspaper. This triptych
depicts a pivotal moment in Japan's military campaigns during
the First Sino-Japanese War (1894–95) when the country's
First Army advanced on Fengtienfu (present-day Shenyang,
Liaoning Province, China). Notably, the artist chose to
obscure the harsh realities of the battle in the background,
while centering a soldier holding a Japanese flag, indicating
that this print was intended to serve as propaganda for the
country's imperial ambitions.

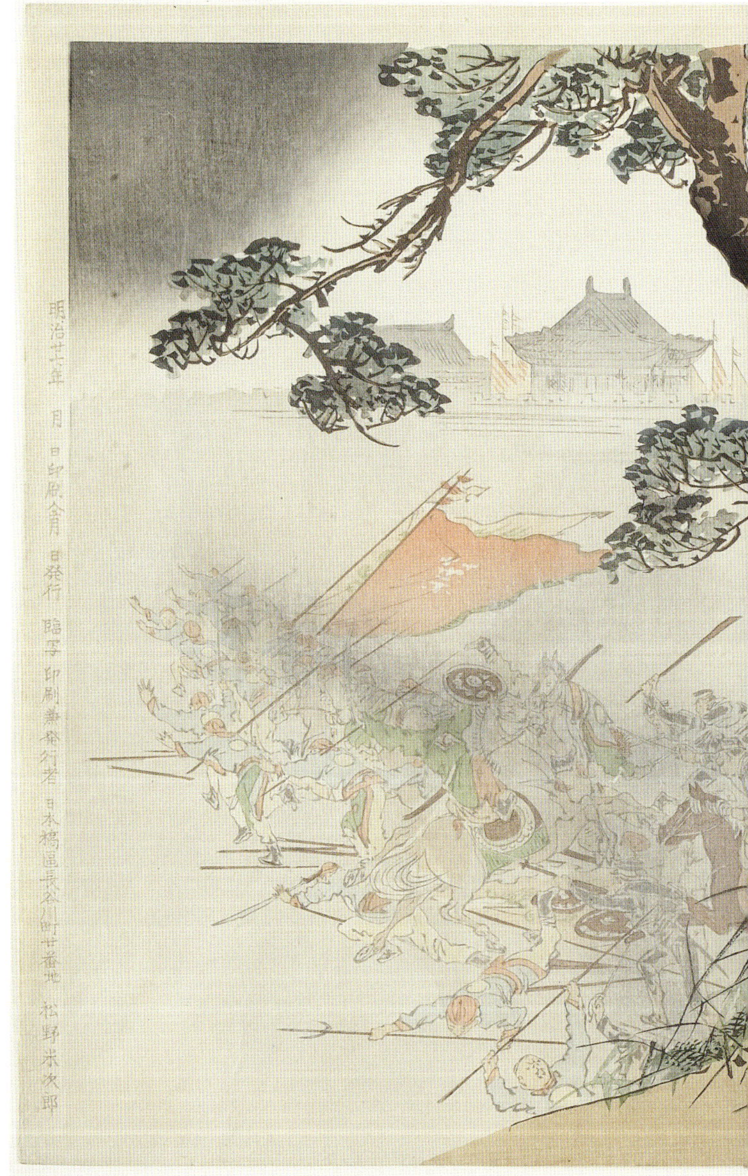

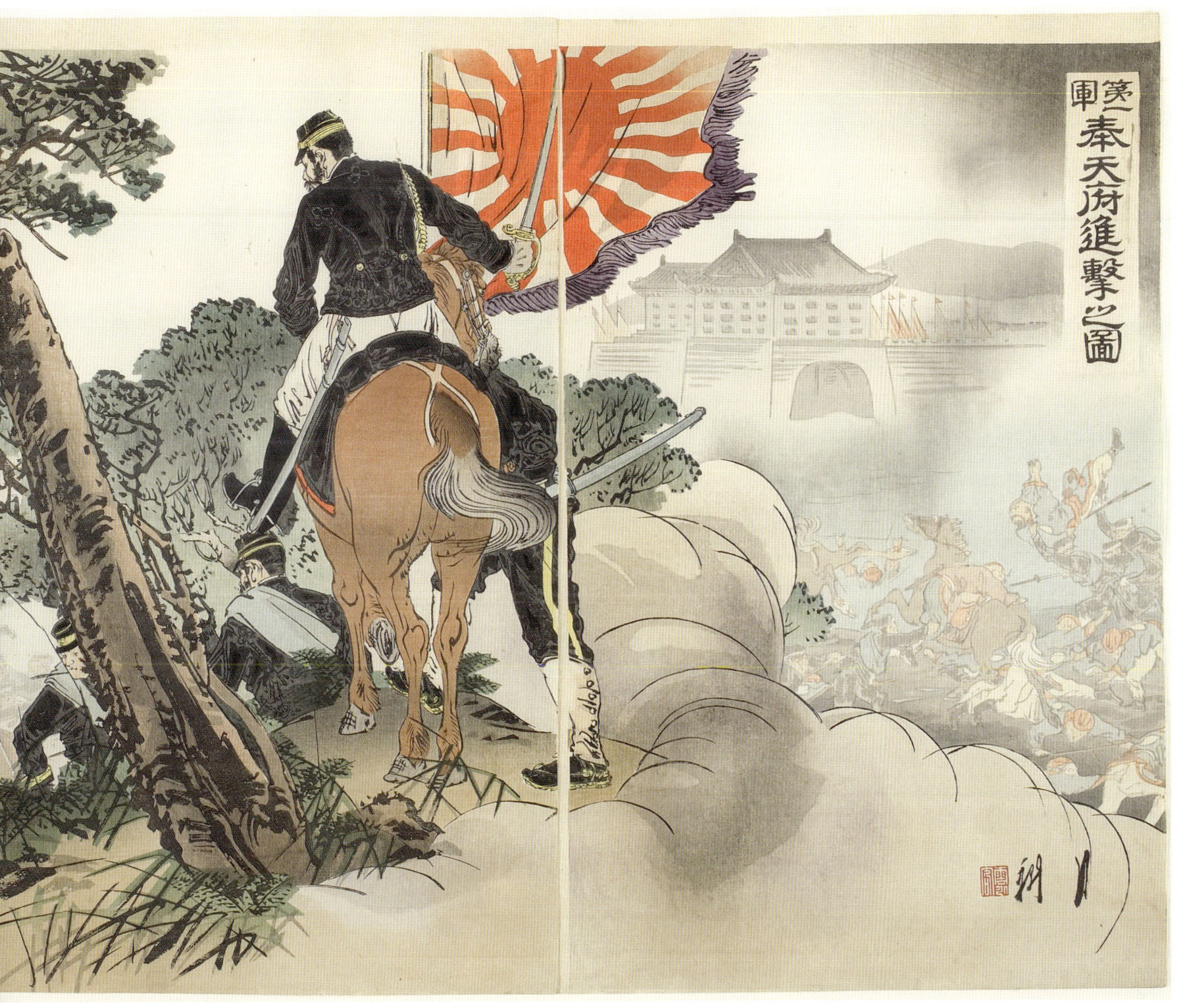
第一軍奉天府進撃之圖

KAMISAKA SEKKA

(1866–1942)

World of Things, 1909–1910

Publisher: Unsōdō
Bound volume: color woodblock prints with silver and gold, textured background (baren sujizuri), and blind embossing (karazuri)
Volume when closed: 30.1 × 22.3 × 2 cm (11⅞ × 8¾ × ¹³⁄₁₆ in.)
Museum purchase through the Eliza S. Paine Fund, the Stoddard Acquisition Fund, and the Harriet B. Bancroft Fund, 2019.15.1

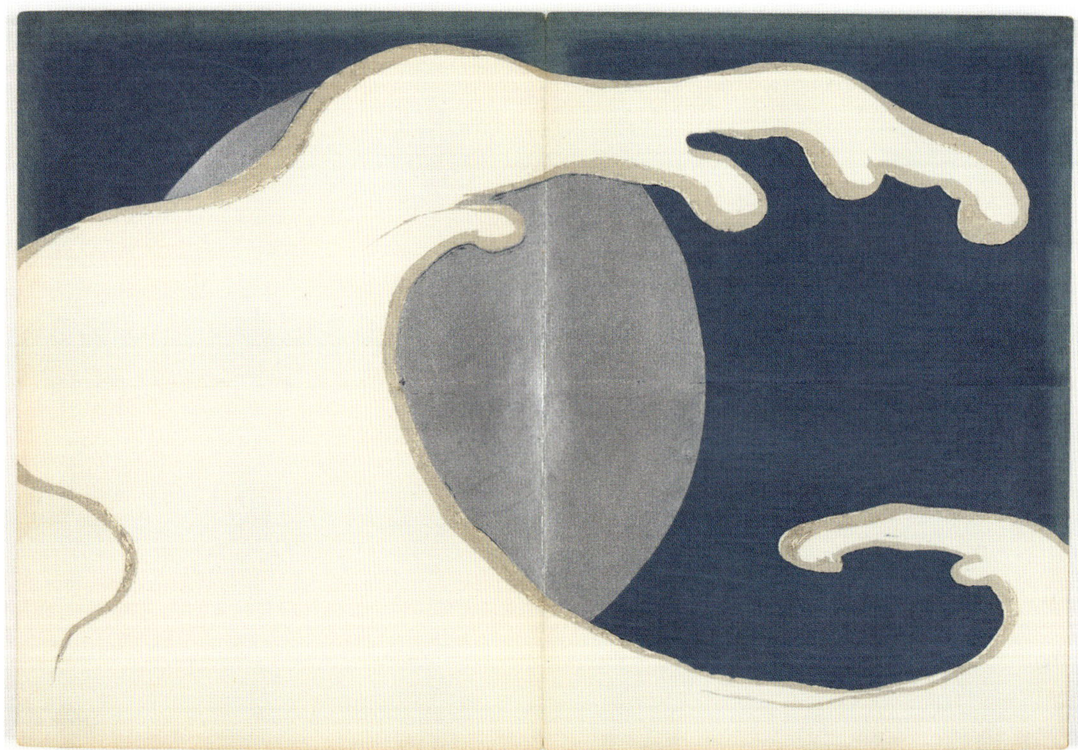

Kamisaka Sekka, a renowned painter, printmaker, and textile designer, was a key figure in the non-hereditary Rinpa school of art, which championed the design sensibilities of early modern masters like Ogata Korin (1658–1716) and Tawaraya Sotatsu (d. 1643). Sekka, considered the last great proponent of this artistic tradition, was first exposed to the tenets of Rinpa art in Kyoto and over the course of his career added his own flair to the designs, including the flowing lines and organic forms characteristic of Art Nouveau, which he studied from 1888 to 1890 at the Glasgow School of Art in Scotland.

His artistic journey culminated in his masterpiece, *World of Things*, a three-volume album that combines woodblock printing, hand painting, and shimmering metallic materials. Sekka was skilled in *tarashikomi*, a technique loosely associated with Rinpa which involves applying aqueous ink onto an already saturated surface to create an irregular, mottled effect.

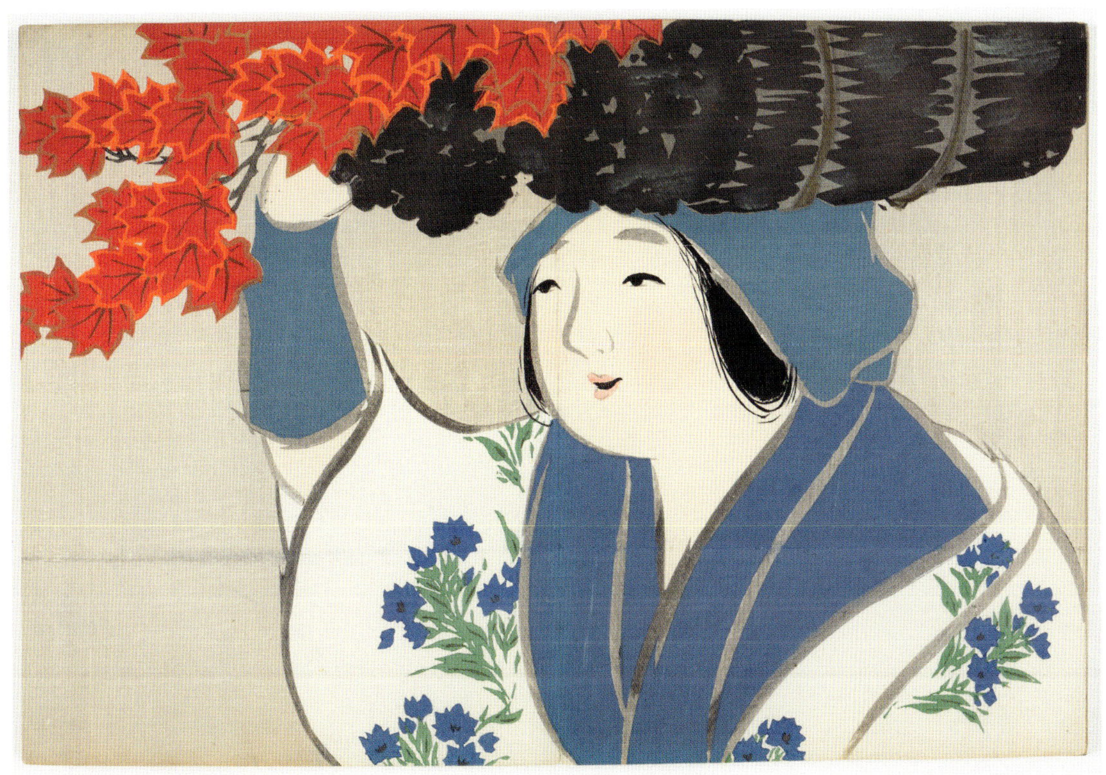

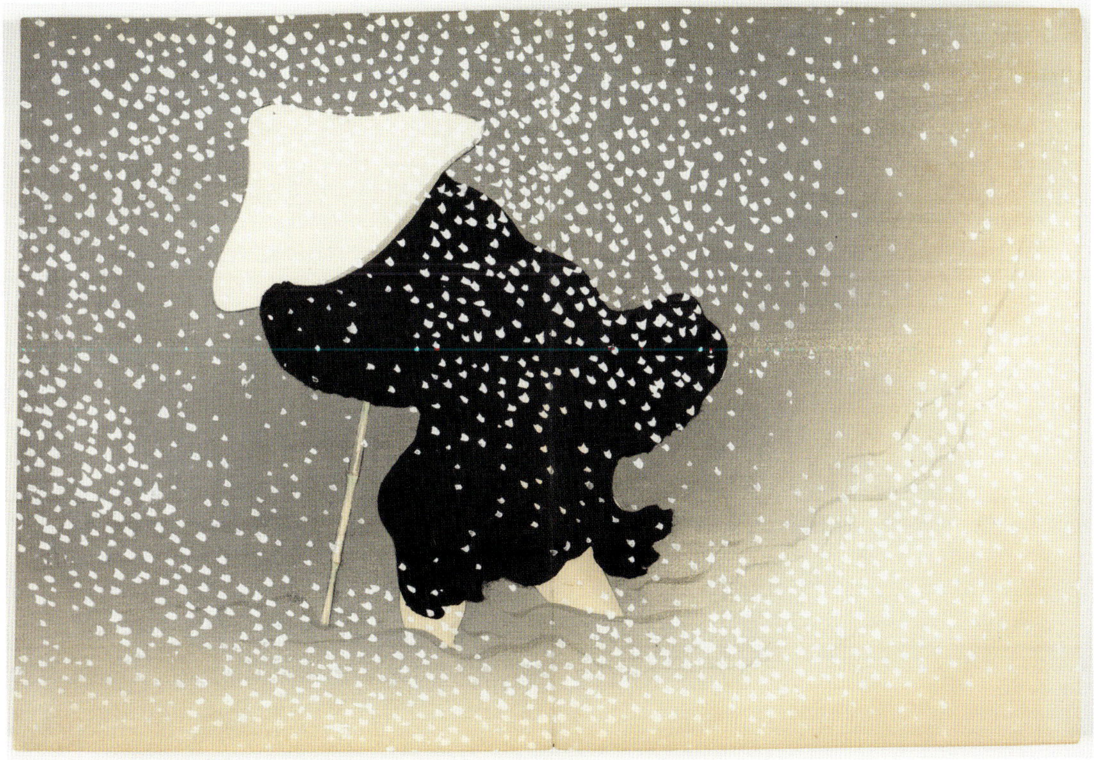

HASHIGUCHI GOYŌ

(1880–1921)

Woman Applying Make-up, 1918

Woodblock print: ink and mica on paper
Ōban: 55.7 × 39.2 cm (21¹⁵⁄₁₆ × 15⁷⁄₁₆ in.)
Stoddard Acquisition Fund, 1996.41

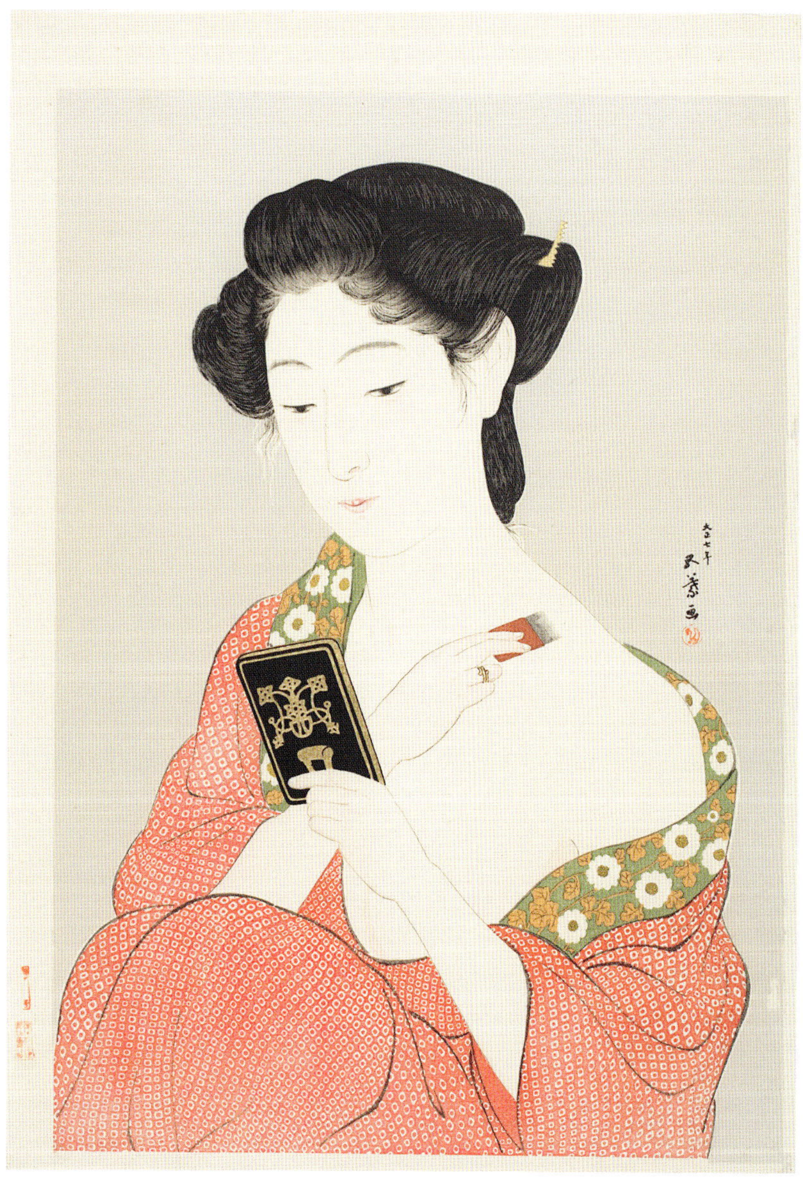

Known for his portrayal of women, Goyō's masterful balance of line and subtle modelling brings his subject to life while a glimmering mica background enhances her mystique. Although this model resembles archetypal beauties from *ukiyo-e*, the woman's downcast eyes and serene expression also recall the repose of Raphael's Madonnas, a subtle nod to Goyō's training in *yōga* (Western-style) painting. This is Goyō's first self-published print.

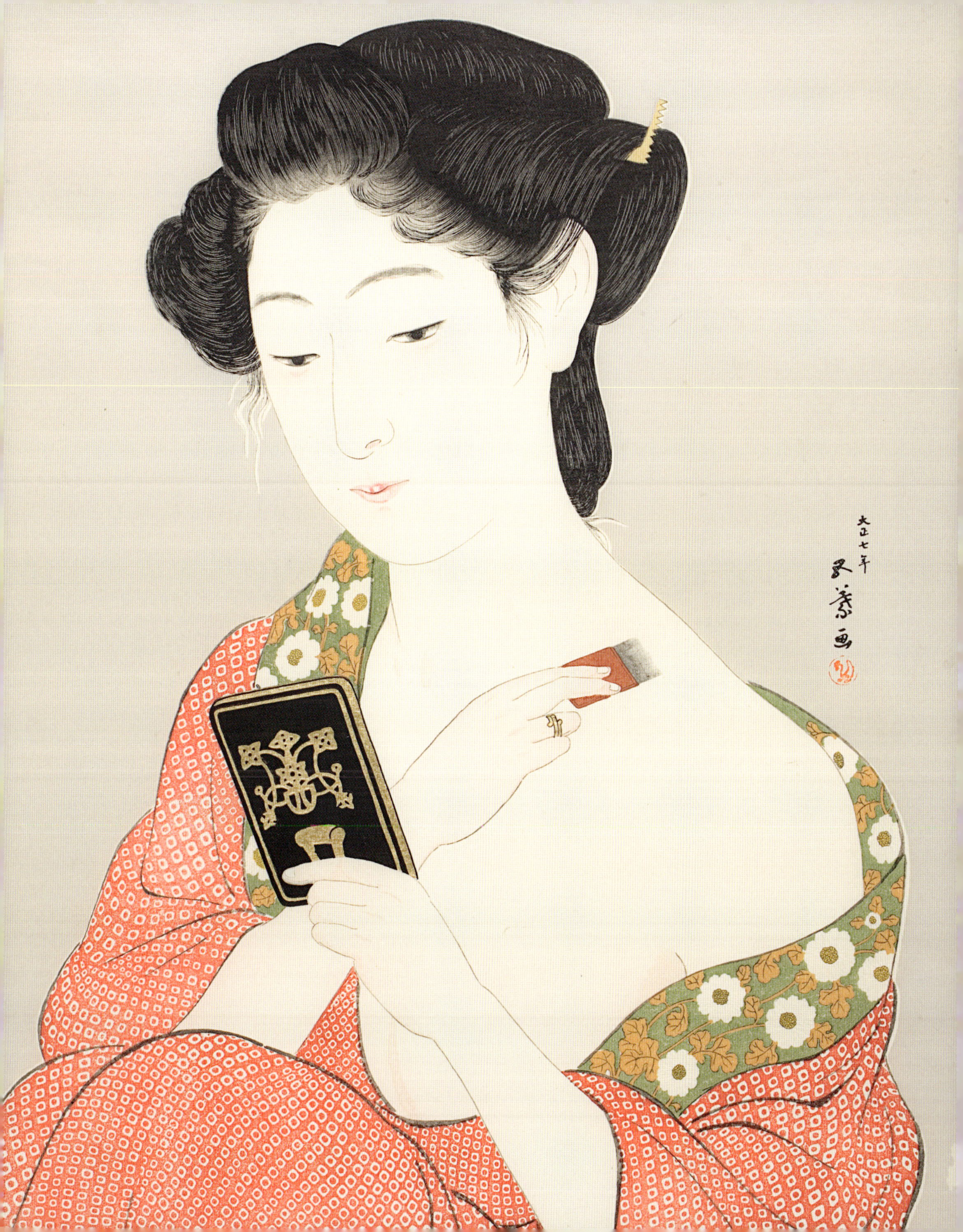
大正七年
五葉画

YAMAMURA TOYONARI (KŌKA)

(1885–1942)

Dancing at the New Carlton Hotel in Shanghai, 1924

Woodblock print: ink and color on paper
Sheet: 42 × 28.6 cm (16⁹⁄₁₆ × 11¼ in.)
Stoddard Acquisition Fund, 2000.26

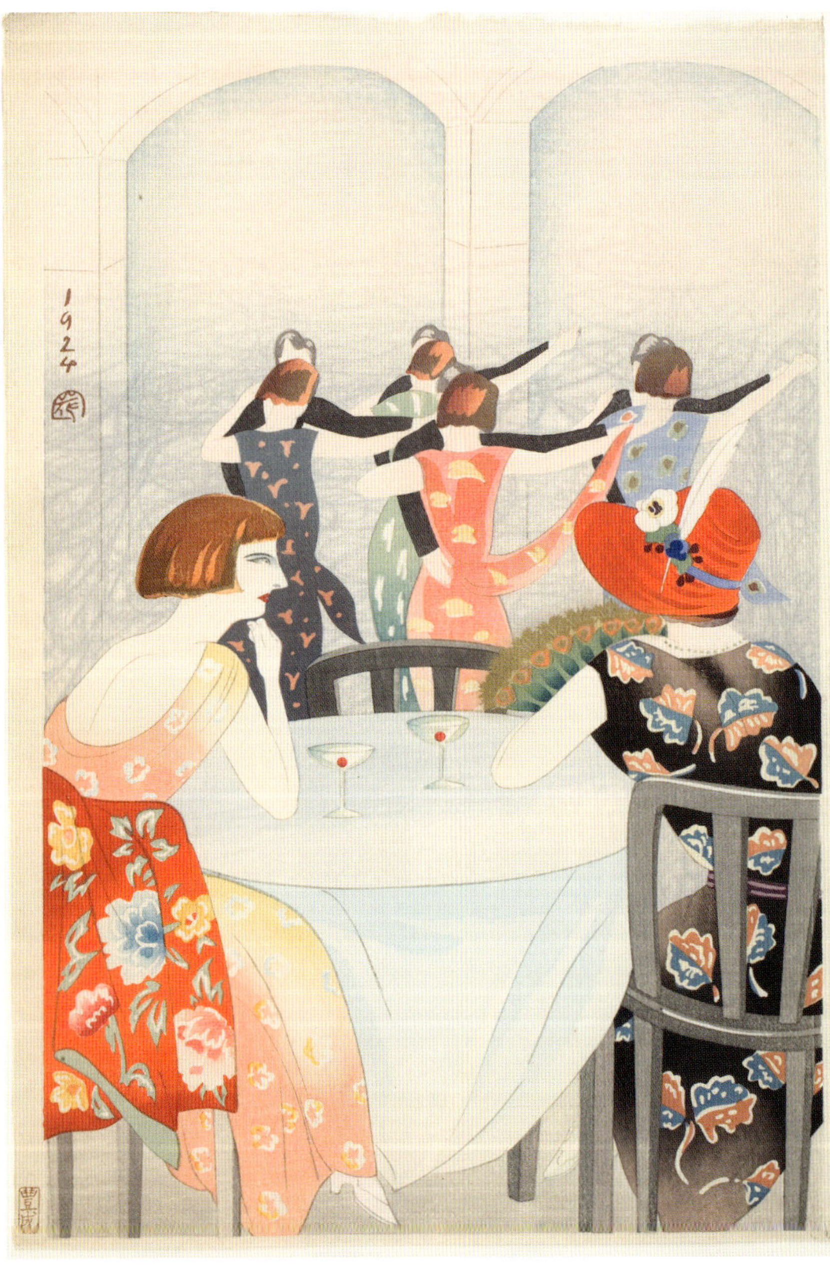

Yamamura Toyonari (Kōka) captured the effervescent zeitgeist of the Roaring Twenties in this scene set in the New Carlton Hotel, a trailblazing establishment that was the first to offer regular performances of jazz music in Shanghai. The two figures in the foreground, with their fashionably bobbed hair, elegant slinky gowns, and cocktails in hand, epitomize the modern, liberated women of the era, a striking departure from the traditional *bijin* archetype that dominated *ukiyo-e* or contemporaneous *shin hanga* prints. The figural forms and the subtle dusting of mica on the rich blue background evoke Art Deco poster design, enhancing the overall impression of luster, glamor, and cosmopolitan sophistication.

OHARA SHOSON (KOSON)

(1877–1945)

Crow Perched on a Snow-covered Branch, ca. 1925

Publisher: Daikokuya Heikichi
Woodblock print: ink and color on paper
O-tanzaku: 35.8 × 19 cm (14⅛ × 7½ in.)
Alexander H. Bullock Fund, 2008.18

Ohara Shoson (formerly Koson) initially studied Shijo-style ink painting—a style recognizable for its Western-influenced naturalism achieved through traditional Japanese painting media—before becoming a respected teacher at the prestigious Tokyo School of Fine Arts. It was there that he first met Ernest Fenollosa, an esteemed American collector, scholar, and curator who recognized Koson's talent for creating *kacho-e* ("bird and flower pictures"). Fenollosa encouraged him to export his bird prints to enthusiastic American art collectors, and later helped to establish the artist's reputation internationally. This depiction of a solitary crow perched on a snow-laden branch stands as a testament to Koson's keen eye for detail, judicious use of negative space, and ability to imbue his prints with charm.

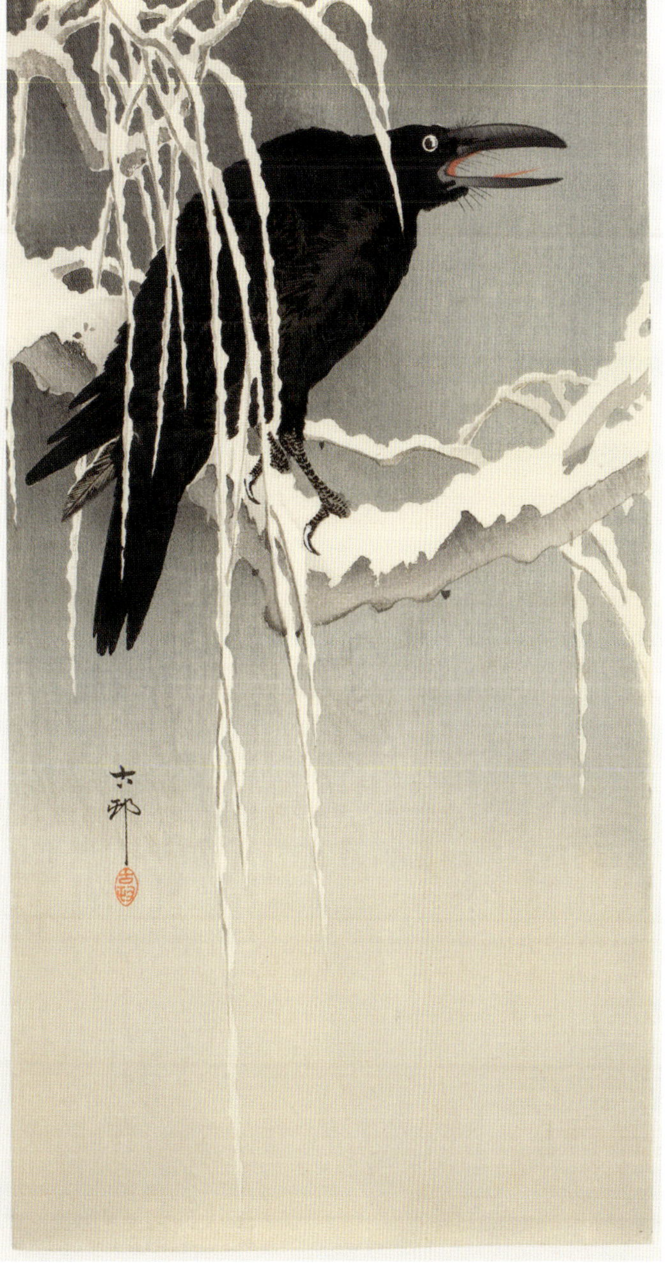

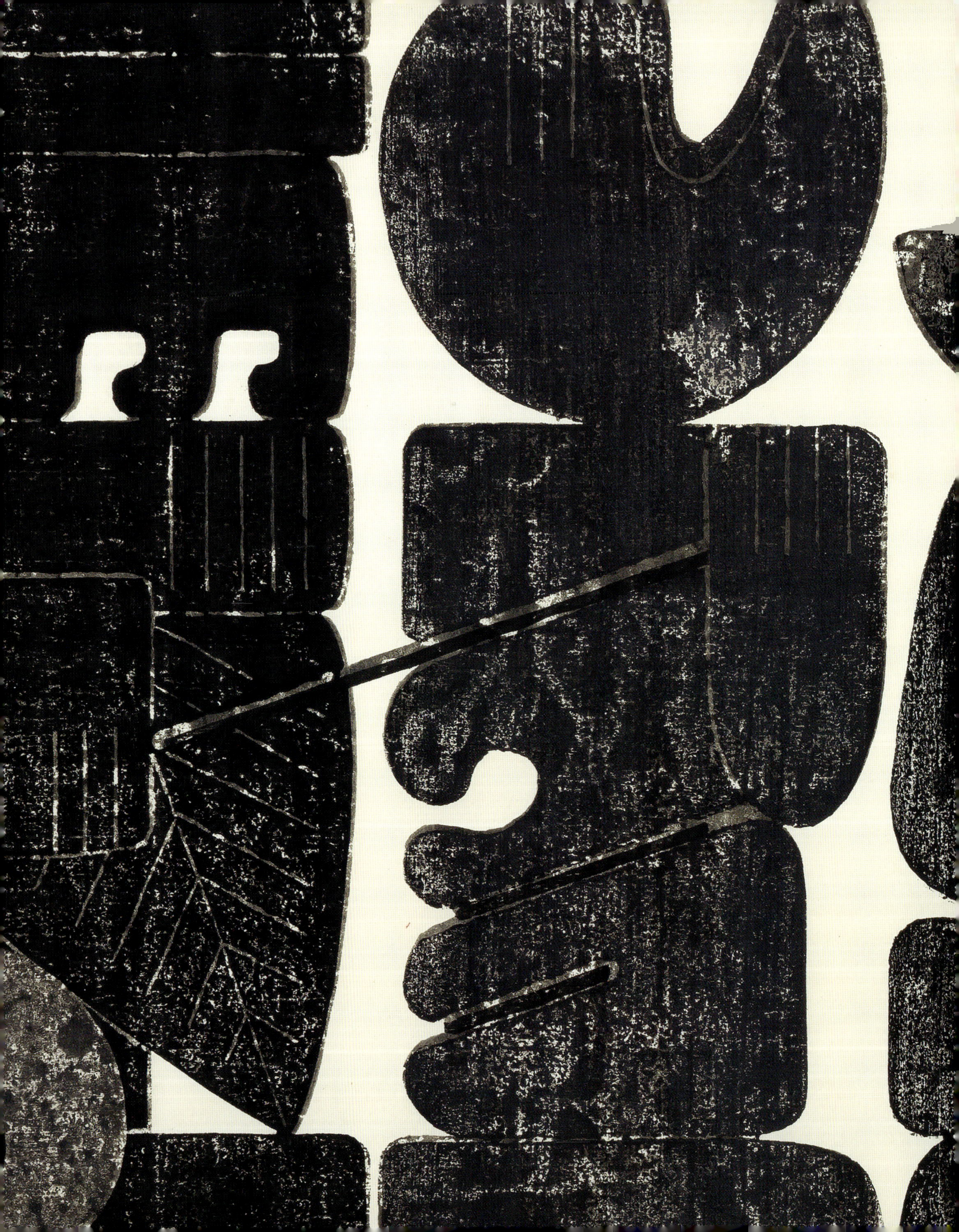

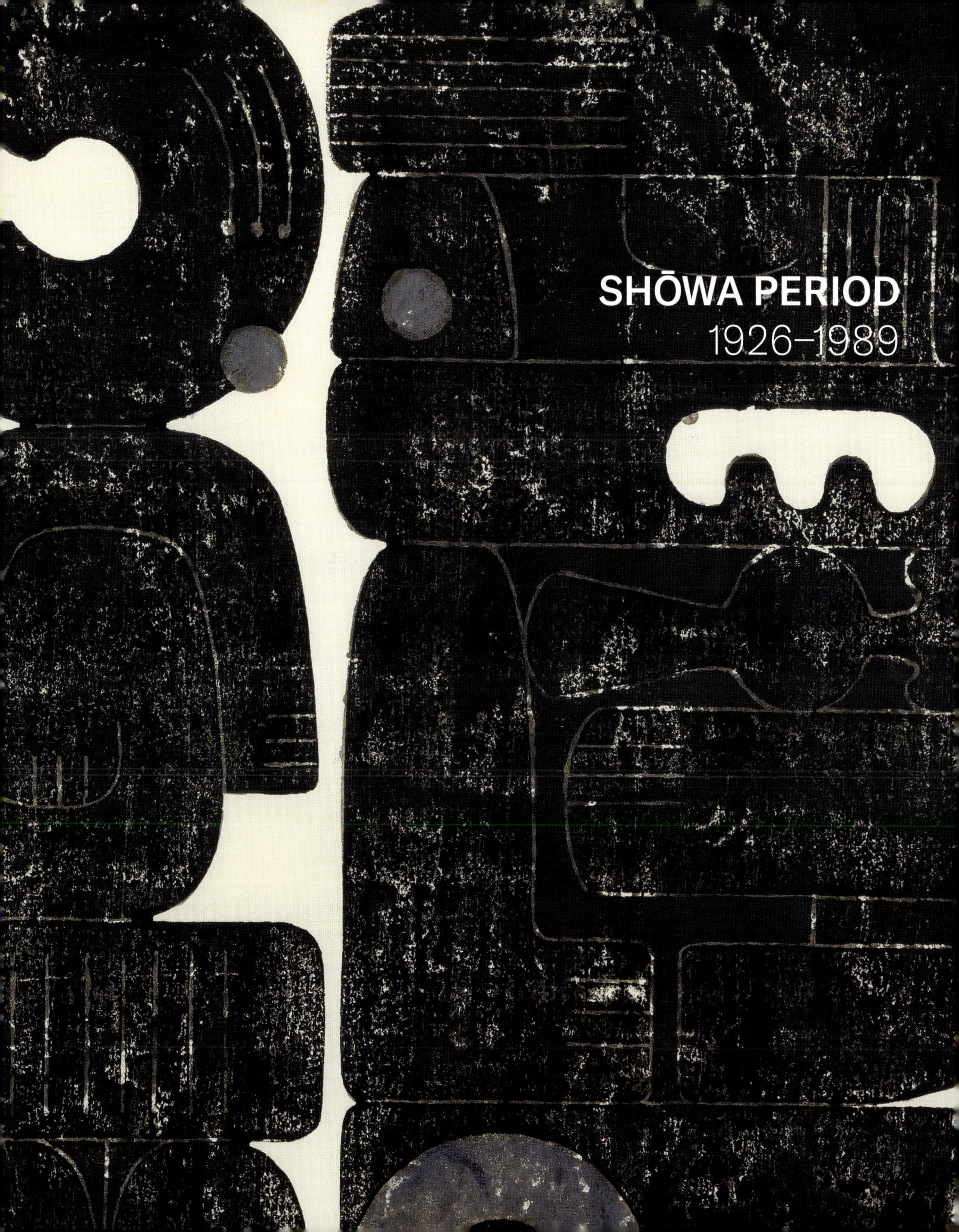
SHŌWA PERIOD
1926–1989

YOSHIDA HIROSHI

(1876–1950)

Three plates from the series "Twelve Tokyo Subjects", 1926

a) *Sumida River – Mist*

Woodblock print: ink and color on paper
28 × 41 cm (11 × 16⅛ in.)
Harriet B. Bancroft Fund, 1998.52

b) *Sumida River – Evening*

Woodblock print: ink and color on paper
28 × 41 cm (11 × 16⅛ in.)
Harriet B. Bancroft Fund, 1998.50

c) *Sumida River – Tokyo*

Woodblock print: ink and color on paper
28 × 41 cm (11 × 16⅛ in.)
Harriet B. Bancroft Fund, 1998.51

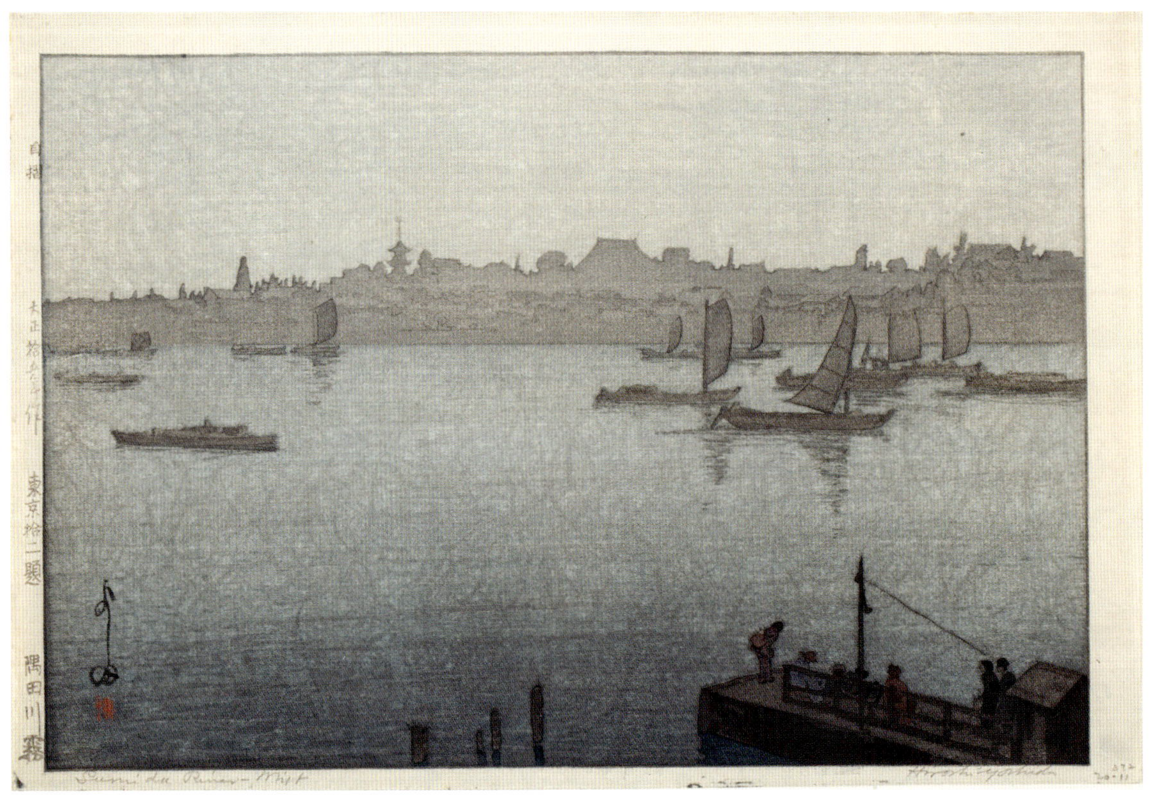

a

Yoshida Hiroshi initially trained in Western painting styles (*yōga*) both in Japan and for a brief time at the Académie Colarossi in Paris in 1899. Hiroshi's time in Europe had a profound impact on his artistic development, as he explored innovative ways of depicting light, color, and atmosphere in his work, drawing inspiration from the techniques and philosophies of the impressionist and post-impressionist movements. Upon returning to Japan, Hiroshi collaborated with the influential publisher Watanabe Shōzaburō to create *shin hanga* ("new prints"), which sought to revitalize the declining *ukiyo-e* tradition by incorporating elements of Western-style naturalism and perspectival devices.

These three prints depicting the Sumida River in Tokyo (originally from a series of twelve) exemplify the balance that Yoshida struck between modern and traditional sensibilities. On the one hand, they evoke the nostalgic charm of *meisho-e*, the "famous place pictures" that were popular during the Edo period. On the other hand, Hiroshi's exploration of changing light on the landscape —achieved through the use of *baren-suji* and layers of ink—resonates with Claude Monet's iconic series of paintings depicting the façade of Rouen Cathedral under different lighting conditions (which he likely saw while in Paris). These prints are among the first Hiroshi produced after establishing his own print workshop in 1925.

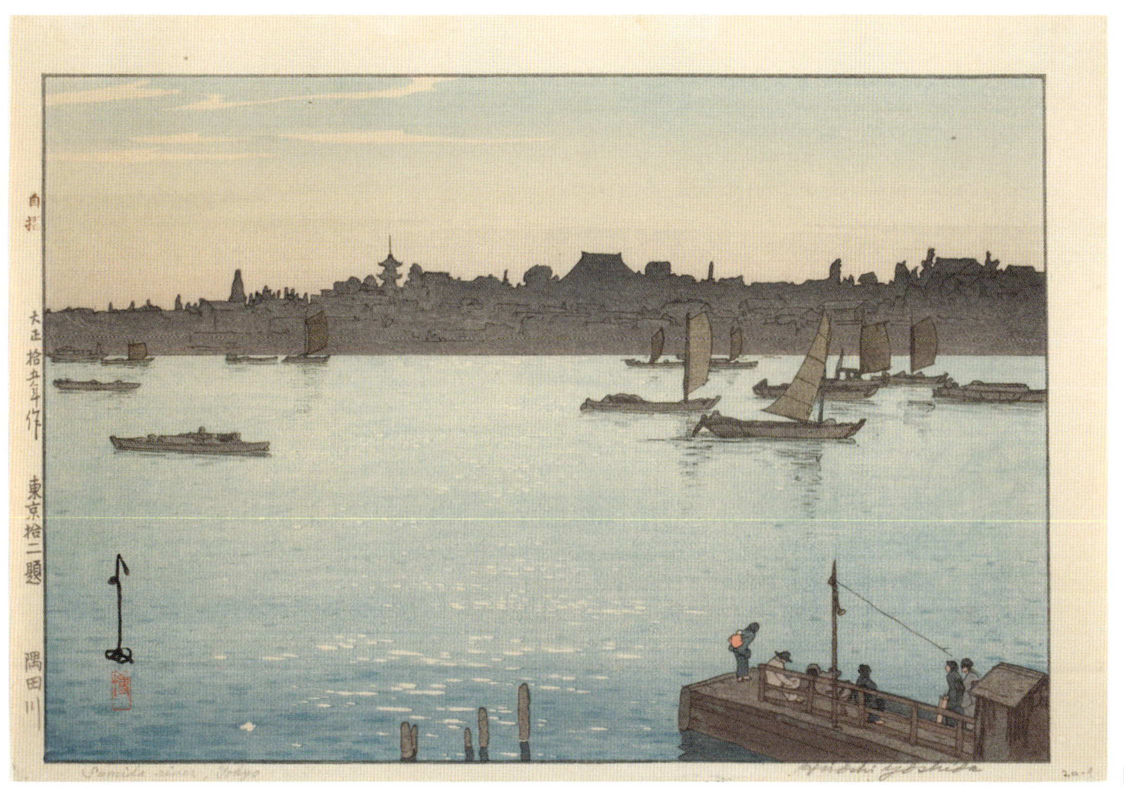

b

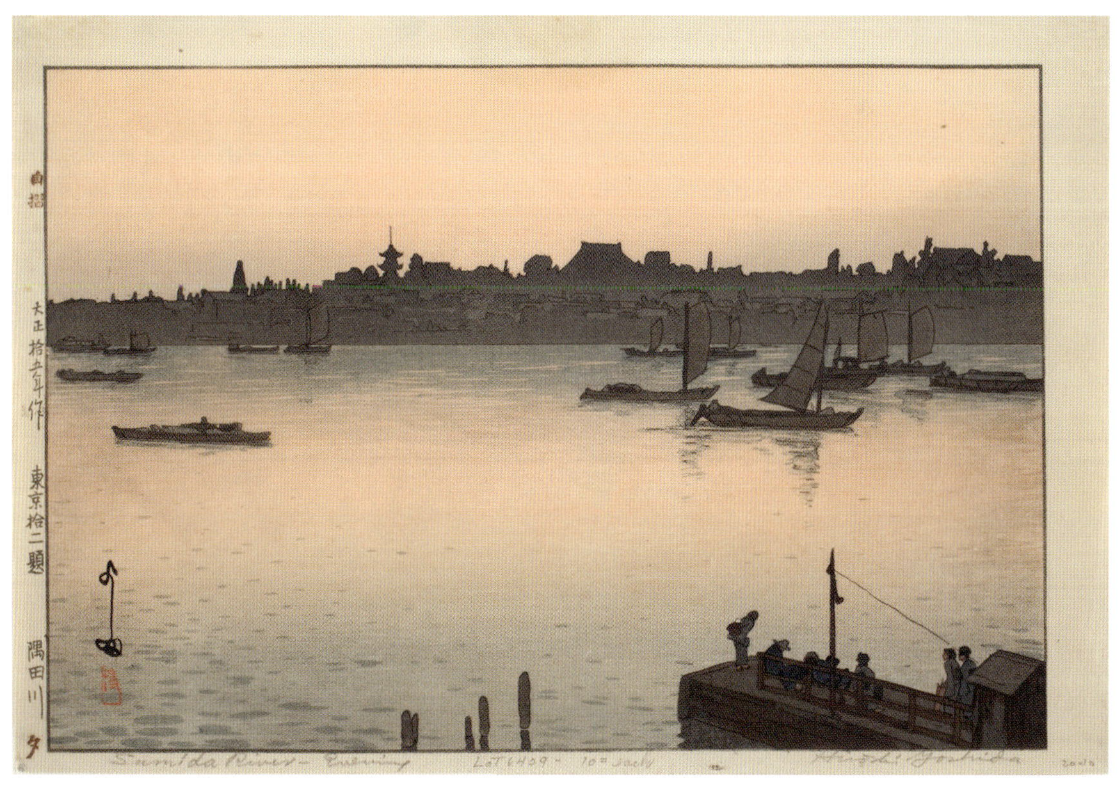

c

KAWASE HASUI

(1883–1957)

Spring Rain at Gokoku Temple, ca. 1933

Publisher: Doi Hangaten
Woodblock print: ink and color on paper
39.2 × 26.7 cm (15⁷⁄₁₆ × 10½ in.)
Harriet B. Bancroft Fund, 1997.144

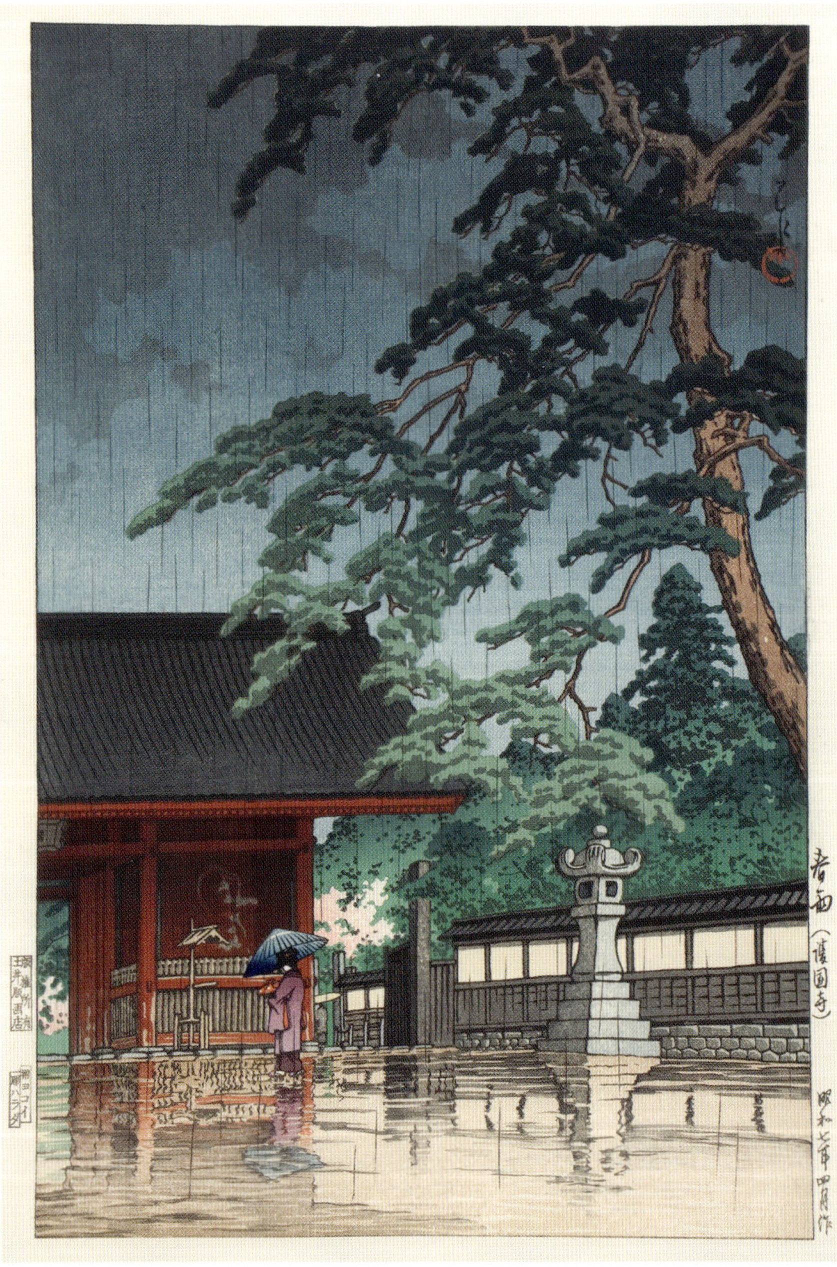

After studying Western-style painting under Saburosuke Okada in his mid-twenties, Kawase Hasui trained under renowned Nihonga painter Kaburagi Kiyokata at age 29, who gave him the artist name Hasui, meaning "water gushing from a spring." These early influences profoundly shaped his later woodblock print designs, which cemented his legacy as one of the most celebrated artists of the *shin hanga* ("new prints") movement. He is best known for his collaborations with Watanabe Shōzaburō, resulting in over 600 woodcuts.

Hasui's designs are characterized by atmospheric weather conditions and pastoral quietude, elements that imbue his prints with a sense of serenity and introspection. His works invite viewers to reflect on the beauty of nature and the harmony between manmade structures and their surroundings. *Spring Rain at Gokoku Temple*, a later collaboration with the Tokyo-based publishing company Doi Hangaten, captures a tranquil moment in Tokyo after a rainfall. Rendered in vivid jewel tones, the print highlights Hasui's exceptional attention to detail, with glistening reflections on damp pavement and subtle gradations in the overcast sky.

ITO SHINSUI
(1898–1972)

Pupil of the Eye, from the second series of modern beauties, 1936

Publisher: Watanabe Shōzaburō
Woodblock print: ink, color, and mica on paper
28.7 × 24.4 cm (11⁵⁄₁₆ × 9⁵⁄₈ in.)
Bequest of Charles B. Cohn in memory of Stuart P. Anderson, 1985.144

Hajime Ito earned his artist's name "Shinsui" while under the tutelage of Kaburaki Kiyokata. Translating to "deep water," it referenced his unwavering dedication and diligence. At eighteen years old, he joined the ranks of the *shin hanga* movement under the guidance of publisher Watanabe Shōzaburō (1885–1962). Ito specialized in *bijinga* (pictures of beautiful women). In this close-up portrait, Shinsui captures his model in a dreamy state as she adjusts her green hairpin, her gaze drifting to the left. The application of mica powder, the blush on her *oshiroi* makeup, and the *shibori*-dyed waves on her kimono add subtle dimensionality to the design.

This is a *sashiage*, a print produced early in the process as a color proof. It served to guide the printer and publisher in bringing the artist's vision to life, though colors and details may be adjusted during the final printing to perfect the result.

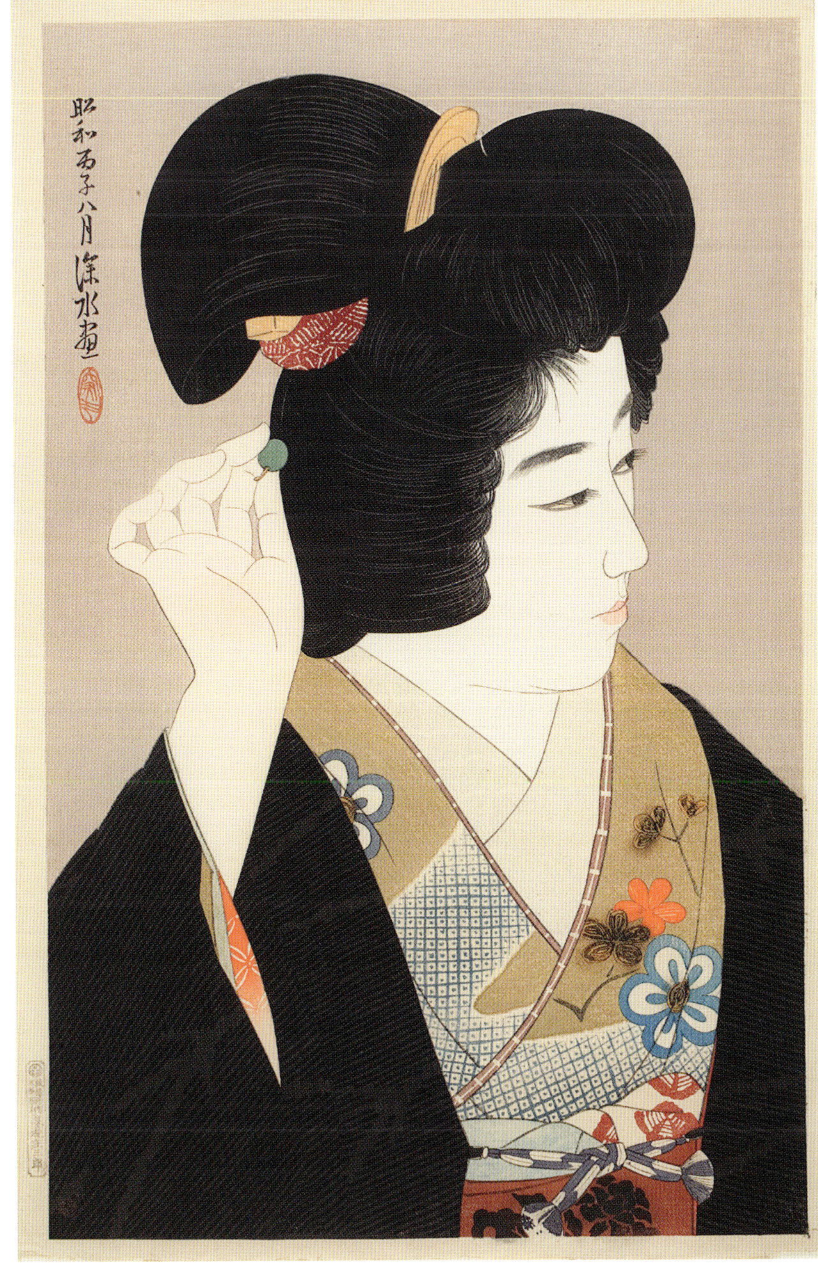

UN'ICHI HIRATSUKA

(1895–1997)

Sukiya Bridge, from the series "Scenes of Lost Tokyo", 1945

Woodblock print: ink and color on paper
20 × 28 cm (7⅞ × 11 in.)
Members' Council Fund, 1987.79.5

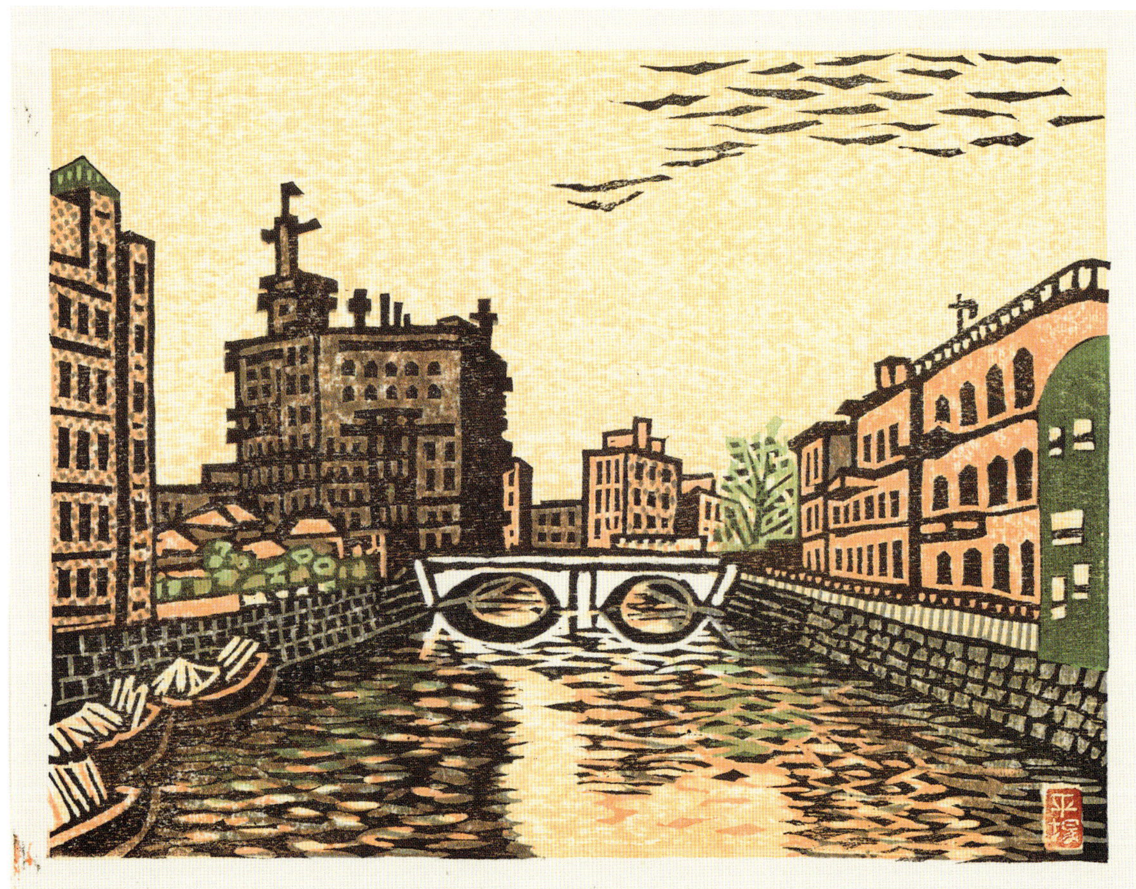

This design depicting Sukiya Bridge first appeared in the series "One Hundred Views of the New Tokyo" (*Shin Tokyo Hyakkei*) (1928–32), a collaboration between eight *sōsaku hanga* printmakers to commemorate public work projects in the capital. Later, it was reprinted in 1945 as part of "Scenes of Last Tokyo," which featured images of beloved Tokyo landmarks as they appeared before they were damaged or destroyed by Allied air raids during World War II. The introduction to the series explains that the project was initiated as a means for participating artists to reflect on the city's permanently altered urban landscape and to inspire hope for rebuilding what was lost. Unlike the warm yellow daylight glow of the 1930 impression, the light in this 1945 version has a peachy tone reminiscent of sunset.

The prints in this series were published with both Japanese and English titles in order to appeal to both Japanese audiences and the Allied Occupation forces stationed in Japan after the war. It is possible that the title "Scenes of Last Tokyo" was printed by mistake instead of "Scenes of Lost Tokyo."

YOSHIDA TOSHI

(1911–1995)

Stone Garden, 1963

Woodblock print; ink and color on paper
34.9 × 24.1 cm (13¾ × 9½ in.)
Gift from the Judith and Paul A. Falcigno Collection, 2010.95

The following three prints represent the Yoshida family of printmakers' departure from the representational style and traditional *ukiyo-e*-inspired designs of the patriarch, Hiroshi (1876–1950). His sons, Toshi (1911–1995) and Hodaka (1926–1995), and his daughter-in-law Chizuko (1924–2017), depict the serene beauty of Buddhist temple landscaping while incorporating elements of abstraction and minimalism in ways that are unique to each of their oeuvres.

The first two prints, by Yoshida Toshi and Yoshida Hodaka respectively, depict Zen temple rock gardens, which have long been a wellspring of artistic inspiration in Japan. These minimalist landscapes, meticulously crafted with carefully arranged rocks, raked white gravel, and greenery, are designed to facilitate deep meditation and introspection. In contrast, Yoshida Chizuko's print portrays the stone road leading to the eighth-century Muroji Temple in Nara prefecture. The 1.8-kilometer path, believed to have been constructed during the Kamakura period (1185–1333), comprises hundreds of steps winding through a beautiful cedar forest. This path provides access to the temple as well as a tranquil and meditative journey.

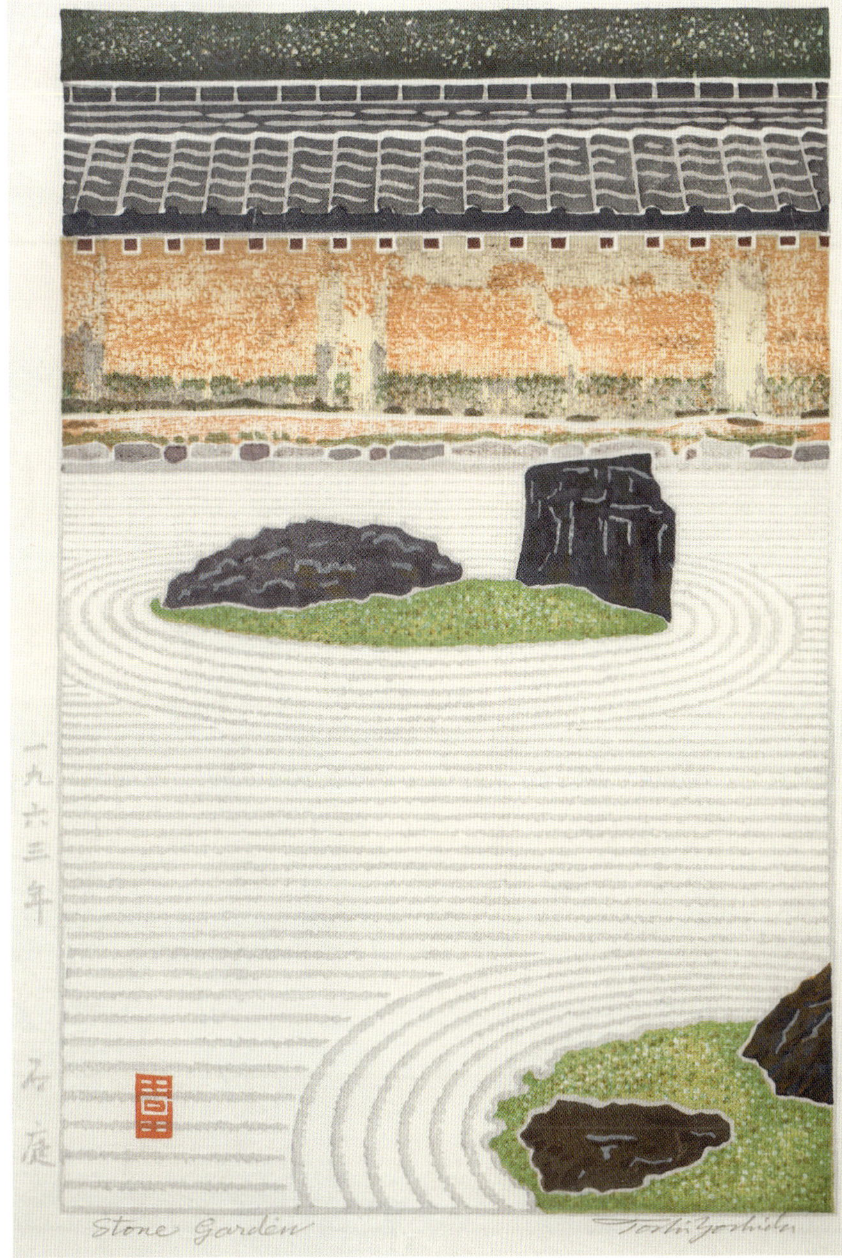

YOSHIDA HODAKA

(1926–1995)

Ryoanji Garden, Kyoto,
1952

Woodblock print: ink and color
on paper
19.1 × 12.1 cm (7½ × 4¹¹⁄₁₆ in.)
Director's Discretionary Fund,
1954.4

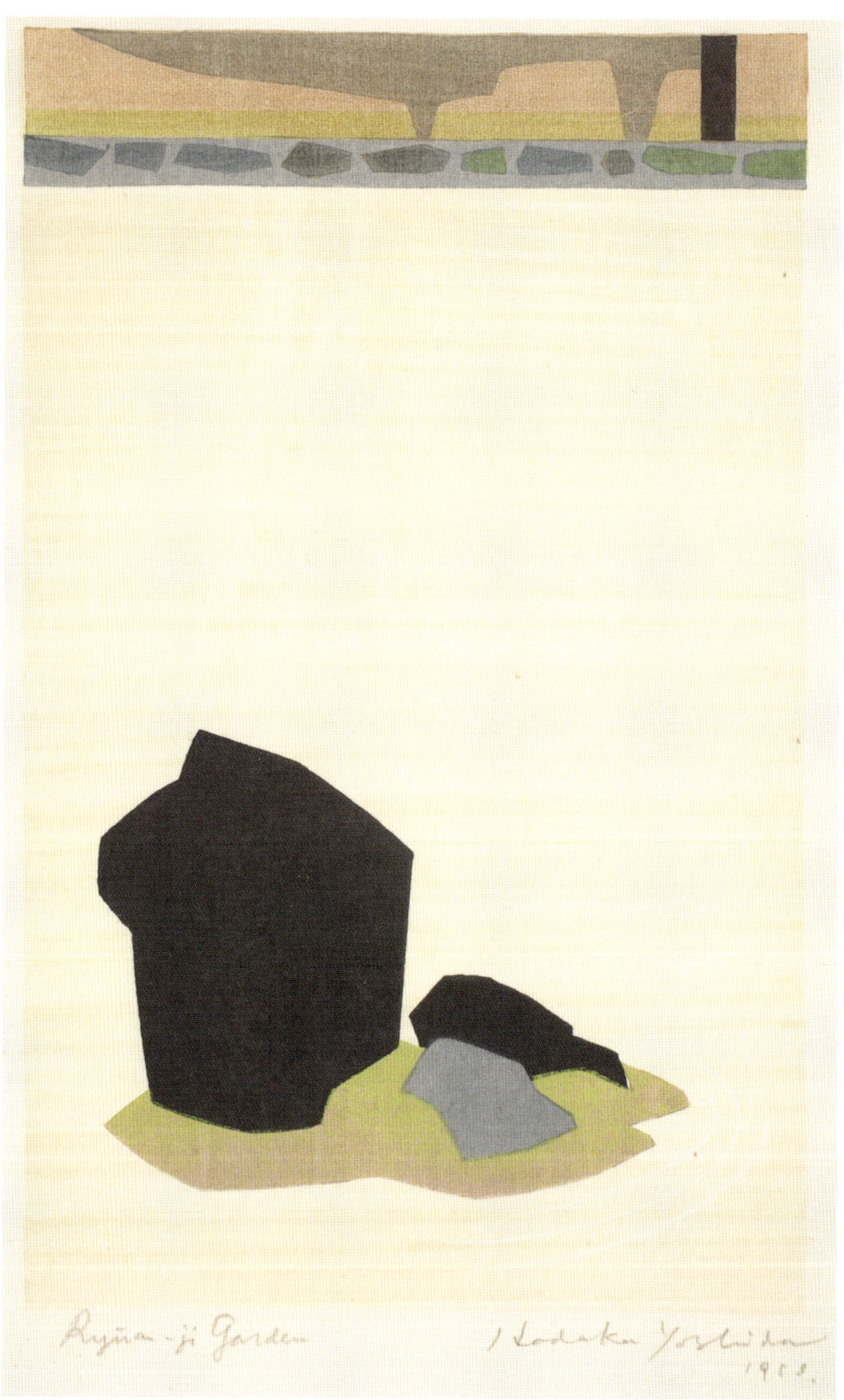

YOSHIDA CHIZUKO

(1924–2017)

Muroji Stone Road,
1953

Woodblock print: ink and color
on paper
19.1 × 11.9 cm (7½ × 4¹¹⁄₁₆ in.)
Director's Discretionary Fund,
1954.5

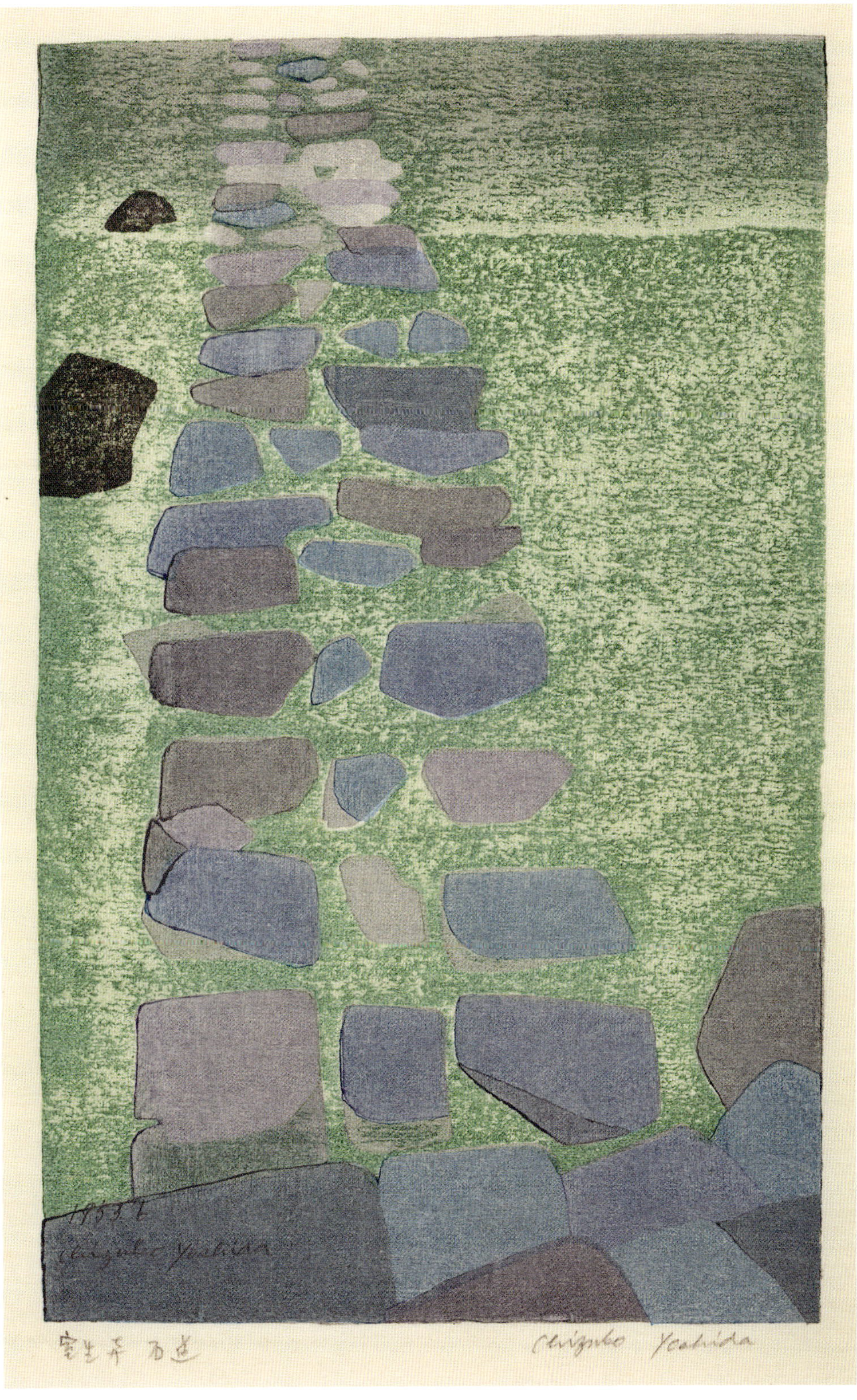

YOSHIDA HODAKA

(1926–1995)

Ancient People, 1956

Woodblock print; ink and color on paper
54.6 × 68.6 cm (21½ × 27 in.)
Harriet B. Bancroft Fund, 1962.33

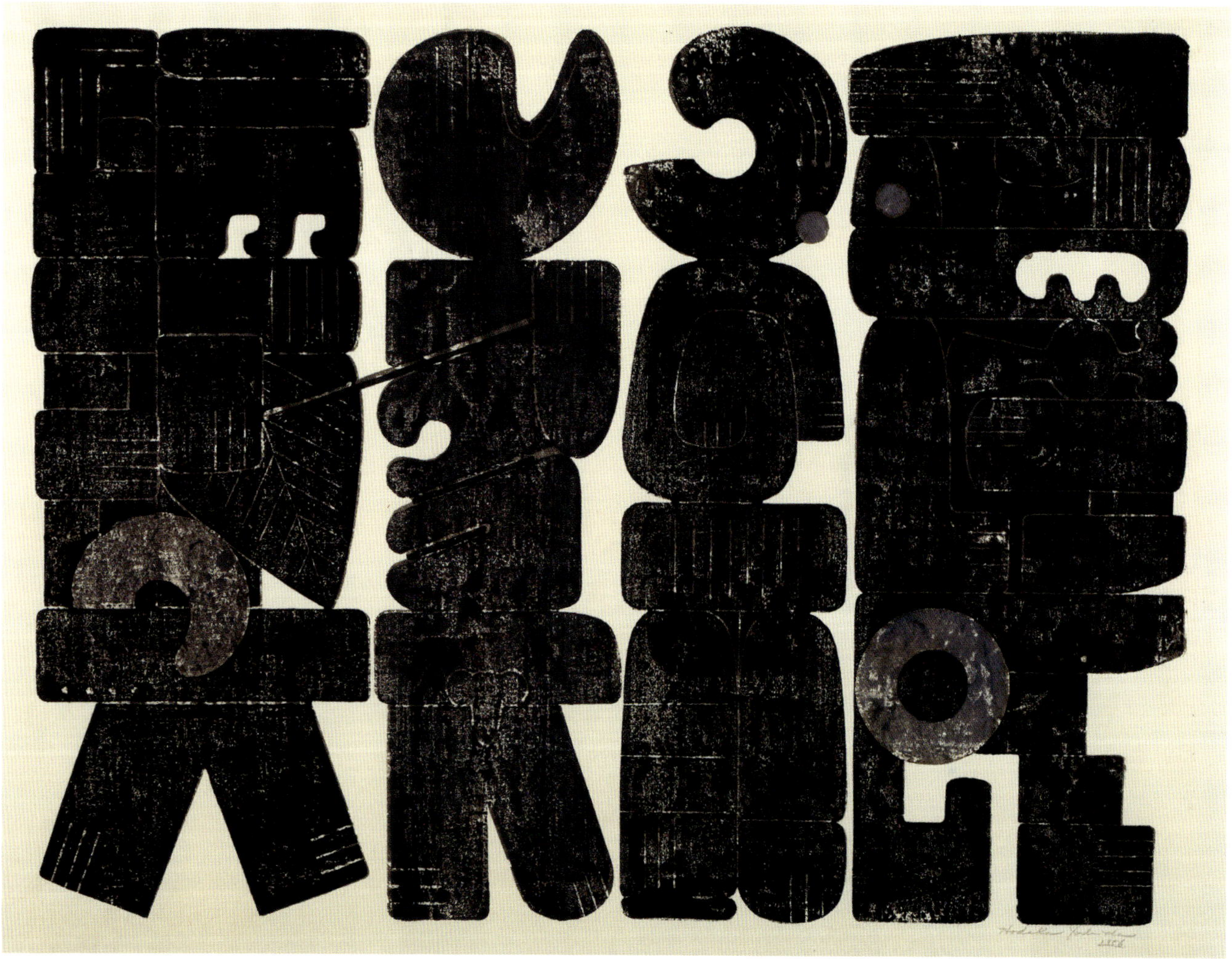

Unlike his father Yoshida Hiroshi (1876–1950), Yoshida Hodaka championed the visual languages of abstraction, surrealism, and primitivism. His trip to Mexico in 1955 marked a pivotal moment in his artistic career and inspired a series of self-published works, like the one seen here, influenced by the visual cultures of the ancient Americas, later referred to by scholars as "primitive energy prints." Their forms reveal Hodaka's reverence for artists like Joan Miró (Spanish, 1893–1983) and Paul Klee (Swiss, 1879–1940), two prominent figures in the development of abstract art in the early twentieth century.

SEKINO JUN'ICHIRŌ

(1914–1988)

Sunset in Kyoto, 1969

Woodblock print: ink and color on paper
82 × 55.2 cm (32⁵⁄₁₆ × 21¾ in.)
Gift of Daniel Catton Rich in memory of Bertha James Rich, 1969.145

From a bird's eye view, the onlooker peers down upon a rooftop in Kyoto, contributing to a long tradition of using urban landscapes as a subject in Japanese prints. Jun'ichirō's masterful manipulation of perspective flattens the architectural space into an abstraction, challenging the viewer's perception and inviting them to explore the intriguing interplay between two- and three-dimensional representation. The light emanating from the window illuminates the surroundings, creating a captivating focal point that anchors the eye within the landscape and draws the viewer deeper into the scene. The strategic pops of bold red, white, and blue hues are subtle nods to the influence of Mondrian, and other De Stijl artists whose work is often characterized by the use of primary colors and rectilinear shapes.

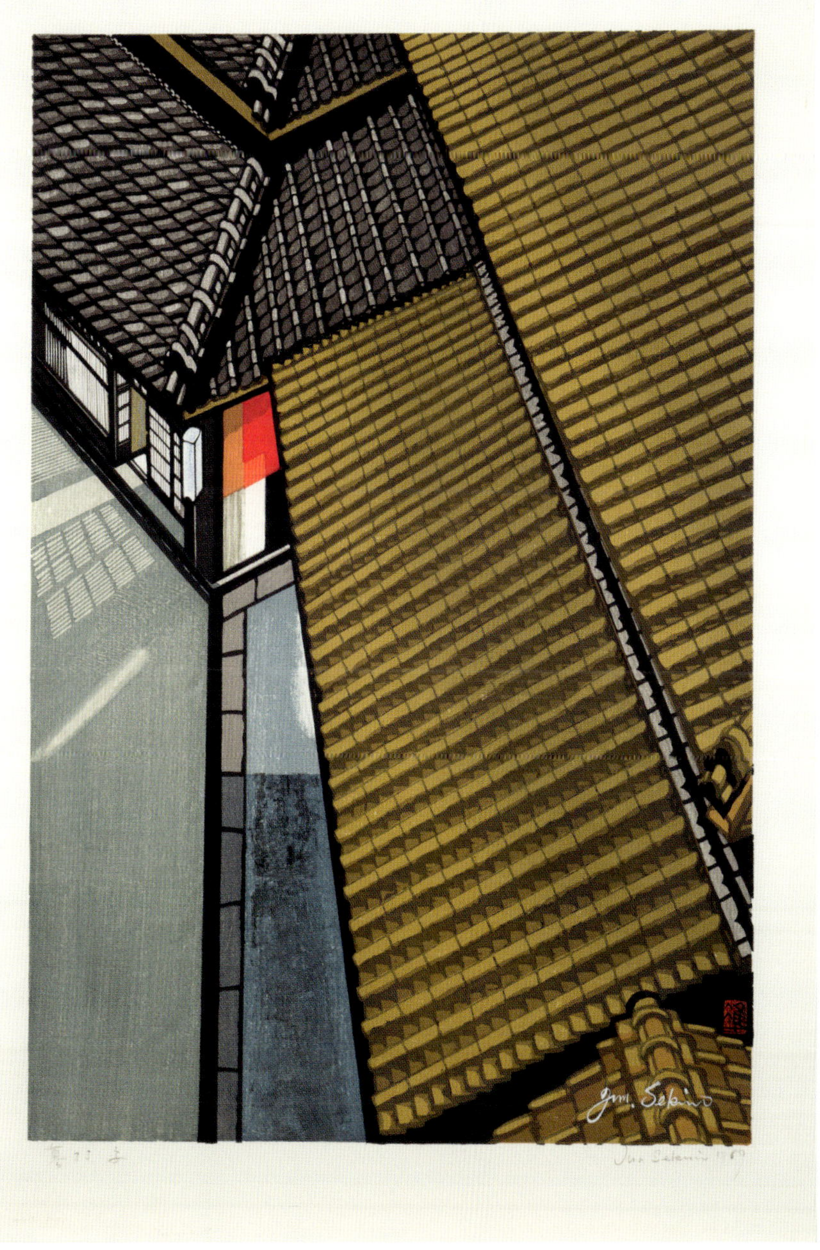

UMETARO AZECHI

(1902–1999)

Stand on the Snow Gorge, 1956

Woodblock print: ink and color on paper
Sheet: 59.1 × 40.8 cm (23¼ × 16¹⁄₁₆ in.)
Bequest of Barbara Milliken, 2014.643

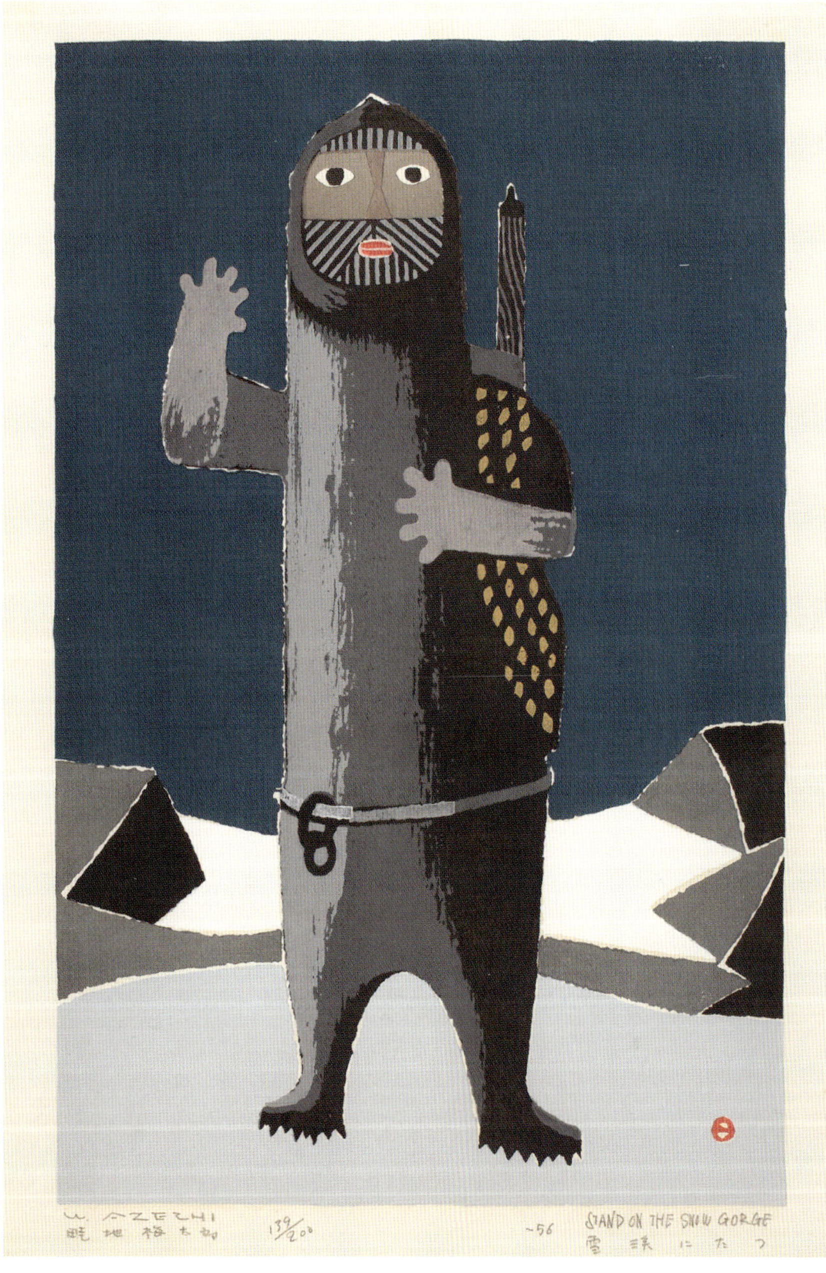

Umetaro Azechi became involved in the *sōsaku hanga* ("creative prints") movement while under the tutelage of Unichi Hiratsuka. During this time, Azechi developed a signature style that involved using a flat, straight-end chisel to scrape the edges of lines on the block, giving them coarse, organic properties. This technique imbued his prints with a distinctive texture and a sense of raw, natural energy.

Azechi's passion for mountaineering deeply influenced his artistic output, with his most celebrated prints depicting figures in alpine terrains in a palette dominated by blue. *Stand on the Snow Gorge* features a friendly-looking mountain man (*yama-otoko*) on a snowy summit, with gear slung over his shoulder and raising his hand in greeting. The figure's spiked boots, resembling bear feet, anchor him firmly to the icy rock, conveying a sense of strength and stability in the face of the harsh mountain environment.

MUNAKATA SHIKO

(1903–1975)

Tengu no saku, from the series "Wandering Away from Home: Compositions on Yoshii Isamu's Tanka", 1963

Woodblock print: ink on paper with hand-coloring applied on the verso
40.3 × 33.5 cm (15⅞ × 13³⁄₁₆ in.)
Stoddard Acquisition Fund, 1998.75

Munakata Shiko was known for applying pigments to the backs of his woodblock prints, allowing the colors to seep through to the front. This innovative approach drew inspiration from exposure to the stencil prints of the Mingei folk art movement, with which he became involved around 1936, as well as the bold palette of Vincent van Gogh's paintings.

From 1958 until his death, Shiko created a series of calendar prints titled "Wandering Away from Home" that utilize this distinctive technique. Commissioned by Yaskawa Electric Corporation, the series showcases compositions inspired by the poems of Yoshii Isamu. This print created for January 1963 portrays a *tengu*, a supernatural entity from Japanese folklore often characterized by a long nose and wings. In Japanese mythology, *tengu* were believed to embody the dual nature of life, symbolizing both good and evil, or the delicate balance between gods and *yokai* (supernatural beings).

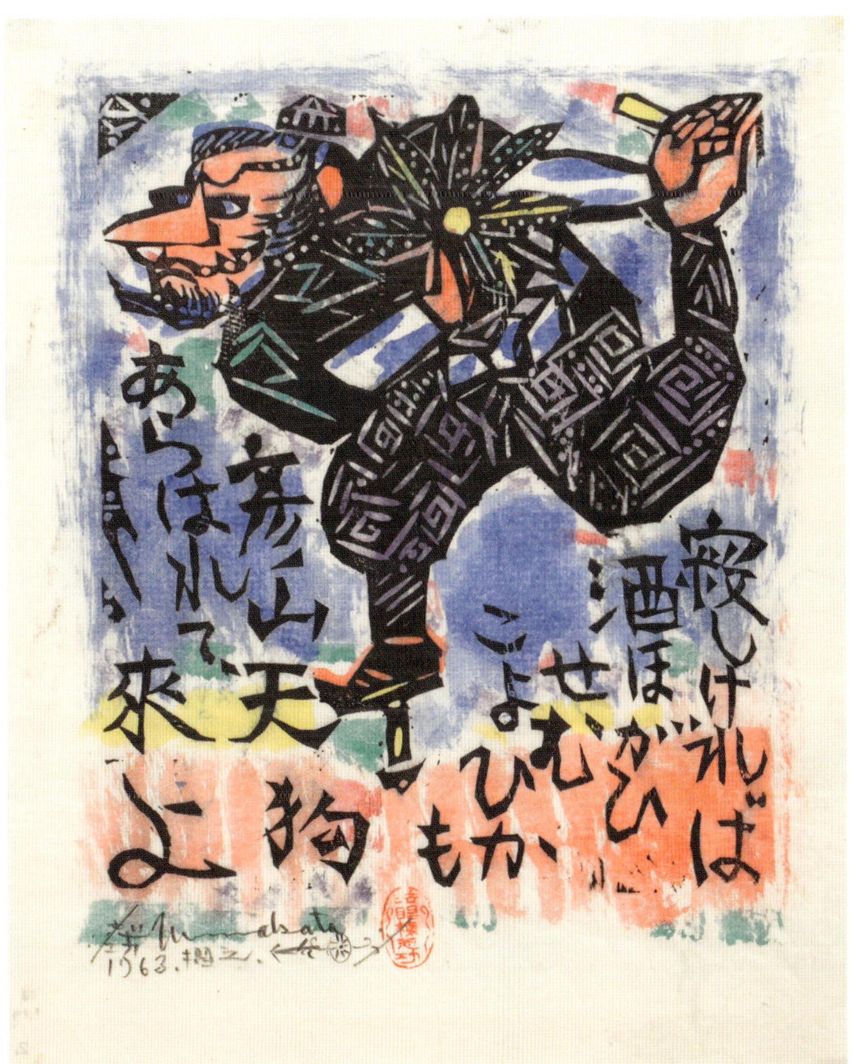

SAITŌ KIYOSHI
(1907–1997)

Clay Image (Haniwa), ca. 1955

Woodblock print: ink and color on paper
55.6 × 37.1 cm (21⅞ × 14⅝ in.)
Gift of Mr. and Mrs. David Milliken, 1999.46

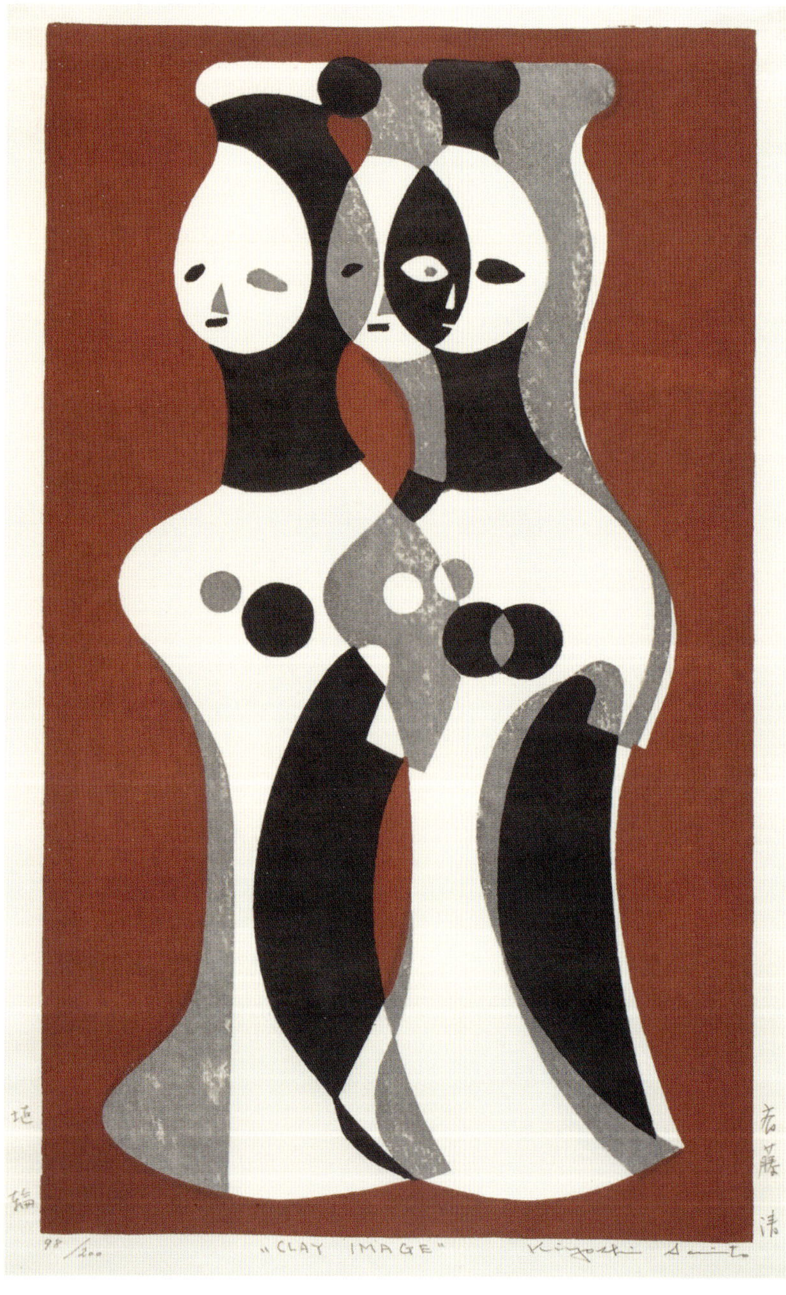

Several major excavations of Yayoi (300 BCE–300 CE) and Kofun (300–552 CE) archeological sites between 1880 and 1940 unearthed a wide range of ancient artifacts such as ceramics, bronze mirrors, bells, and weaponry. These discoveries captivated artists like Saitō Kiyoshi, who sought to reinterpret and celebrate these ancient forms through the lens of modern artistic sensibilities.

Kiyoshi often found inspiration in *haniwa*—funerary sculptures from Japan's Kofun period, typically representing warriors, shrine attendants, and animals—which he encountered while working at the Tokyo National Museum. By 1951, he had produced over thirty woodblock prints, such as the one seen here, inspired by these enigmatic artifacts. In these works, Kiyoshi often abstracted the forms to their geometric essentials, deftly incorporating influences from cubism and European primitivism. As is characteristic of his mature style, the prints are executed in a palette of rust red, black, white, and grey.

MATSUBARA NAOKO

(Japanese, active in Canada, born 1937)

Inner Strength, 1964–68

Woodblock and plastic wood, black ink
111.4 × 77 cm (43⅞ × 30⁵⁄₁₆ in.)
Harriet B. Bancroft Fund, 1989.31

Reflecting on her formative years at Kenkun Jinja, the Shinto shrine in Kyoto where her father served as the chief priest, Matsubara has spoken of the joy she experienced while gazing at the various shapes of aged pines, giant oaks, and gingkos she encountered there. Trees came to represent strength, resilience, and personal growth in her work, as suggested by the title of this monumental print, and her use of the woodblock medium took on extra poetic significance as she sought to express the "life" of the woodblock. Matsubara went on to create several portfolios of woodcuts about trees, including "Solitude" (1971)—inspired by a visit to Walden Pond and the writings of Henry David Thoreau—and later "In Praise of Trees" (1984).

Matsubara began making this print by carving directly into a soft pine block but was not satisfied with the initial result. She filled the carved parts with plastic wood (a type of moldable, wood-like material), and began to experiment with texture. This innovative use of plastic wood allowed her to create unique textures and add depth to her print.

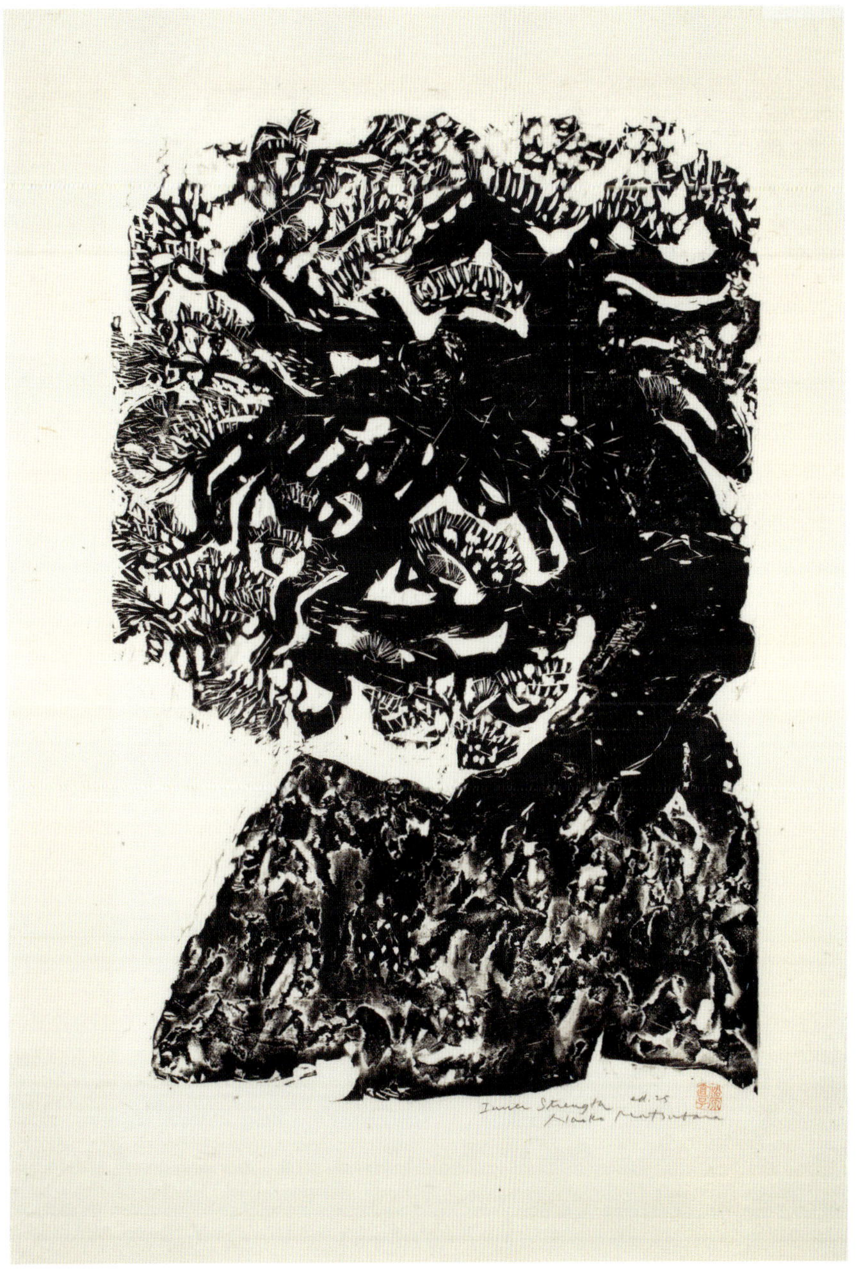

NAKAYAMA TADASHI

(1927–2014)

Afternoon of Decorated Horse (B), 1967

Woodblock print: ink and color on paper
64.3 × 57.1 cm (25⁵⁄₁₆ × 22½ in.)
Gift of Mr. and Mrs. Felix Juda, 1967.49

Nakayama Tadashi initially trained as an oil painter before transitioning to woodblock prints. In *Afternoon of Decorated Horse (B)*, the central figure of the bucking horse is composed of smaller, intricately arranged shapes that evoke the appearance of a shimmering mosaic or gilded icon, revealing the influence of Byzantine art on his work. The abstract and surreal nature of the composition, with its fragmented forms and dreamlike quality, also draws comparisons to the works of European surrealists such as Joan Miró (Spanish, 1893–1983), who often employed biomorphic shapes and vibrant colors in his paintings and prints. These elements invite the viewer to engage with the image on an emotional and subconscious level, exploring the interplay between recognizable forms and abstract elements to create a sense of mystery and intrigue. The palette is characteristic of Nakayama's mature style, distinguished by rich earth tones and bold, jewel-like hues, often enhanced by adding metallic pigments.

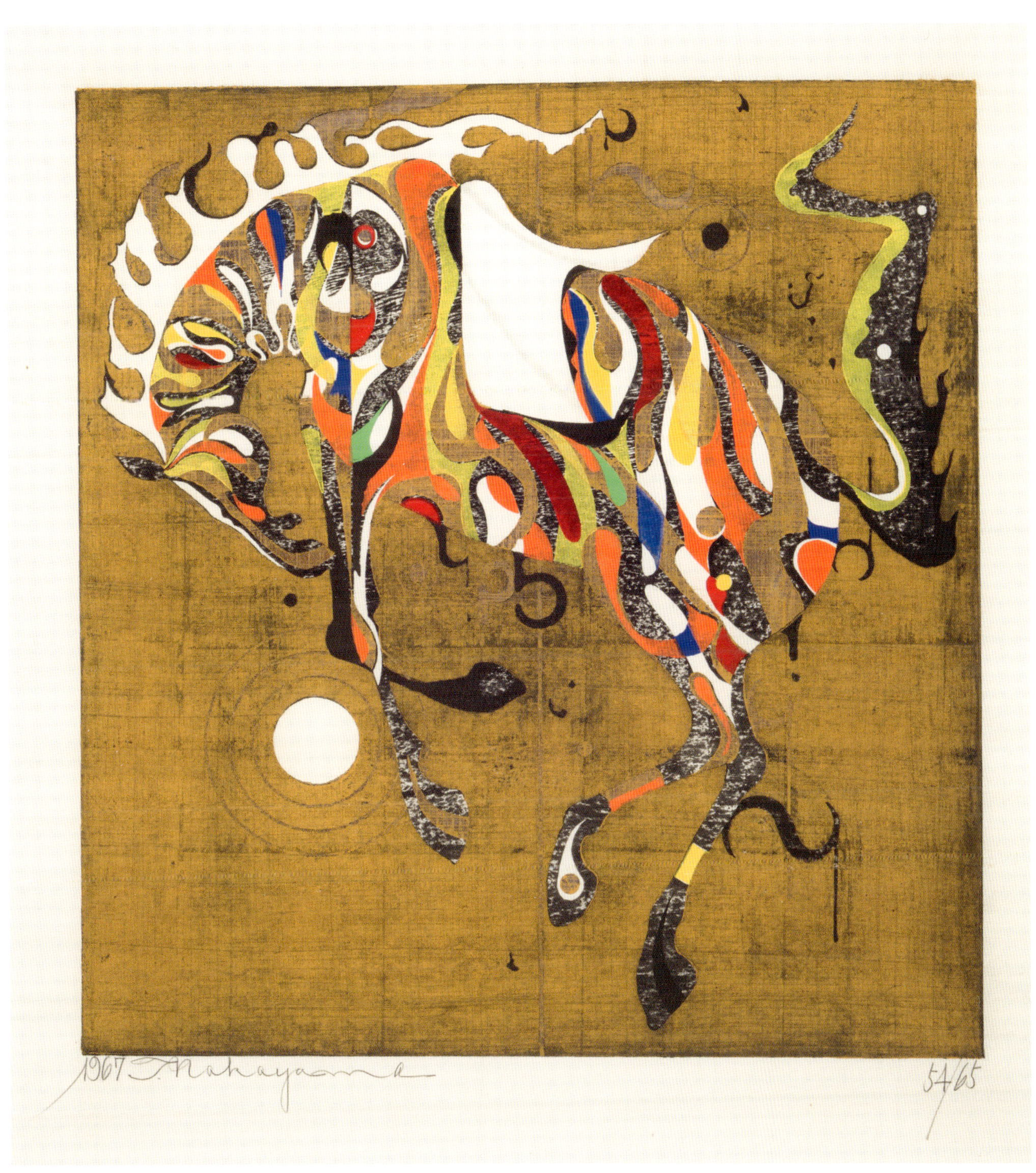
1967 T. Nakayama
54/65

MAKI HAKU
(1924–2000)

A self-taught printmaker, Maki Haku honed his relief printmaking skills at the monthly meetings of Ichimoku-kai, a group committed to advancing the early twentieth-century Japanese *sōsaku hanga*, or "creative print," movement. His work often features Chinese characters, English words, and other phonetic symbols that are magnified and abstracted to the point where they become illegible. This approach forces the viewer to consider the form of the characters and their evocative potential alongside their literal meaning. The deep embossment of the two works shown here is a signature characteristic of his work and is achieved by pressing dampened paper onto plywood blocks enhanced with cement paste.

76–11 (Wind – D), 1976

Wood and cement block relief print on paper
84.5 × 44.5 cm (33¼ × 17½ in.)
Gift of The Wise Collection, Joanne and Douglas Wise, 2011.386

76–15 (Cloud – C), 1976

Wood and cement block relief print on paper
84.5 × 44.5 cm (33¼ × 17½ in.)
Gift of The Wise Collection, Joanne and Douglas Wise, 2011.387

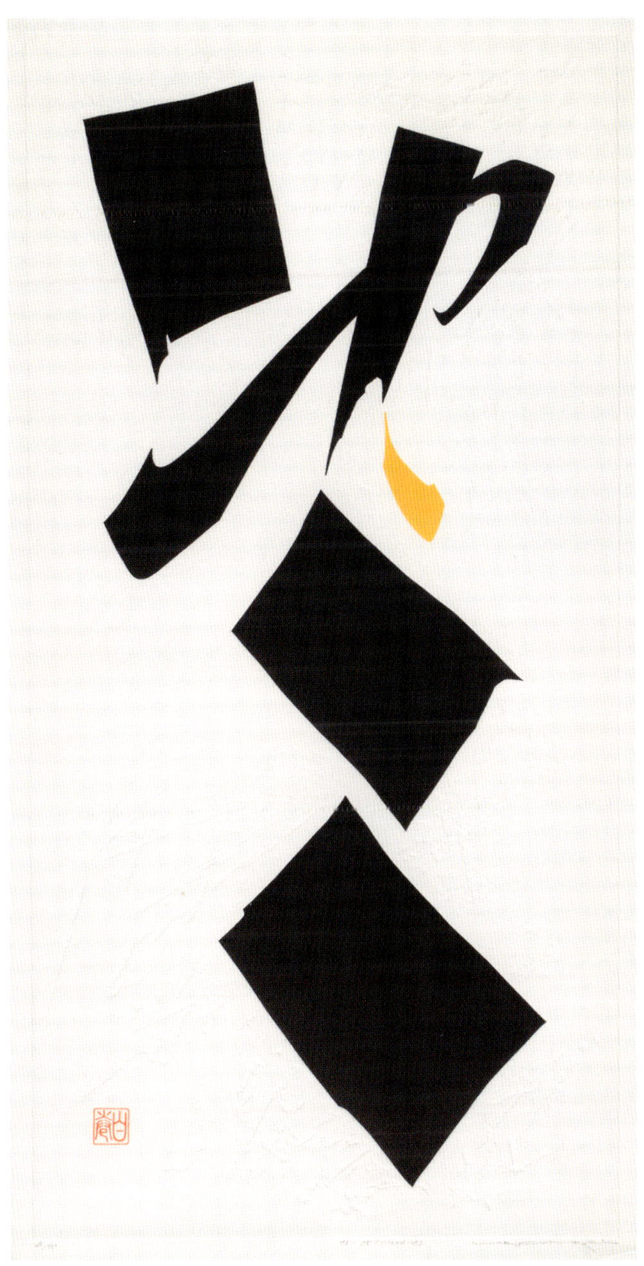

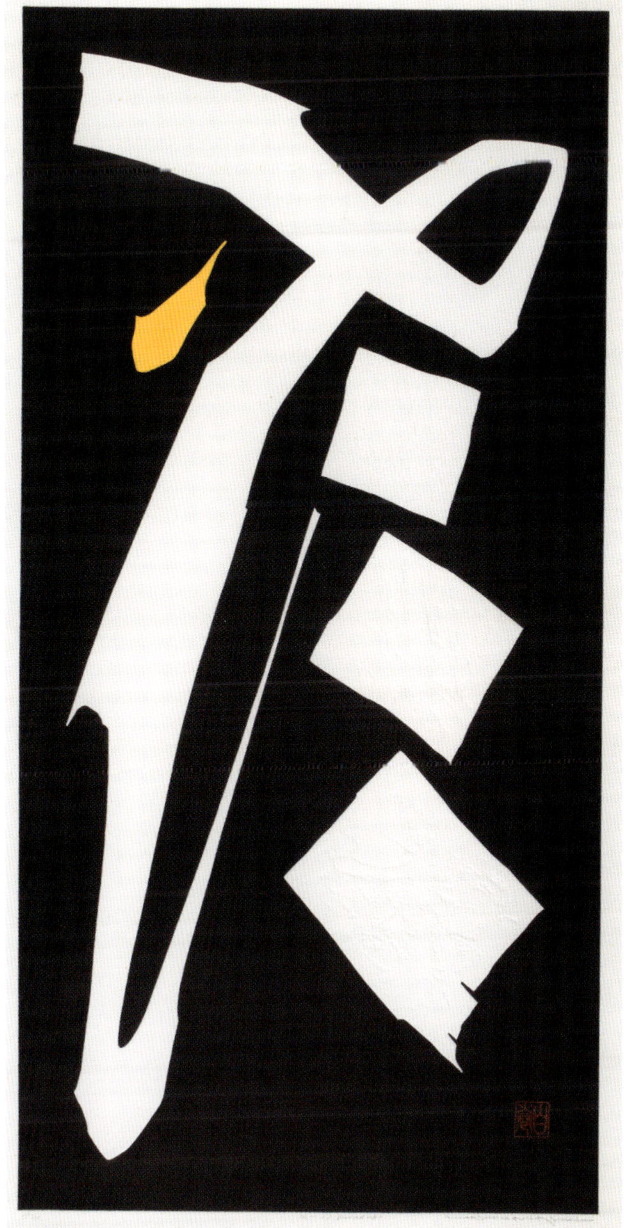

MASAMI TERAOKA

(Japanese-American, born 1936)

Today's Special, from the series "31 Flavors Invading Japan", 1981

Woodblock print: ink and color on paper
28.2 × 42.4 cm (11⅛ × 16¹¹⁄₁₆ in.)
Harriet B. Bancroft Fund, 1987.97

Masami Teraoka's "31 Flavors Invading Japan" series marks
an early endeavor to integrate the collaborative production
techniques of *ukiyo-e* into his practice. Here, he also employs
the visual language of these Edo-period prints in particular, as
seen in the Prussian blue background and the evocation of the
idealized *bijin* (beautiful woman) of Japan's early modern period.

Inspired by Pop Art's focus on cultural icons, Teraoka
juxtaposes icons of Japan's floating world with that of 1980s
American media, drawing a powerful parallel between the
cultures, both which were driven by consumerism and fostered
ideals that conversely promote both conformity and hedonism.
The figure's blond hair and Western facial features can also be
considered a commentary on the way women are consistently
affected by capitalism and media-driven ideals on appearance.

The poem beside her reads: "She's about to lick / A scene
from today's life."

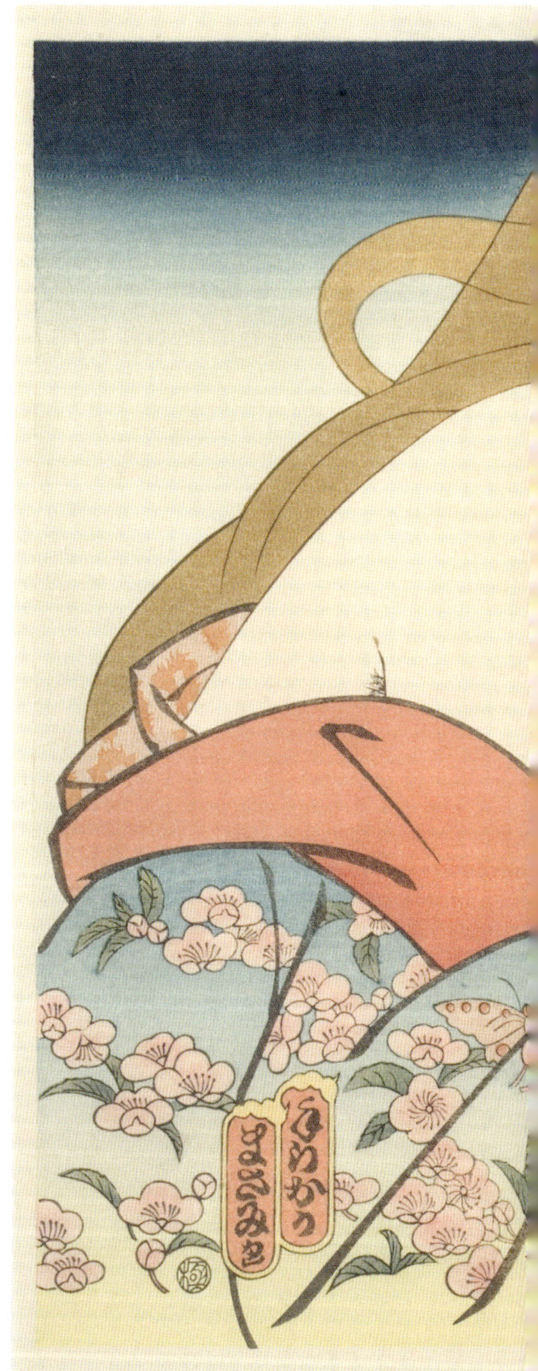

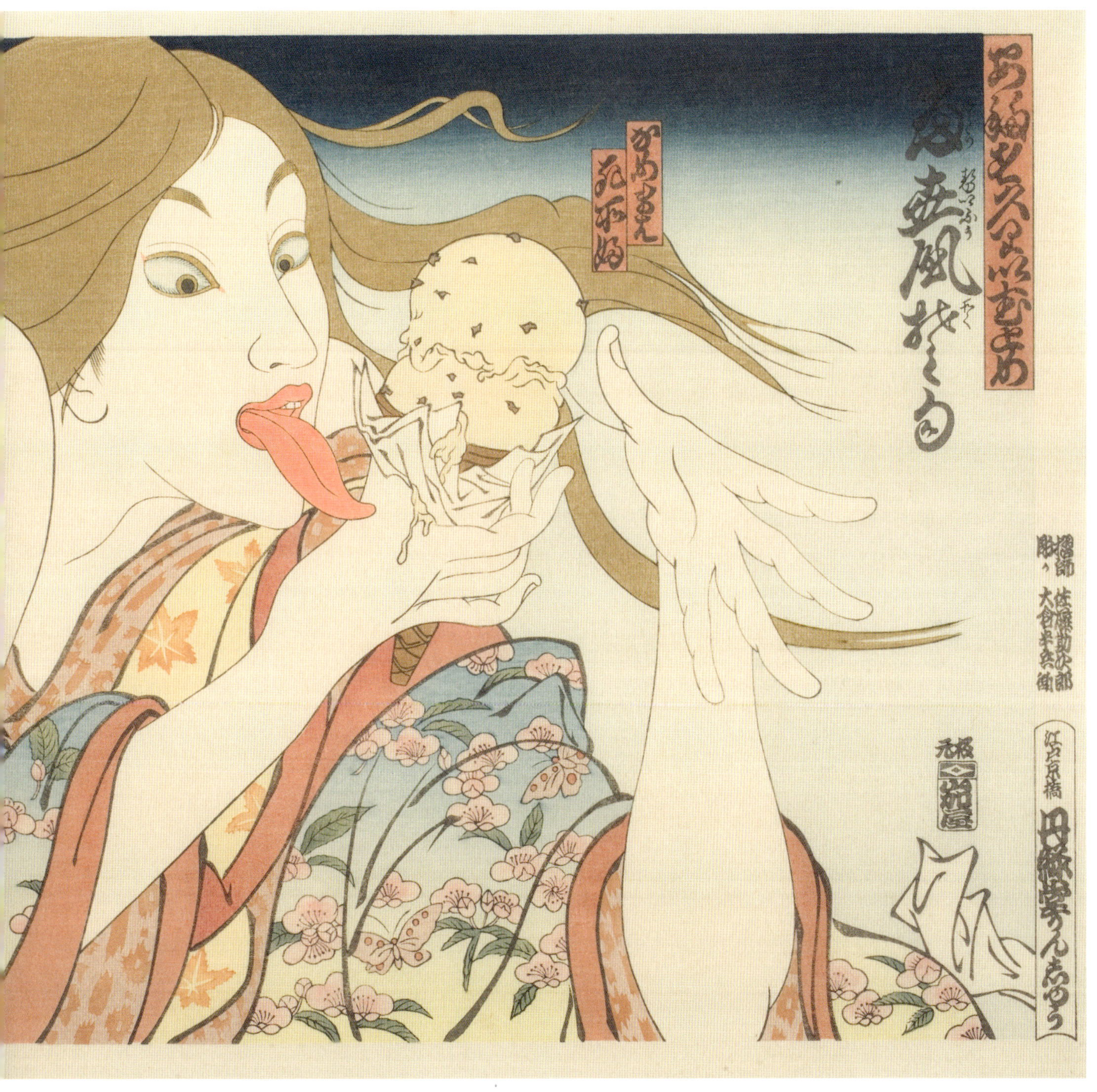

GLOSSARY OF TERMS

aiban: A somewhat rare print size, roughly halfway between *chūban* and *ōban*, measuring approximately 34 × 23 cm (13 × 9 in.).

aizuri-e: A type of print that primarily uses shades of blue.

baren: A hand-printing tool used to apply pressure and transfer ink from the woodblock to the paper.

baren-suji: The patterns or marks left on a print by the *baren* during the hand-printing process.

benizuri-e: Prints that primarily use shades of red or pink due to extensive use of safflower.

bijin: Literally "beautiful person," often referring to beautiful young women.

blind printing: A printing technique that creates a raised, embossed effect on the paper without the use of ink.

bokashi: A printing technique that creates a gradation of color or tone.

chonin: Townspeople during the Edo period in Japan, often a reference to the wealthy merchant class.

chūban: A somewhat common small print size, measuring about 25 × 19 cm (10 × 7 in.), created by dividing an *ōban* in half along its short axis.

courtesan: A high-class prostitute or entertainer in Japan during the Edo period.

e-hon: A term for illustrated books or albums.

gampi: A type of paper made from the bark of the *gampi* tree, known for its smooth texture and translucency. It is often used for high-quality woodblock prints.

geisha: A professional female entertainer skilled in traditional Japanese arts, such as music, dance, and conversation.

gilding: The application of gold leaf to a substrate for decorative effect.

hashira-e: Pillar prints, notable for long vertical formats reminiscent of scrolls. Sizes vary, but they are typically around 73.6 × 12.7 cm (29 × 5 in.).

kabuki: A form of traditional Japanese theater known for its elaborate costumes, makeup, and exaggerated acting style.

kacho-e: Prints featuring birds and flowers, and sometimes other flora and fauna.

kara-zuri: An embossed printing effect.

kira-zuri: A printing technique that involves scattering fine mica flakes on the print while the ink is wet, creating a subtle sparkling effect.

koban: A fairly rare small print size, measuring about 23 × 17 cm (9 × 7 in.), created by dividing an *aiban* in half along its short axis.

kozo: A type of paper made from the bark of the mulberry tree, commonly used for Japanese woodblock prints. It is known for its strength and durability.

meisho: Famous places or landmarks depicted in prints (known as *meisho-e*).

mica: A mineral used in the *kira-zuri* printing technique to create a sparkling effect on prints.

mitate-e: Prints that parody or reinterpret well-known scenes, stories, or characters.

murasaki-e: Prints that primarily use shades of purple.

mushi-e: Prints featuring insects, often depicted in a detailed and naturalistic style.

nishiki-e: Literally "brocade pictures"; refers to full-color woodblock prints.

Nihonga: Literally "Japanese painting," the term was introduced to distinguish those practicing in traditional Japanese styles from *yōga*, or "Western painting," during the Meiji period.

Noh: A form of traditional Japanese theater introduced in the Muromachi period (1336–1573). It began as an aristocratic art form, and is characterized by opulent costumes, masked performers, and musical accompaniment.

ōban: The most common print size, approximately 39 × 26.5 cm (15¹⁹⁄₃₂ × 10¹¹⁄₁₆ in.).

ō-ōban: Larger than *ōban*, roughly translates to "extra large print"; usually around 46 × 30 cm (18 × 12 in.).

okubi-e: Prints featuring large, close-up portraits of actors or courtesans.

rōnin: A samurai who had lost his master due to death or disgrace and was expected to commit seppuku. Many *rōnin* during the Edo period drifted into criminal activity.

samurai: The warrior class of feudal Japan, known for their strict code of honor and loyalty to their lords.

shin hanga: The "new prints" movement, which revitalized traditional Japanese printmaking in the early twentieth century.

shogun: The military ruler of Japan during various periods, who held the real power while the emperor served as a figurehead.

shunga: A genre of Japanese woodblock prints and paintings that depicts explicit sexual scenes. The term *shunga* translates to "spring pictures," a euphemism for erotic art.

sōsaku hanga: The "creative prints" movement, which emphasized the artist's involvement in all aspects of the printmaking process.

sumizuri-e: Prints created using only black ink.

surimono: Privately commissioned woodblock prints, often featuring poems and distributed as gifts.

tan-e: Hand-colored prints; often characterized by the presence of orange-red lead-based pigments. Popular in the second half of the seventeenth century.

uki-e: A genre of woodblock prints that employ Western-style linear perspective to create a sense of depth, often featuring landscapes or architecture.

ukiyo: The "floating world," a term referring to the pleasure-seeking urban lifestyle during Japan's Edo period (1603–1868).

ukiyo-e: Pictures of the "floating world."

urushi-e: Prints that incorporate lacquer or varnish for a glossy effect.

wakushū: Adolescent boys who sometimes served as apprentices or assistants to kabuki actors and were often objects of sexual attraction.

washi: Literally meaning "Japanese paper," it refers to traditional handmade paper made in Japan.

woodblock print: A type of relief print made by carving an image into a wooden block (in Japan, typically made of cherry wood), inking the block, and transferring the ink to paper by applying pressure.

yakusha-e: Prints depicting kabuki actors, either in character or as themselves.

yōga: Literally "Western painting," it is a term developed in the Meiji period to distinguish paintings by artists studying European and American traditions from those studying Japanese ones.

Yoshiwara: The designated pleasure district in Edo (present-day Tokyo) during the Edo period, where courtesans and geisha entertained clients.

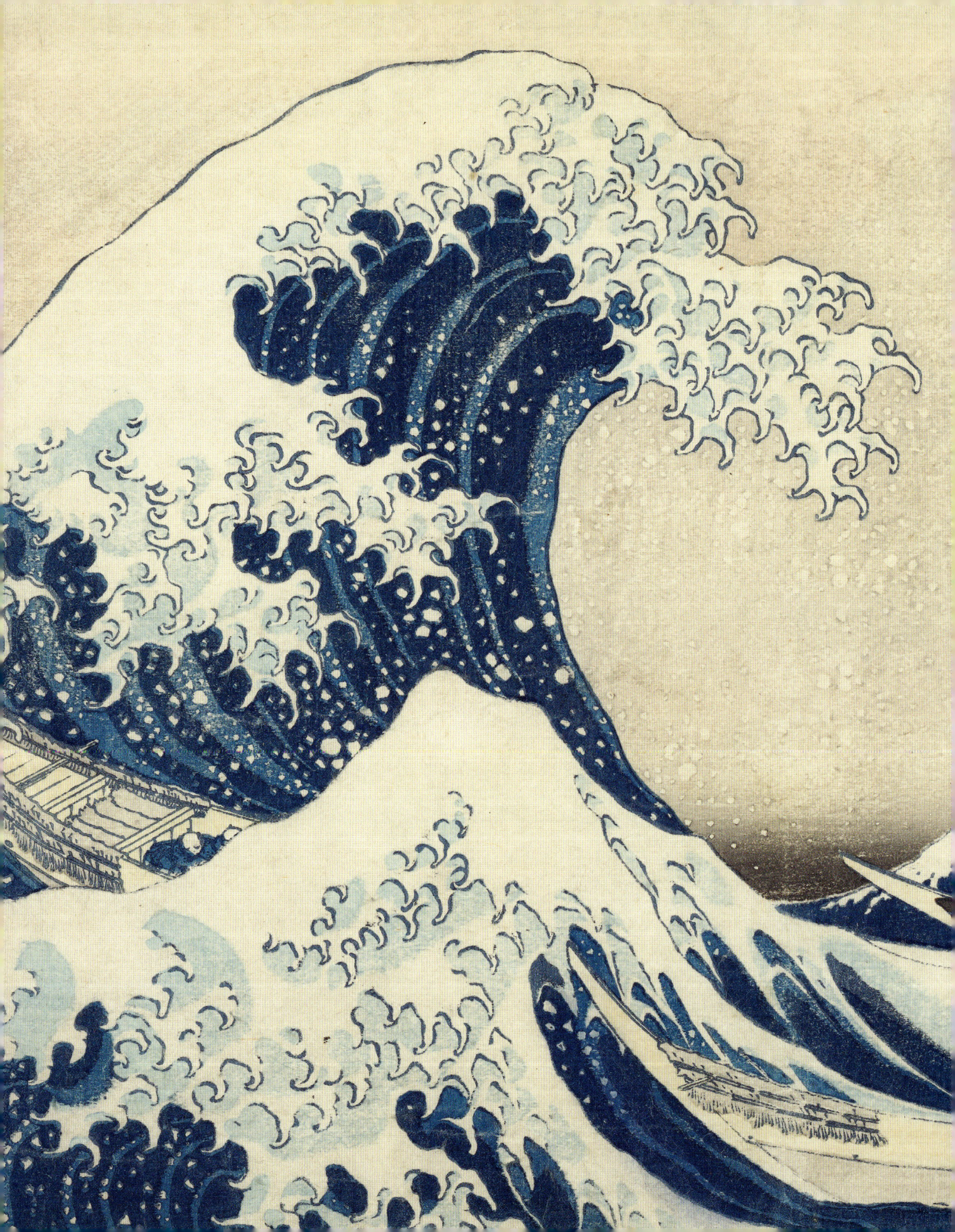

<h1 style="text-align:center">INDEX</h1>